Finding Gold

Also by the Author

The Wood Fire Handbook

Finding Gold

My life-changing treasure hunt with nature

Vincent Thurkettle

First published in Great Britain in 2026 by Short Books, an imprint of
Octopus Publishing Group Ltd
Carmelite House
50 Victoria Embankment
London EC4Y 0DZ
www.octopusbooks.co.uk

An Hachette UK Company
www.hachette.co.uk

The authorized representative in the EEA is Hachette Ireland,
8 Castlecourt Centre, Dublin 15, D15 XTP3, Ireland (email: info@hbgi.ie)

ISBN: 978-1-80419-418-8
eISBN: 978-1-80419-419-5

A CIP catalogue record for this book is available from the British Library.

Typeset in 11.25/16pt Heldane Text by Six Red Marbles UK, Thetford, Norfolk

Printed and bound in Great Britain.

13 5 7 9 10 8 6 4 2

This FSC® label means that materials used for
the product have been responsibly sourced.

Treasure above all those who care for you.
This book is dedicated to my family, and the wonderful
collection of friends I found scattered alongside
the world's gold-bearing rivers.
The gold we found is mostly gone and forgotten now.
But you endure in me, and in these pages.

CONTENTS

OPPOSITES ATTRACT

Gold is born when neutron stars collide. It is an element and is immortal. The 244,000 tons of this bright yellow metal that we have taken from the earth and stored as treasure are older than our planet. Throughout history, almost every human civilization has prized it as wealth or ornament. In this digital age we are still enchanted by this alluring metal, perhaps even more so. The lustrous glow of pure gold is as captivating as it ever was. As the Greek poet Pindar observed, 'Gold is the child of Zeus, neither rust nor moth devoureth it, but the mind of man is devoured.'

I was born in late November in the middle of the 20th century, soon after my parents had collided. As a self-aware organic structure, primarily made up of carbon, calcium and water, my existence is fleeting. I am not in any way rare. There are presently over eight billion humans on planet Earth, weighing 316 million tons. And if not the moths, something will devour all of us. If all of the gold ever discovered were to be shared out equally, we would each receive about 29g – six wedding rings.

Our love affair with gold continues; we are opposites in every way.

LIVING WITH GOLD FEVER

'There's gold, and it's haunting and haunting,
It's luring me on as of old;
Yet it isn't the gold that I'm wanting
So much as just finding the gold.'

—Robert Service, 'The Spell of the Yukon'

If anybody had told me how hard it is to find gold, would I have listened? I hope not.

The siren call of gold is unique; there is no platinum, silver, diamond or sapphire fever – only 'gold fever'. This magical metal is enchanting, never fading or tarnishing. The gold jewellery of ancient peoples still looks like new: gold is almost indestructible. But what is it about gold that lured me away from a decent, comfortable job to go hunting for it, to leave my office and the security of home for a life based on hard work, danger and chance? Was I belatedly joining the 'tenderfoots' and 'sourdoughs' that flocked to the spectacular gold discoveries of the 19th century simply to take part in the great lottery that goldfields offer?* I don't think so. I never expected to get rich. For me, even from the very beginning, it was all about *finding* the gold.

There is a delightful subtlety here, an interesting divergence between *owning* gold and *finding* gold – both are ancient and compelling, but are completely different.

Gold that is *owned* and then hidden is a primal insurance against troubled times: often much better than money in the bank. It helps to explain gold's staggering value with a simple comparison. In the UK a standard pack of butter weighs 250g – a lump of fatty golden material worth roughly two house bricks or one roofing tile. The same sized bar of gold would buy the whole house. For the very rich, the vast wealth that can be stored in a tiny volume of discreet and mobile gold coins, bars or jewellery has always been attractive.

Gold that is *owned* and not hidden serves to display love or status, hopefully creating respect and admiration – envy even. Amazingly, with all the technology and sophisticated investments of this age, we still fall back on gold. It is available and legal. We can own gold and still want to. Gold has such power over some people that it is almost a faith, or a drug. Maybe this is the root cause of gold fever.

Of course, my gold obsession may all be my mother's fault. When I was very young, we lived in a caravan in a clifftop field in the far west of Wales, above the magnificent Newgale beach in Pembrokeshire. My father was in the Royal Navy serving as

---

*   'Tenderfoot' and 'sourdough' were names for prospectors. Beginning with the Californian gold rush of the 1800s, gold miners would often keep sourdough starters with them so they could bake their own bread.

a helicopter engineer and my mother was at home with me. Although very young, she had an extraordinary love of literature and was determined to pass this on to me. We meandered through many of the children's classics, but it was the work of Jack London that stood out for me. I was thrilled by the gritty realism of *White Fang* and enthralled by *The Call of the Wild*. Unusually for a six-year-old, I had already felt this myself – especially when sent out into the woods to hide.

Whatever arrangement my mother had with the local authority, she was not confident of the legitimacy of our home-schooling. Whenever the school inspector was due, I was told to go off and play in the woods, somewhere out of sight. And this was fine with me. I had an oilskin coat that came down to my wellington boots and a sou'wester hat – I was prepared for any weather, and I loved the freedom. It is possible that my mother exaggerated the frequency of visits by the school inspector, a simple ruse to give her some peace. I am loath to admit it, but I may have been a lively and difficult child.

I know we were poor at the time, as the family took on any work that was available. When my father was home, my parents would grab the chance to go fruit or potato picking to help make ends meet. I clearly recall one incident that I am now deeply sorry about. Unable to afford a Christmas tree, my father had cut us a gorse bush. My mother crouched beside it with a roll of cotton wool, pulling off and fluffing up little fibrous snowflakes. Jolly and festive, she encouraged me to help her decorate our tree. But it was not a real Christmas tree – I knew it and I said so. I refused all of my mother's gentle encouragement to join in. I was it seems, a stubborn and precocious little boy. No wonder I was sent out in all weathers to avoid the 'school inspector'.

Life often loops things around. The Greeks felt that the gods play with us, who knows? But it is a pleasing irony that I now have a field growing eight thousand Christmas trees. They provide me with an income in winter when gold prospecting is too hard due to the cold, the dark or the rivers being in flood. My mother and father helped me plant these trees, both still doing fieldwork into their eighties, but now with a son who was much better company, I hope.

If I could meet my younger self, how would I advise him, and would he listen?

Many years ago, I bumped into Ian Stephen, a friend and good gold prospector from the south of England. He was parked beside a Scottish river in a large campervan and spotted me first and invited me over. He had retired long ago, and it was always interesting to catch up with him – brimming with stories of his recent gold adventures. With some difficulty he climbed back up the steps into his vehicle, and I noticed that he now had an artificial leg. While I was still working out how to diplomatically ask about this, he cheerfully told me. Apparently, he had been working somewhere in the Yukon, welding up a large machine, and had damaged his leg. This wound then went gangrenous, and nobody was more surprised than he was when they cut it off. The writer Robert Service would have written a poem about Ian.

I commented that he seemed to have taken it all rather well, and asked what his wife, Beth, thought about it. He went quiet and murmured, 'She died earlier this year.' I felt a wave of compassion for Ian and said what a rotten year he was having, losing one leg and his wife in the space of a few months. He paused, clearly upset, and then surprised me by being unexpectedly sanguine about these recent tragedies. He said that he had had such a great life that he was content and accepted these catastrophic losses. Suddenly, he glanced up and stared at me intensely over the rim of his coffee mug. As if passing a great secret, he then offered this wisdom: 'Vince, if you will take the advice of an old man it is this. Make your memories while you're young, as you'll live on them when you're old.' I listened carefully and it was just as well, for we never met again.

I do not need to advise my younger self – Ian did.

My three children grew up with all this too, and it was sweet to have my family join with me in the slow harvest of the precious dust. My daughter married a gold prospector, and I sometimes take young couples out to find the gold for their wedding rings. This feels good, the pinnacle of the martial art – wild gold, love and ancient tradition woven into two rings, new heirlooms with an old story. And the gold we find is virginal. It has never been touched before and is utterly pure, as old as time itself and yet as fresh as their new love. This 'green gold' is innocent and has no links to the tragedies of human past; no ghosts of war, murder or brutality stain the bright atoms. And gold pans have a timeless rhythm. They cut through the water barely making ripples, just enough to brush away sand and leave the gold – like winnowing wheat from chaff.

I think I would have been content to stay with my rusting old gold pan, scything each temperate river for grains of gold, but then I met Ken Williamson. He had dived on a shipwreck back in the late 1970s and filled my head with new possibilities. But, essentially, just one bold idea: that there was still far more gold hidden in that shipwreck of his than could ever be found in a stream or river.

I soon realized that Ken's world of treasure could only be a dream for me while I remained in full-time employment, salaried with the jam-tomorrow promise of distant retirement and a Civil Service pension.

Don't ever let me give the impression that living with gold fever is easy. Quitting work was hard – I liked my job, and the boss was fine. But – and this might be the most important thing I ever write – there has not been one minute of any day when I wished I was back at my desk. It is good to dwell on that thought for a moment, as it is so very important.

And things have been tough from time to time. I told my mother at one point that I was living on roadkill and stolen firewood – a slight son-to-mother exaggeration. All the same, having had a comfortable salary for over 28 years, it was a nasty shock when it stopped. The reality was chilling: I had to succeed, or my bank account stayed empty.

They say that the two keys to success are perseverance and a positive attitude. To this I would add 'imagination'. It is vital to visualize success and imagine what it will feel like. This thought then becomes your close companion, a secret friend who will push you on through the hard times. And curiously, I now look back upon the darkest hours with great fondness. There is as much pride to be had from overcoming adversity as from success itself. But I have to say, success does feel pretty good! I had imagined my cupped hands full of gold coins and rough nuggets, and one day this dream of treasure became reality.

Yet truly there was something else too. Through my seeking gold, I had glimpsed a secret world, fey, free and beautiful. I had seen that the old-timers and the dreamers were all still out there – a world community of cheerful optimists, often living on little more than hope. They are welcoming and warm-hearted, gold fever flowing through their veins like a health-giving spice. I like these people. They are a global family and often refer to themselves as such. To be at one with the world's gold prospectors is an honour.

Often it is assumed that the desire to *find* gold is simple avarice, but it is not. I first went out gold prospecting almost 50 years ago now, and in all that time I have met hundreds of other people out searching. But only a handful, a very few, were there purely for the money. For me, it is in the desire for the challenge. I am thrilled to have my hunter-gatherer genes wide awake and passionate. Gold prospecting is an exciting lifestyle choice – a treasure hunt with nature, new friendships, an adventure as big or small as you wish: a family weekend by a warm summer stream or hunting storm-lashed rocks for a shipwreck. I find luxury boring. I have never wanted to be passive, sedated by comfort, a rabbit caught in the headlights of endless on-tap entertainment. Life is too short, and I want to feel alive.

I would note, however, that my introduction to gold was quiet and unexpected. I was totally happy without it – too poor to own any and ignorant of the fact that it could still be found. But from first contact, wild gold whispered to me and wove a lifelong enchantment.

At first, I was simply enthralled by the very idea that gold and treasure were still out there, ownerless and available – finders keepers, more or less. It was like I had suddenly found out that

Treasure Island was real and, even better, I had met someone who could take me there. As described in the brilliant lines by Robert Service, quoted earlier, from the very beginning I was haunted by gold and wanted to find some.

My first steps into the world of gold prospecting were careful and measured, like a toddler tottering over an unfamiliar floor. I would research a gold-bearing area, sort out the necessary permissions and then spend a day or two panning to see what it felt like. Did I like the place, could I find gold, were the people nice? And if it went well, it might be a year or two before I was tempted away to a new river. These small steps, each relaxing and pleasant, steadily improved my skill with a gold pan and built invaluable experience.

Gold is astonishingly good at hiding and it took me years to learn the language of water. And this is the real art of gold prospecting: to be able to 'read' a river. To stand quietly by the gentlest flow and visualize the river in flood, reading the signs for where the gold should be. Gold is so heavy that it will only move in a torrent, a sudden snowmelt or when a downpour raises the river water to frightening levels. I have watched these events and they are awesome – tree trunks and bushes tumbling along in the swirling, muddy current sweep away bridges. Huge rocks are torn from the deep riverbed and thump along like a giant's footsteps. The whole valley trembles with the power of it all – the riotous anarchy of a river in flood. These are the times when the valley is worn deeper, and gold nuggets find a new home. Even years after the turmoil has subsided, a truly skilful prospector can see this – something like tracking a huge, enraged animal. I feel that this ability is close to being a martial art, as it is both learned and felt.

This is the Zen form of gold prospecting: to use only cheap and simple tools, and combine them with knowledge, skill and intuition. I have seen loud people arrive with a mountain of equipment and find nothing, in too much of a hurry to stop and contemplate the river, to listen, to read the riparian pages for clues. And it's all there: the river's full history is written in its banks if you learn how to read them.

1

THE OLD MINES AND
THE PROSPECTOR

'Life shrinks or expands in proportion to one's courage.'

—Anaïs Nin, *The Diary of Anaïs Nin*

The events that led to my unlikely meeting with a gold prospector unfolded slowly. It was a case of serendipity for which I am ever grateful. A terrifying experience, while exploring an old mine, led to my being more cautious when underground, and this prudence resulted in my meeting with the man who would open my mind to gold, and change my life.

At 19 years old, I was studying rocks and soils as part of a 3-year woodland management course. I soon found that geology fascinated me. But even more intriguing were the captivating minerals within ancient mine workings. Long before I had any idea that natural gold could still be found, I was delighted by the perfect symmetry of quartz crystals and the spectacular colours of the metallic copper ores. These minerals are the flowers of rocks, and I found them enthralling. In obedience to the laws of chemistry and crystallography, deep in the earth their petals silently unfold, and they are beautiful.

In pursuit of this new passion for weird and wonderful rocks, I hitch-hiked around Iceland and across southern Norway to collect specimens. In Iceland I sought the double-refractive spar, the sunstone once used by the Vikings as a navigation aid. (On cloudy days, the crystal takes the scattered rays of light and mutually aligns them. The light is then focused into two images, which is thought to have enabled these ancient seafarers to find the sun's position.) I also wanted a sample of the stunning pearl-lustred mineral heulandite. There were few other travellers, and the Icelanders often gave me food or took me home to show me their way of life. A hunter once spent much of the afternoon showing me the rifles he used when out stalking seals or geese. It seemed to help that they thought my name was ancient Icelandic: the Kettle clan feature in their sagas.

In Norway I was after ruby-coloured pyrope garnets and hoped for a specimen of native silver from the Kongsberg mines. Again, the people were warm and welcoming, and this time they seemed to like that I was English. I had one long lift with an old man who quietly told me what it was like to live under occupation during the Second World War; he cried, many of his family had been killed.

My collection of mineral samples grew quickly, and I was pleased with it. But I soon discovered that scouring heaps of old mining waste for good specimens was a pretty hopeless task – hundreds of collectors had been there before me. However, underground was so much better. Few people ventured into an old mine's maze of long-abandoned shafts and tunnels, so finding good samples here was relatively easy. As long as one had a reasonable knowledge of ropes and lights, and the ability to find the way out again, underground was definitely best.

I had learned basic rope work from the rock climbers at college, so was able to explore even quite difficult mines. I do have a fear of heights, which could have been a problem. But I was pleased to find that, when underground and blanketed in a darkness so thick I felt I could touch it, I could never see how high I was. My head-torch beam only ever lit the rock face in front of me. Thus, there was a curious illusion of safety. However, while confidence born of competence is a wonderful thing, over-confidence will get you killed.

With three friends, I went to an abandoned mine in the Borrowdale valley to find samples of the humble mineral graphite. We opted not to be roped together. At the time, climbers were divided on whether a party should be roped together or not. There were equally well-reported accounts of a falling climber pulling the others over the precipice with them, or conversely, the others saving the person who had fallen. Happily, the day had gone well, and on the way out we were relaxed about a vast shaft that had been cut near the mine's entrance. The chasm stretched across the full width of the tunnel and there was no way around it. Nevertheless, it seemed easy to traverse, as there were plenty of hand- and footholds along the shaft's rough side walls. Once the first man had reached the far side, I started my climb across.

I was a little over halfway when the suitcase-sized rock I was gripping came loose, and I started to fall backwards into the shaft. In a moment of God-given clarity, I twisted and pushed on the rock and sprang forwards. My arms and upper body just made it to the void's edge and the first man dived to grab hold of me. Then, with the lower half of my body still hanging in the mineshaft, we listened in silence as the huge rock fell and fell. It crashed thunderously into the shaft's walls as it plunged away into the darkness. Each violent contact made a chilling sonorous boom that echoed back up to us. Several seconds later, there was a long distant rumble as the rock finally came to rest.

Perhaps in shock or adrenalin-fuelled, we laughed and joked about it at the time, as the third man made a most careful – and roped – crossing. But later that night, in the quiet of my small room, the immensity of what had just happened terrified me. I lay quite still, while my mind replayed again and again the sound of the falling rock. But for the twist and leap, and my friend's lightning reactions, I would still have been holding that rock during its descent – conscious until my body cushioned a blow with the side wall.

While still keen on minerology, and prepared to go collecting underground, I was now wiser and much more cautious. I read that the Carrock mine in Mosedale held three rare minerals that I wanted: wolframite, scheelite and apatite. But there was a problem: the mine was still being worked. I visited the site, met three of the miners and asked if I could go in. They said that officially I could not, but what I did when they weren't there was up to me. While a little ambiguous, I felt that this was tacit approval. They were decent, interesting men, and I sat with them and watched as they lit a small fire and placed a sheet of corrugated iron above it. Then they poured a bucketful of glittering black sand – crushed wolframite – onto this hot plate to dry it. The work seemed very primitive. Either this ore of tungsten was really valuable, or these men were desperate, and I couldn't work out which it was. I learned that they blasted the face of the massive, mineral-rich quartz vein they were working late in the afternoon, just before leaving. I decided to come back in the middle of the night, when the air was clear of fumes, and I would have a safe hour or so to look for mineral specimens.

At about 2am, I arrived at the newly shattered working face and was delighted. The explosives had fractured a huge white quartz vein that was criss-crossed with long blades of jet-black wolframite and pale-green hexagonal apatite crystals. But I hadn't even started collecting a few samples, when two faint lights appeared in the tunnel far behind me. Suddenly unsure of my assumed permission, my mind raced through the options. There was still time to move deeper into the mine and hide. But an awful recollection of the nightmare-inducing mineshaft incident flashed into my mind, and I opted for honesty. I took a deep breath and walked back along the tunnel towards the oncoming lights – *mea culpa.* I would take whatever punishment they saw fit and hoped that my candour would mitigate its severity. As I walked, I did think it odd that the miners hadn't mentioned a night shift.

When I reached them, I was surprised not to be greeted by a torrent of abuse. A hesitant conversation soon established that these two men were just mineral collectors like me and had no more right to be in the mine than I had. Like a comedy scene, on spotting each other's lights, we had both nervously assumed that the other had authority and that there might be consequences for trespassers. How incredibly improbable that the three of us chose to visit this remote and tiny tungsten mine at the same time on the same night! But it proved to be a crucial encounter that nudged me onto a new course. This meeting changed my life and shaped all that was to follow for the next 50 years. Now feeling relaxed and with my specimens gathered, I was pleased to be invited back to the older man's house a short drive away to join them for an early breakfast.

His home was old and beautiful – a large stone farmhouse with an enormous kitchen paved with dark-grey flagstones. We sat down to eat around a scrubbed wooden table beside a huge Welsh dresser. In place of bowls, plates, cups and saucers, the dresser was packed with rocks and multicoloured crystals; the display of museum-quality minerals arranged along its shelves was breathtaking. My eyes drifted across the collection, enjoying the beauty of each piece, and then came my Damascus moment. I was puzzled by an incongruous line of clear resin paperweights that sat along the very top of the dresser.

On seeing that I had noticed them, my host brought one down and carefully handed it to me. And there, embedded within the clear resin dome, was a constellation of gold. A glorious scatter of bright star-like flakes and iron-stained grains of rough dust were now suspended in the space between my hands. It was like looking into a crystal ball and seeing my future. Awed, I held the paperweight reverently in both hands as if it were fragile, totally absorbed in the magnitude of my first contact with natural wild gold.

I knew the history of gold-fevered hopefuls who had raced across the world during the great Victorian gold rushes. But that was over a hundred years ago. And yet the man beside me had found all this gold. I sat spellbound as the prospector took down each treasured paperweight, one at a time, and told me its fascinating story. On seeing that I was enthralled, this generous man then told me all the locations where he'd found the gold, one of which was in the stream below the very mine where we had just met.

It has been a lifelong regret to me that I didn't make a note of this man's name. He introduced me to gold prospecting and changed the course of my life. The circumstances of our first meeting, deep in the mine, were a little tense. However, there had been plenty of time to exchange addresses during breakfast later on, yet I had missed the opportunity. Regrets are usually for the things we have not done, and such is the case here.

2

THE GOLD STAR

'The alchemists in their search for gold discovered
many other things of greater value.'

—Arthur Schopenhauer, *Counsels and Maxims*

The catering staff at my college must have been surprised to find
three dustbin lids missing one morning. And possibly just as
surprised when they reappeared two days later. After meeting
the prospector in the mine the weekend before, I was now itching
to go and try my hand at gold panning. This was during my third
year of studying in England's Lake District – a singularly beautiful
area absolutely riddled with fascinating old mines. One of which, I
now knew, was shedding a little natural gold into the river below.

With wellington boots and the improvised bin-lid gold pans
safely stowed, a couple of friends and I signed out the college
minibus and set off westwards towards the mountains. At that
time, my family home was in the intensively farmed south of
England – a predominantly lowland landscape of barren rye-
grass fields that stretched across the southern countryside like
oversized bowling greens. But up here in the north, ancient
drystone walls, themselves rich in mosses and lichens, divided
small fields of breathtaking beauty. Dozens of unfamiliar

wildflowers were alive with bustling insects – such an abundance of life and energy. I revelled in the, to me, unfamiliar fecundity of 'unimproved grassland' and was delighted now to become acquainted with it. I soon found that I liked the people up here too. It seemed that their very character had been shaped by this mountainous and glaciated land, as were their distant Scandinavian ancestors. These were hardy folk, straight-talking and self-reliant, and they immediately had my respect.

The single-track road that winds and twists up into the Mosedale valley is exactly the sort of road that should lead to a gold mine. To its left flows a sparkling, crystal-clear river that splashes and tumbles back down and out of the valley. The rough potholed road is like a dark-grey mirror image of the river itself. It snakes between huge erratic boulders that were dropped as the last Ice Age ended, and the valley's glacier receded. Up to the right, there are shrubby patches of exquisite juniper forest, and to the left, small, sodden flushes of sphagnum bog – where insect-eating sundew plants lie waiting for their prey. There is something primal about this dale, a striking natural beauty and sense that humans don't come here much. Wilderness is rare in England, and this timeless valley is a gem.

That day, as we approached the mine at the end of the road, we chatted excitedly in the minibus, childlike, likening ourselves to the pioneers of the world's great gold rushes. How pleasing is the innocent naivety of youth: the whole world is out there, fresh and ready to explore. This is one reason why I've always been happy to be referred to as 'childlike', even when it has not been meant as a compliment. To me, the term suggests an open mind and the confidence to play and explore. It intimates that the full weight of convention and the pressure to conform have not yet settled on someone and smothered their personality; whereas to be called 'childish' is another thing entirely.

The road might have been built solely to service this old mine. It was rough and, as nobody lived at the far end, otherwise pointless. It ended abruptly beside the last workings, where the main valley splits into two. The river sweeps away to the left and to the right a ragged ravine cuts up into the hillside. The mine itself was small, just a scatter of semi-derelict buildings and a steep scree of barren rocky waste, the signature of all ancient mines in these mountains. The mine's dilapidated state was a tragedy, for a place so important to Britain during the two world wars and the Korean War in the early 1950s. The mine had produced vital supplies of tungsten – the metal used in armour-piercing ammunition and high-quality steel – but like a homeless veteran, ragged and forgotten, it now seemed an embarrassment to the authorities. The last miners were laid off in 1981, some years after our trip, and with a total disregard for the tiny mine's industrial heritage, the whole site was levelled soon after my last visit.

At the time of this first visit, the ore deposit was still being worked, so we parked well away on a patch of short-cropped grass near the river. This time, there was a chance that the miners might object to visitors and we thought it best not to crowd them. The intrusion by a noisy band of claim-jumping greenhorns might prove to be too much. However, if they were watching us that day, I suspect that baffled amusement was more likely. The comical sight of three scruffy youths pulling metal dustbin lids out of the back of their vehicle, and then racing down to the river's edge, must have been at least a little entertaining.

It was late spring, the snow had gone from all but the most northerly facing crags and the air seemed amazingly clean. The sun had a brightness and warmth, almost forgotten during the long, dark months of winter. Arriving at the riverbank, we found the water deeper and less inviting than we had imagined. Recent rain had seeped through the blankets of peat bog that lined the valley bottom and stained the water a light brown. But the main thing that stopped us and caused doubt to enter our minds for the first time was where to start . . . We now knew that tiny flecks of natural gold from the quartz veins high above us had worked their way down into the river's sands and gravels – but where? In the college bar the evening before, it had all seemed so easy. I had watched cowboy films in which prospectors just washed gravel and then picked out the gold. But now, while we stood gazing at the river and the thousands of tons of sand and gravel scattered along the valley bottom, a reality far colder than the water itself washed over us.

Fairly quickly, we decided to give the main river a miss, as it looked too difficult. A tiny stream flowed down past the mine before joining the river, and this little beck seemed much more approachable. Besides which, we reasoned, it was more likely to have caught gold as it cut through the mountain exactly below the mineralized veins. The small and manageable banks of gravel also seemed less daunting.

Standing in the stream's small pools of bright water, we dipped the dustbin lids low and scooped in as much gravel and streambed sand with our hands as we could lift. There was an easy, natural rhythm to swirling everything around and letting the larger stones wash over the dustbin lid's rim, but no gold appeared. We tried again and again for over an hour, but not a solitary speck of gold revealed itself in any of our makeshift pans. We were mystified. Albeit improvised, we had gold-panning equipment and were in a gold-bearing stream – so why no gold?

My two companions decided to give up on panning and went back to the main river, saying they might have a quick swim instead. Slightly upstream there was a fabulous place where the river had worn a plate of hard rock into a long chute that plunged down into a deep pool. For a moment I thought about joining them. But I remembered holding those paperweights: I had cupped gold fragments from this mine in my hands. Somewhere close, possibly right under my feet, lay dust or flakes and maybe even little nuggets, and I wanted to find some.

Working alone felt easier, as I could focus on my washing technique and the stream around me. When small clouds of muddy silt washed from my pan, tiny fish approached, perhaps hoping some grub or worm would float down to them. A pair of dippers went past and totally ignored me – beautiful chocolate-brown birds with a white breast. A little while later, a small group of the native Herdwick sheep wandered down to drink or watch me, I wasn't sure which. This was so very different from the hard, dark and dangerous underground world of mineral collecting – bucolic and safe, with sunshine, fresh air and a host of welcome visitors.

I worked steadily for another hour or so, enjoying the rhythm and peace of it all. I found that I was getting more heavy stones left in my pan as my washing technique improved, but still no gold. Then something rather wonderful happened. A ring ouzel appeared and sat flicking its tail on a large rock just upstream of me. This blackbird-like thrush, with its white bib and desolate song that has none of a blackbird's rich melody, makes its home in the mountains. I had never seen one before, nor have I since, which is surprising given how much time I've spent in similar places. Perhaps the American mink that escaped, or were released, from fur farms into the countryside now kill them.

The magical bird flew off, and I looked up to see a young woman and child approaching. They were weaving their way down through the tangled clumps of last year's dead bracken; this year's lime-green fronds were just starting to uncoil. They watched without comment for a minute or so; then the woman settled down and started talking to me. Sitting in a long, loose dress with her knees pulled up and her arms wrapped around her boy, she told me how much she liked this place and how good it was to bring her son here. After avoiding the obvious question for a few minutes, she finally asked me what on earth I was doing. I had been ready to be defensive, but there was a gentleness to her and no hint of mockery. So, while feeling that I was giving away a great secret akin to the treasure of the Sierra Madre, I told her all about the mine and the gold. And how I was sure that gold was in this stream somewhere, and why I had chosen to use a dustbin lid as a gold pan. She stayed awhile, watching quietly, and then took her child and wandered off. Later, when I had finished and went up to my rucksack, I found that she had left me a tiny gold star taken from the bracelet she was wearing. There was also a short note on a scrap of torn cardboard: 'Now you have gold!'

And indeed I had. Already I loved this gold prospecting. I felt energized by the optimism of that first day, the rough and tumble of it all and the quiet time. I was enchanted by feeling at one with the stream itself, and with my visitors – the dippers and ring ouzel, the inquisitive Herdwicks and the quiet young woman and her child. I felt that a door had just opened for me. I liked nestling into the streamside with its ferns and cropped grassy bank, with boulders splashed white with the dippers' droppings, and my absurd gold pan and water-filled wellies – I felt at home. I was hunting without killing, and it didn't matter to me that I had failed to find even the tiniest speck of gold.

On the way home, I sat quietly in the back as the minibus bumped along down the valley and then away eastwards, towards the sprawling college. I wanted to think. I had a growing sense of a new purpose in life; a golden seed was stirring in the earth of my mind. I knew already that my passion for collecting minerals had been eclipsed by this elusive yellow metal. I marvelled that 'gold fever' was so easily caught. I took out the small gold star and studied it closely. Then looked at the scrap of cardboard with its all-too-brief note, and sighed. Again, I had failed to exchange details and wished that I had asked for her name.

3

FIRST GOLD

'You will be thrilled, and there is no other thrill to
compare with it, when you find gold glittering in your pan.'

—Lois de Lorenzo, *Gold Fever and the Art of Panning
and Sluicing*

During the weeks that followed the extraordinary meeting with
the gold prospector and my enchantment with the precious
metal, my studies suffered and I came second to last in my final-
year exams – something I was not happy about. Nevertheless,
the siren call of gold held me in a glittering dream, longing for
the end of term and the chance to go prospecting again. But this
time it would be different, I promised myself: I would be in a river
absolutely full of gold, *Bonanza*-rich. And the dustbin lid would
stay at home, serving only its designed purpose, for I would be
properly equipped with a real gold pan!

I recalled how the first paperweight that had been gently taken
down from the huge Welsh dresser contained, appropriately,
Welsh gold – some bright grains and a small, rough nugget. The
prospector had found them in the mountains of Snowdonia and
surprised me by describing exactly where. His directions seemed
Tolkienesque: to go to Dolgellau, a market town set back from a

large sandy estuary and then follow the main river far upstream. A narrow single-track road would lead me through a dark forest of massive conifers and I should continue along it as the river climbed up into ancient oak woodland. Here, a second river joined the main flow and both plunged over high cliffs. On the narrow isthmus, just below the waterfalls and before the two rivers converge, there was an abandoned gold mine. He told me that his gold had been found exactly below those old mine buildings. While this might sound fanciful, his directions turned out to be true and would not be the only time an incredible story led me to find gold.

Although I had very little money, I already had some skill in bushcraft and could live frugally. My plan was to hitch-hike to Snowdonia and then to live rough in the oak woods for as long as my food lasted. I rather liked hitch-hiking and enjoyed the serendipity of a series of random encounters that sooner or later would bring me to my desired destination. Also, the people who stopped to give me a lift had mostly turned out to be interesting and generous. So, after the long trips around Iceland and across Norway, I thought that getting over to Wales would be a piece of cake and I hoped to arrive there later the same day.

The morning went well and I travelled over England easily, being given long lifts by cheerful people. But in the early afternoon I crossed the border into Wales, and it started to rain. Hitch-hiking became hopeless, as even the kind people who usually offered lifts didn't want a wet traveller and his sodden pack in the car. As dusk fell I gave up and looked for a safe place to sleep overnight.

I had noticed an empty road worker's hut propped up on pallets. While the door was securely locked, I reasoned that I could sleep comfortably out of the rain underneath the hut itself. A thousand mosquitoes had had the same idea. It was a wretched night, made worse by the steady rain finally forming a small stream that ran through my rough bed.

The next morning dawned bright. I was cheered by the promise of a lovely day and crawled out, hoping to dry off quickly in the early sun. I had received a few bites on my face during the night and the one on my eyelid had swollen so much that the eye was half-closed. I made my way back to the road and resumed trying to hitch a ride. A couple of cars slowed as if to stop and then, when close, sped off again. Initially, I put this down to a playful mischief on the part of the drivers. But then I realized that it was more likely to be because I looked like a smallpox victim – well, chickenpox at least. I was wondering how to deal with this when I met a tall, cheerful young Dutchman who was also hitch-hiking to North Wales. We walked and talked together for a couple of hours, and having had no joy at getting a lift, decided to stop in a roadside café for a late breakfast.

I like Dutch people and have generally found them to be great optimists and, helpfully, to be excellent English speakers – this man was both. He was, however, louder than the dozen or so other customers having breakfast. This hardly mattered as we chatted away, until I asked him what he did for a living.

'My father and I fuck hamsters,' he said breezily.

I froze, stunned with embarrassment and the café fell silent. I stared at him and whispered, 'You don't, really you don't!', my mind reeling in an attempt to make sense of his highly unlikely statement.

'Yes, we do!' he protested.

Suddenly I understood, and desperate for him not to repeat his earlier assertion, I urged, 'Breed! You *breed* hamsters!'

He shrugged. 'It's the same thing.'

I tried to explain that it most certainly was not and hurried to finish my breakfast. I needed to get away from the room full of people who were now quietly listening for the next stunning confession from the bedraggled, spotty youth with a droopy eye, or his perverted friend.

Outside, we parted and I continued to make my way across Wales, content to be alone. I had learned to speak Welsh as a boy, but progress was slow as by now I had forgotten how, and I couldn't pronounce the name of the village I was trying to get to – Ganllwyd. Being able to say where you want to go is a basic need when hitch-hiking. But the fates were kind and by nightfall I had muddled my way to the southern edge of Snowdonia and made a much more comfortable camp beside a river within a grove of enormous western red cedars.

The Afon Mawddach was even more beautiful than the Lakeland prospector had said it was. Alongside this mighty river, a narrow, metalled road threaded an almost parallel course up into the valley. As I walked along it, I noticed that the road's edges were crumbling, as if nature was anxious to reclaim this place. In no hurry, I dawdled, enjoying the patterns of ever-changing light. The road ran through patches of brilliant sunlight, then plunged into deep shadow beneath huge conifers – pines, more cedars, and European and Douglas firs. The steep-sided valley had provided the shelter that these wonderful trees needed to reach such a great size.

The cool forest smelled of morning at first, earthy as the damp ground and thick layer of fallen conifer needles scented the air. Then, as the sun rose higher and its early summer strength bore down upon the upper canopy, the trees' foliage released the perfumes of honey-sweet resin. These filtered down to me on warm drafts of air through the tangled branches. Pleasing and evocative – I was reminded of a family holiday in southern France, camping on a beach among umbrella pines.

The silent road weaved its way upstream, while alongside it, the noisy river was largely hidden from view by thick rhododendron bushes. Not able to see it as I walked, I could nevertheless hear the many sounds of moving water; an aquatic symphony, slowly changing as I passed rapids and small waterfalls. When the might of the river was hushed as it moved sluggishly across deep stretches, it seemed that the full orchestra had paused for a soloist to perform. Only then could I hear the high trilling notes of a tiny rivulet as it bubbled and splashed down to join the main current – a virtuoso pianist in the never-ending concert. At last, sorry to break the musical spell but frustrated at not being able to see what I was hearing, I left the road to push through the bushes and look.

Way downstream, this river was much like any other. It meandered through rich grassy meadows grazed by tail-flicking cattle lazily looking for shade. A broad expanse of calm water, its surface was scuffed with breeze-ripples and edged abruptly with a thin line of water-worn boulders and yellow flag iris. Beyond this colourful margin the acres of verdant, flower-rich pasture began. But up here in the forest, the young river was vibrant and cut through the tree-covered mountainside with all the energy of an athletic 20-year-old.

When I'd struggled through the dense tangle of rhododendrons, I came out onto a small beach. A pair of goosander ducks panicked and burst from the water. Flying low, they quickly disappeared up through a gorge. Here before me, the whole river was forced through a narrow rocky chute and roared as it plunged in a single thick column into a deep, dark pool. There was no spray from this waterfall, but a Jacuzzi-like mass of bubbles rose in a boiling arc to burst quickly on the water's glassy surface. A recent flood had left a pile of pebbles on the downstream edge of the pool, forming a narrow, curved beach. High above me on the far side behind some boulders, the same storm had lifted and jammed three enormous logs and a mass of small branches. Unlike the goosander, clouds of zigzagging gnats ignored me completely and continued their wild dance in the patches of sunlight. Below the pool the river spread to its full width, and now shallow, the whole surface was corrugated as it passed over a long bed of cobbles and away out of view. I loved this place. I stood silently, drinking in its freshness, intoxicated by the sheer energy – raw nature, absolutely alive and visceral. It was timeless, untouched, with no trace of human activity. And somewhere, deep in the dark, down below this cacophony of beauty, was gold.

But this was not the place where my Lakeland prospector guide had successfully worked. I knew that I had to push on upriver and find the fabulous waterfalls he had so carefully described. I could still see him talking quietly in the first light of morning, his hands slowly turning the Welsh gold paperweight as he remembered his own time here.

Although I had not yet read Thoreau's *Walden*, nor Johnson's *Rasselas*, and the more cheerful aspects of Stoicism were still unknown to me, I had an instinctive understanding of what it meant to have 'enough' – to be content with having only what is actually needed. My light pack was a testament to this empathy with minimalism, and I swung it back up on my shoulder to do battle once more with the rhododendrons and continue upriver.

Back on the road, I scuffed along, thoroughly enjoying myself, and mused on why I liked Wales so much. I decided that it was because half of my childhood had been spent in South Wales – in the Rhondda valley, the Vale of Glamorgan and the far west of Pembrokeshire. To me the soft Welsh accent was home, a now subliminal comfort born of blissful years growing up there. Carefree days spent exploring woodlands and birdwatching with my friend Meurig, or up on the grassy hillsides looking for a landslip crevasse to build a den in. From our homes in the small town of Pencoed, we boys could cycle all the way to a castle by the sea at Ogmore. Then cross the river on ancient stepping stones to the vast sand dunes beyond to play French foreign legion. Children were so free back in the 1960s. The risks were mostly the same as they are today, but the perception was different.

Now high in the Mawddach valley, I passed a row of abandoned cottages, and the road surface changed, and became a potholed gravel track that cut into the slope. The trees were different too. The massive shady conifers from the lower sheltered slopes had been replaced, and the track now passed beneath the dappled light of oak woodland. These small, heavily branched old trees clung to the steep hillside, some so covered in moss that it seemed as if they had grown green fur. High up, delicate ferns grew in the trees' forks and along large horizontal branches, forming a curious silhouette – like a series of dainty, narrow roof gardens. Dun-coloured clusters of lichens had grown thick in the clean air, obscuring the bark-like patches of camouflage. On the occasional birch, tangled strings of usnea lichens hung like unwashed scraps of an old man's beard. To me, the whiskers of usnea always seem pagan, like a tree-worshipping druid's offerings, and are the signature totem of wild places.

The newly unfurled oak leaves were still olive green, not yet casting as much shade as they would in full summer. I was delighted to see that beneath these trees lay a carpet of blueberries. Although the fruit wouldn't ripen during my stay, it was good to see them anyway. They had been a staple food during my trip to Norway, along with the small trout I had caught in roadside streams.

From somewhere above the track, a large brown bird took off and flapped slowly, then glided away skilfully between the trees – *a buzzard*, I thought. Relieved that the predator had gone, a wood warbler began its curious song. Like a glass marble being dropped from height onto a hard tiled floor, each note is separate and clear at first, but then they quickly speed up and blur together before dying away. There were few rhododendrons among the oak woodland, allowing me clear views of the auspicious, gold-bearing river below. The track bore away and rose higher onto the shoulder of the hillside, then curved to the right and arrived at a bridge.

I stopped; this was unexpected, it was barely a crossing point. Steel beams had been laid across a deep gorge and narrow iron sheets had been welded onto them, making two parallel tracks that were spaced for the wheels of a vehicle. Between the tracks, expanded steel mesh filled the gap, but had come loose in places where the weld had broken. A single scaffold pole served as a handrail on either side. The crossing over the ravine was like some final test: *should you be here? This place is only for the strong – or at least, only for those with no fear of heights.* Annoyingly, my unease wasn't assuaged by the fact that this unique bridge was obviously built for vehicles and could clearly take my weight. The problem was that I could see straight through the steel mesh, right down to the jumble of sharp rocks far below. Fear is both a safety mechanism and a curious thing, as it is often completely irrational. I stared at the stony track on the far side, gripped the handrail and slowly shuffled across.

Much relieved to be back on firm ground, I looked up at the waterfall at the head of this gorge. It was white and delicate, falling in long cascades like a bridal train. Masses of spray filled the air as the water tumbled down a steep cliff. A small rainbow had formed in the drifting mist – finally, I was here!

The Eldorado I had trekked so far to find was now beneath my feet. I set off quickly to look for the other great waterfall that I had been told about. And suddenly there it was, like the muscular rugby-playing groom. This fall was formidable, at least four times bigger than the first one. It fell as one solid curtain of glassy water, roaring as it plunged into the vast pool below.

Like the remains of an ancient castle, a group of long-abandoned mine buildings sat high above the waterfall's plunge pool. Stone-walled but roofless, they had been patched some time ago with sheets of corrugated iron. A narrow watercourse, a leat, had been constructed to bring water down from above the falls and power an enormous water wheel (now missing). This clutter of derelict buildings was the sad, skeletal remains of the once mighty Gwynfynydd gold mine.

Unlike my brief trip to pan for gold with a dustbin lid beside the Carrock mine in Mosedale, I had done my research this time. I had learned that in the mid-19th century, the world enjoyed one stupendous gold rush after another. It mattered not the hardships faced, nor the great distances – thousands flocked to California, Australia, South Africa and New Zealand. Amid the hubbub, when the whole world was mad with gold fever, the Welsh struck gold too. In 1862 miners working lead in this valley found their crushing equipment had become coated with gold. Within a few years there were 18 gold mines operating in southern Snowdonia. The amount of gold produced was modest at about 100,000 ounces a year, just over 11 bucketfuls, but it was pleasingly home-grown and was soon a favourite of Queen Victoria herself.

By the time I had finished exploring the peninsula between the two rivers, it was getting late, and I needed to make camp. I had expected there to be other people in such a strikingly beautiful place, but in fact I had seen nobody else all day. I chose a bushy gap between two mounds of dirt to set up a simple shelter. Here, I pitched a dull-green, rectangular tarpaulin across a length of twine and made up my bed – a thin foam mat beneath an old army sleeping bag.

That first night was testing. While blissful in the twilight of dusk, the camp's dynamic changed once it was dark and a fresh breeze had blown up. The tarpaulin was small and open at both ends, so that my feet and head were barely beneath it. Lying in the total darkness, I could not shake the awareness that I was very far from the comfort and safety of Ganllwyd, the nearest village. I imagined this haven with windows lit and light spilling out onto the road, friends chatting and laughing as they walked home from a pub, and I felt lonely. The ominous night touched my feet and crowded behind my head – *something could easily grab me*, I thought. I reasoned that if my feet were seized, I could kick and repel whatever it was, but my head was another matter.

It is difficult to defend yourself when attacked from behind. This whole unsettling line of thought was not helped as the rising wind began to rattle some of the corrugated iron on the old buildings. It sounded much like an old mine door was being forced open, but by what? Folklore is rich with tales of the creatures that dwell in the depths of abandoned mines . . . Eventually, exhausted from my long day, I eased into sleep. And the imagined nocturnal beings that came up from within the mine chose to leave me in peace.

I was blessed with a fine summer's morning, dry and bright. I didn't know if anybody would have a problem with my camp, so I opted to keep a low profile. As there is nothing like a campfire to give your position away, I got up at dawn to boil enough water for the day and make my bread, so that I could put out the small stick fire before it attracted any attention. I brought the river water up to a rolling boil three times: I had been taught in Scouts that this would purify it. I then made two loaves with self-raising flour and baked them in the pot in which I had just purified my water. One loaf was savoury and studded with scraps of bacon that had been twisted around sticks and set beside the fire to cook. The second was sweetened with a little brown sugar and raisins. Beyond these simple rations, I had chocolate, apples, peanut butter, cheese, small tubes of condensed milk, instant coffee and powdered milk. The condensed milk was not for the coffee, but to go with the peanut butter – a wonderful high energy hit I had learned to use while mid-winter camping.

I think that my mother would have liked my meagre camp. She had raised my brother and me to be as independent as possible, as fast as possible. Her father had died when she was 16 years old, and this monumental loss devastated her. Just as she was beginning to know this fine man, he was gone, leaving her and her mother alone and adrift. Should history repeat itself, she was determined that we boys would be better equipped for life.

With the day now unfolding and my cooking fire safely doused, I sat down to read a small yellow book, *Gold Fever and the Art of Panning and Sluicing*. This wonderful little guide was written by Lois de Lorenzo, a woman from Minnesota who had spent years gold hunting with her husband and three sons, and it held all the information I needed. While it had somehow seemed inappropriate to read the book at home, now I was camped in the goldfields I could savour every word.

This all happened in the late 1970s, when knowledge was precious and not always available. The time before the internet was so very different from now – like the age of horse transport before the motor car. Although I had been able to find plenty of information on the history of this area, geologically known as the Dolgellau gold belt, I hadn't at first been able to find anything helpful on how to actually pan for gold; not even my library could help. I did, however, learn that massive amounts of gold had been discovered at Sutter Creek in California and reasoned that there must be a touristy bookshop there. I sent a letter with ten dollars enclosed asking for any information, addressed simply to: The Bookshop, Sutter Creek, Sacramento, California, USA. Rather like some desperate soul putting a message in a bottle and hurling it out to sea, I didn't really expect a reply. But to my delight, two small books arrived three weeks later, the better of the two being de Lorenzo's book, *Gold Fever*.

My pan had also been difficult to find. There was no market for gold pans in England. I had traipsed from shop to shop in the small city of Norwich, feeling increasingly self-conscious as I asked for one. The question invariably then needed a lengthy explanation of what a 'gold pan' actually is. And each time the shopkeeper's expression quickly changed from polite curiosity to open amusement. To help them understand what I was looking for, I mentioned that cowboys used them in films. But I think that instead of being helpful, this led them to believe that they were dealing with a simpleton with a penchant for westerns.

In a small gift shop on a narrow, cobbled street, the solemn man behind the till unexpectedly answered, 'And how many would you like?' Thinking that I was being lined up for yet more gentle ridicule, I decided to brazen it out and boldly asked for two. He nodded and still po-faced disappeared out the back of the shop, shortly to return with two steel 12-in gold pans. My astonished face must have betrayed my incredulity, and he burst out laughing. He explained that he had bought a stack of pans back in the early 1960s, when there was a fashion for outlandish presents. And he hadn't sold one in more than a decade.

I finished reading the little yellow book and gathered together a small trowel, one of my Norwich gold pans and a pair of tweezers to pick out any gold nuggets I found. The peninsula I was camped on was shaped like a huge slice of cake, with each cut side falling steeply to a river. At the apex, an animal track led down to where the two rivers met. The book said that gravel deposits at such confluences could be very gold rich!

While I didn't doubt the book on this point, it seemed that my confluence was the exception to the rule. I dug little test holes and washed each gravel sample gently at the river's edge, while searching attentively for a nugget – but none appeared. The day passed and finally I drifted back up to my camp, puzzled by this failure. I slept unexpectedly well and had an easy second night. No ghouls threatened, as I was now comfortable here and felt I belonged in this hallowed place. The next day, I tried other likely places that the book had assured me would have gold, but still no nuggets.

There is a therapeutic peacefulness in gold panning. Long hours of quiet repetitive work with the promise of a prize. It is quintessential slow living. Nothing much happens for several hours, but the time passes quickly and pleasantly enough. Grey wagtails were nesting in a small cliff on the far bank, and between washing pans I would watch them feeding their young. Dippers went past, pausing on their favourite white-splashed rocks before noticing me and moving on. I saw the shadows of trout, their bodies waving slowly in the current like tresses of aquatic weed, always in the upstream side of a pool. But I set no lines to catch them. Looking back, I am not sure why now – I had caught a great many in Norway. I think that I was so focused on finding gold, I had no time to fish. A few years later, I found a way to catch small trout by setting my gold pan as a trap. Something I have never seen anybody else do!

The third day of panning and prospecting came and went much like the first two – pleasant but barren. I had now settled into a camp routine of gathering very small dead sticks in the evening, ready for my domestic morning of boiling water and baking bread. My covert fires needed to be fed very dry twigs to be smokeless. My first choice was thin alder, ash or hazel, if I could find them. The best fuel of all were those sticks brought down with a flood and left high and dry up on the bank. The violence of the river in spate had often stripped the bark off, which allowed them to dry more quickly. I avoided oak and birch, which have a strong-scented, tangy smoke – like kippers. It is usually the whiff of woodsmoke that gives away a fire's location, not the light of the flames. After a million years of evolving with fire, humans can pick up the slightest hint of woodsmoke hanging in the air.

I had an interesting lesson in field craft one night, when my camp was visited by an actual nocturnal being. I was woken in the small hours by urgent rustling in my food bag and at first thought it must be some trick of the wind. But as I focused, it was definitely an animal noise. I reached for the pencil-thin torch I carried and lit up the bag. The rustling stopped. It is a beginner's error to be casual about food storage, but I thought that I had taken reasonable precautions. My supplies were in a plastic bag that was hanging from the tarpaulin's ridge line by a short length of thin twine. Suddenly, a tiny face appeared in the beam and a small dark mouse looked down at me. In less than two seconds it had made its escape plan and leaped out, all four legs spread apart like a free-fall parachutist. It landed easily and fled away into the darkness.

How the mouse had got into the food bag was a wonder. It must have climbed under the tarpaulin along the horizontal ridge line upside down, and then down the vertical twine and into the bag. But more impressive was how it had known the food was there, before it made the incredible climb. It took such a risk, having to creep past a sleeping giant to get at the suspended treasure. And the elegance of its escape, most impressive. That mouse was something else, the bravest animal I have ever met.

I may have learned a good lesson on safe food storage from the mouse, but I had fortunately improved upon the badger's half-hearted toilet habits. To deal with the more unpleasant part of wild camping, I had dug a small hole to use as a latrine, as badgers do. But then I put a match to the used toilet paper, as Scoutmasters do and badgers do not. And while badgers leave their toilet holes open, I put a large flat rock over the hole when not in use, to hide it and prevent the unpleasantness of accidentally stepping into it. The loo paper was certainly a luxury, but light to carry and took up little room in my pack. I had never found that leaves were any good – that's a myth. If paper hadn't been an option, I would have chosen small rounded pebbles, but only those worn very smooth! Sphagnum moss works as a wet wipe if that is felt necessary.

I brushed my teeth by the river using only a pea-sized blob of toothpaste, then spat this out under a rock high up on the bank, so that it did not enter the waterway until a flood – I was keen not to pollute this pristine water. I didn't wash as such, but would take a break to swim around midday or whenever it was warm enough, so that there was the time and warmth to dry and fully recover from the chilly river – I had no wish to go to bed cold. I have found that the slightly acidic water in most upland areas does a great job of cleaning my skin and hair. My clothes didn't seem to get dirty, not to my nose anyway.

On the fifth day, I was resigned to spending more pleasant hours in the fruitless search. I knew that in most endeavours, perseverance is the key to success. While there is a time to quit, most people quit too early. That said, there is the constant need to be aware of the subtle difference between dogged determination and stubborn stupidity. Yet I already knew there was gold here . . . I had held that paperweight and gazed at the scatter of bright gold flakes, suspended in the solid resin – and those pieces had been found somewhere close by. And if further encouragement were necessary, I was working just below the ruins of a large abandoned gold mine.

In the early afternoon I was scraping a patch of iron-stained sand out of a pocket in fractured bedrock. I had long since given up bringing the nugget tweezers to the river, and was now using my eating spoon to clean out the little holes that were too small for my trowel.

A piece of rock about the size of a house brick suddenly broke away, and I froze. A speck of intense brightness lay nestled in a thin bed of fine dark sand. It actually shone, as if a golden light had been turned on within it, the tiniest yellow star in a drab night sky of dirt. I gazed down, mesmerized by this precious thing, so small, so bright. Little more than a flattened poppy seed, yet so powerful. I was overwhelmed by a quiet sense of gratitude. It was as if the river had decided to reward all my hours of clumsy effort. Unlike the characters in cowboy films, I didn't shout 'Yee-ha!' nor leap about and feel the need to dance. Quite the opposite. Just to be there with the glowing marvel was enough, as with a newborn baby.

Interestingly, my reaction would be the same many years later, when I found a pocket of treasure while diving on a shipwreck. I felt totally at peace, a silent reverence, completely absorbed in the majesty of the moment. And I'm not the only one who reacts like this. I once taught a man to use a pan who became quite tearful over a speck of gold I could hardly see. He had spent a small fortune on specialist clothing and prospecting equipment, but hadn't found a single speck of gold after eight months of trying: this modest success meant the world to him.

I did have one terrible moment of doubt: could this be something else – the brassy yellow pyrite known as fool's gold? Was this a deceit, some malicious mineral fragment catching the light and playing a spiteful joke on me? But the yellow book had reassuringly mentioned an old saying in gold prospecting: 'If you *think* it's gold, it isn't. You'll *know* it is.' This truism held. I may have had an attack of the collywobbles, but I knew that this piece, my first-ever find, was gold.

I now wondered how to pick it up; the spoon was far too clumsy an implement and I had left the tweezers at the camp. It was agonizing having to hurry all the way back up the peninsula to get them, but when I returned the little darling was still there, unmoved. It had waited perhaps a thousand years for me to find it, and was content. I moved my gold pan close to the rock as I lifted the little flake up, in case I dropped it. I then placed the glowing speck very carefully in my hand. It seemed elemental, venerable and radiated a unique purity. The tiny piece of natural gold that I held was noble – a heavy element that had formed during a supernovae event or the collision of neutron stars, and which was older than planet Earth itself. And now, after unimaginable time and galactic chaos, here it was, lying peacefully in the palm of my hand.

Over the next four days, I gathered the trapped sand from every inch of that rock and recovered another seven pieces of gold. My food supplies were running low, and I'd found what I had come so far to look for, so my thoughts turned to home. I lit a fire to have one last meal before leaving and was startled to see a young man and woman approaching me. They seemed friendly enough as I babbled a greeting and tried to explain what I was doing; then I urged them to have coffee with me. As I crawled under the tarpaulin to reach my pack, I heard the woman whisper, 'Why is he so friendly?' and the man's hushed reply: 'If you had been up here alone for nine days, you'd be friendly too!'

The journey back to England was a blur – euphoric, I must have travelled in a daze. Once home, my parents looked on expectantly as I opened my pack and took out the finger-sized plastic tube that my gold was stored in. They stared at it blankly, as at first it seemed completely empty but for a little water. When I finally got them to see the tiny cluster of rough golden specks, they were not impressed. My mother was the first to speak: 'Is that it?'

They must have thought that I had a sack full of gold to be so excited, but the few glinting grains were enough for me. Hobbit-like, I had travelled to far-off mountains and rough-camped beside spectacular waterfalls and the crumbling walls of an abandoned mine – and, in the sparkling waters beneath, I had found my first gold.

During the pleasant years that followed this first trip, I visited the river many times. On one amazing day I found over an ounce of gold, a heap the size of a grape, and in a spot I must have walked over 50 times when going back and forth to my camp. It takes time to understand where the gold goes during the thundering floods that shatter gold-bearing rocks and free the precious metal. It also takes patience to listen to the river and to learn to sense where the gold is in a way that is almost akin to dowsing. After a while, I began to find that the first place that caught my eye often had the best gold. This could not have been a subliminal summary of practical experience in the early years, as I hardly had any.

Also, on the visits that followed I began to meet other people – river wardens and, occasionally, other gold panners. The officials seemed amused by my simple pan, trowel and infectious enthusiasm – they asked me to stay clear of the gravel beds used by breeding salmon and sea trout and wished me well in my quest. At this time, there were only a handful of people who panned for natural gold in Britain. They were a slightly eccentric community of loners, each a fully rounded character with his or her own story. I liked these people – who included Mike and the ever-cheerful Colleen, Geraint and Fran who ran a café, Eric the shopkeeper, strong-as-an-ox forester Meirion and Les who used a motorized sluice with the water authority's blessing. Besides farmers and labourers, there was Colin the rock musician, Trevor the features editor of a national newspaper, and Glyn and Janet who once found a 5-g wedding-ring-sized nugget in a crevice that I hadn't cleaned out properly, which taught me a major lesson!

And then there was Ken Williamson. A total enigma and by some margin the most mysterious of them all, he looked rough and was rough, yet when I visited him at the cottage he rented with his wife, Denise, she showed me the personal letters of thanks he had received from the British royal family. He once dropped a disc of solid Welsh gold into my hand and grinned, then said, 'You're the second person on Earth to hold the gold for the next royal wedding.' It seemed he had worked in Africa too, doing shady stuff for the Foreign Office.

I began to understand that it isn't the destination that is important in life, nor even perhaps the journey itself, but the people I would meet along the way. Of course, finding gold and treasure were important to me, but only as a theme – an inspiration, to guide me away from idleness and the ordinary. If procrastination is the thief of time, then mediocrity is the thief of life. I find that I only remember the very good and the very bad things that have happened to me – and in gold prospecting both are plentiful.

My store of Welsh river gold slowly increased, and I was almost content. But a nagging idea began to form in my mind. If this yield of gold was possible in a well-known and easy-to-get-to place, what might be found in a faraway unknown goldfield? I picked up snippets of rumours that gold had once been discovered high above the Arctic Circle in Finnish Lapland. *Ha!* I thought. *That's it!*

4

LAPLAND'S GOLD

'The most difficult thing is the decision to act.
The rest is merely tenacity.'

—Amelia Earhart, *The Fun of It*

As the plane circled Ivalo airport, I was surprised to see that the entire landscape was white. It was early June, almost the longest day of the year, and I hadn't expected 'the land of the midnight sun' to still be under a blanket of snow. From mid-May to mid-August the sun doesn't set in Lapland, but my dream of finding easy gold in the warmth of the far north's long summer days suddenly melted away: this was serious. I stared out of the plane's small window at the sparkling winter scene below, struggling to think how I would cope. This trip had been carefully planned and fondly imagined for a long time, and yet I had got it wrong. I resolved to adapt to this unwelcome reality: somehow, I would find gold in Lapland.

The plane drifted down and landed comfortably on a small airstrip, a tiny rectangle in the dazzlingly bright vastness of Lapland's gently rolling hills. The pilot then cheerfully announced how pleased he was to have found the runway, as his navigation system had failed a little while ago. Curiously, I felt good about this easy-going welcome to the far north. It seemed like a frontier: laconic, raw and unexpected. I imagined that only tough people could live up here and I wanted to meet them. My simple plan already felt like an adventure, and I hadn't even got off the plane yet.

Since finding my first gold by the waterfalls of that enchanting river in North Wales four years earlier, I had now panned in two other Welsh rivers and three in Scotland. My skill at washing gold-bearing gravel with a small steel pan was steadily improving. But even though I had found a little gold in each place, I was now plagued by the idea that wild gold might be much more plentiful, and easier to find, in a remote location. And Lapland's mighty Ivalojoki river seemed to fit the bill perfectly.

If such a thing is possible, this area could be described as the setting for the world's 'boutique' gold rush. To start with, by world gold rush standards, very little gold was actually found. At the peak of activity in 1871, there were 22 claims being worked by 491 miners who recovered and recorded almost 57kg of gold. It is believed that in addition to this official figure, a sizeable amount was hoarded and smuggled into Norway to avoid paying the gold tax. But even so, the gold found during the Californian, Australian and Yukon gold rushes was measured in tons.

Claims in Lapland at this time were expensive, so most miners were happy to be employed by one of the main claim owners and worked long, hard days through the brief summer. The Ivalojoki gold rush was short-lived. By 1878 there were only 59 miners working on 4 claims. From then on, the diggings waxed and waned. Thirty years after the first gold was discovered in Lapland, only 600kg had been wrestled from the ground – and recorded.

The physical amount of recovered gold may have been modest, but this glorious wilderness has a compelling and unique charm of its own. It is at once strange yet familiar. From the first day I arrived, I felt that I had known this place all of my life – although I had never been there before. Lapland is truly a very special place, the land of the midnight sun and northern lights, of dark forests and bright glittering gold, of vast reindeer herds and singular carnivores – a living Christmas card. And to top it all, this magical land is home to Santa Claus himself! The familiarity I felt was probably caused by having enjoyed English Christmases that were typically festooned with sentimental imagery of snow-covered Lapland. Every home I had known since childhood had been a shrine to these winter scenes, with Christmas cards depicting festive reindeer, Santas and snowy forests.

On that first visit to Finland, I was anxious to succeed in my quest to bring home a good sample of Lapland's gold. I had talked endlessly to family, friends and work colleagues about the planned trip, and now I had to make good on my heroic ramblings. But there was no greed; I knew I would be pleased to find even the tiniest amount of Santa's precious gold – just enough to shine at midnight. I hoped the small glass medicine bottle that I had brought with me in which to store any gold I found would rattle as I walked. Bell-like, a barely perceptible jingle, only heard by those who knew what it was.

My plan was to travel along the Arctic Highway from Ivalo to the tourist village of Tankavaara, where I could get day permits to pan for gold. In particular, I hoped to meet locals who could advise me on the challenging circular route I had in mind, as I intended to walk west along a dirt road for two days to reach the Ivalojoki river and then follow it downstream for a couple of weeks, wild camping and gold prospecting. The river flowed north before curving eastwards and would eventually lead me back to the Arctic Highway and, by helpful coincidence, Ivalo airport.

Now the bus was trundling south, never missing an opportunity to veer off onto side roads to pick up mail and people. We crossed a high treeless plateau, bleak tundra with lines of criss-crossed wooden snow barriers, the planks of which were sun-bleached grey, weather-worn and told of cruel blizzards. Many years later, during a winter visit, my friend Pirjo would stop the car here and show me my first northern lights. She pointed to two long whitish clouds that resembled aircraft vapour trails, glowing silently in the moonlight. They were nothing like the photographs of aurora borealis that I'd seen in books – great curtains of mysterious pale-green or red light. But I knew that Pirjo must be right as she was born up here, this was her home, and the lights were an everyday thing for her. I stared, confused and a little disappointed by this unimpressive reality, when the vapour trails suddenly started moving, swaying slowly like astral snakes and then vanished. Wow! I'd thought. No cloud did that.

Today, the bus crept steadily on and descended through the treeline, where what had been the occasional stunted spruce tree was now joined by pine, birch and willow. For someone like me, from small and heavily populated England, the vastness of this forest was hard to grasp. I imagined the ominous Russian border to the east, fortified for the Cold War and at times only 23 miles from the road. The pristine forest before me ignored all borders and continued almost unbroken for 4,000 miles right across Russian USSR – only ending by the Bering Sea, just across from Alaska.

Beneath the old trees, thick dark-green branches hung from snow-broken spruce to form natural shelters. There could be wolves out there. Comfortable and familiar as this bus was, the land just beyond my window was untamed and wild. The wolf, the bear, the lynx, the wolverine – animals long gone from England's woodlands – shared this forest with the people and the reindeer. Watching the ancient forest drift steadily past, it occurred to me that I would soon be out among it all in a small tent. I wondered when Lapland had had its last wolf attack . . .

Unhelpfully, I had recently read of a hiker in Alaska who had gone missing. They found his feet untouched in his neatly laced-up boots, while everything above his ankles had been chewed to the bone. *But that was an attack by a grizzly bear,* I thought, *and they don't have those up here, and we're too far south for polar bears.* While trying to rationally consider which large carnivores I might meet during the hike, the relative safety of camping by a Welsh or Scottish river to pan gold was starting to seem particularly attractive.

I distracted myself by talking to the neatly dressed man seated behind me. He turned out to be a Finnair pilot who was also travelling to Tankavaara. He mentioned that he had a shelter near the village and generously said I could stay there too – at least until the melting snow had gone, when I could pitch my tent. Feeling blessed at this good fortune, I agreed.

It was early evening when the bus eventually pulled off the main road and into Tankavaara. Shouldering my rucksack, I prepared to follow the pilot out to his shelter, yet found myself gazing wistfully at the wonderfully inviting café. Music spilled out of the large wooden building, each of its planks and logs darkened silver-grey with age. In the entrance porch a tall man with long grey hair and a fine beard smiled, nodded a greeting at me, picked up a broom and began to sweep the wide steps. Dressed in a dark suit with an immaculate striped waistcoat, he worked slowly and seemed like a ghost from a past age. He even wore a traditional pocket watch from a thick gold chain, each link of which was studded with butter-yellow gold nuggets.

I stopped to breathe in this moment like food for the soul: the cold, damp air, my boots squeaking in the slushy snow and the perfectly dressed man with a broom quietly at his chores. My whole body sighed and relaxed: 'Finally, I'm in Lapland's goldfield! And the old-timer over there is the proof.'

The pilot glanced at me curiously and motioned for me to hurry up and follow him back across the Arctic Highway, westwards out into the forest. By now, I had imagined that this quiet man's natural modesty was at play and the 'shelter' he was taking me to was actually a wonderful old cabin. I had once had Christmas with an Italian family who said I could stay with them at their 'cottage' in the mountains, which turned out to be a five-storey chateau.

I followed the pilot for about 20 minutes before he cheerfully pointed across a small clearing, where half a dozen rough planks were tied loosely to a few sloping poles. Modest he might be, but I felt the term 'shelter' had rather exaggerated the protection that his property offered.

As we got closer, I could see that this wooden lean-to covered a deep mattress of spruce boughs, all carefully aligned for comfort with the cut sticks pointing down. In front of the shelter, a circle of blackened rocks and a long cooking pole served as the kitchen. It wasn't what I had expected, but already I liked it. His hideaway shelter was earthy, ramshackle and real – completely appropriate in a goldfield. And clearly, he loved this place.

While unpacking his belongings, he kept up light-hearted conversation in perfect English, yet I sensed a sadness in him. Something upsetting had happened in his life and this place was his refuge, a haven in which to reflect and refresh. This insight led me to like his camp even more, and I felt honoured to have been invited to stay.

Before sleep overtook me that evening, I watched the thin blue smoke drift over us from the last of the smouldering pine-log fire. Despite being nearly midnight, shafts of bright sunlight blazed through gaps in the shelter's patchy roof. The combination was captivating. The white, laser-like sunbeams seared through silent, swirling eddies of the sweet-scented cerulean smoke. Through half-closed eyes, I gazed up at this mesmerizing and soporific display. A tiny 'northern lights' for me alone – aurora minimis!

The mattress was indeed well made, and I slept deeply. When I awoke the pilot was gone, and so was the snow. My wristwatch said that it was morning, although the word loses all meaning in a place of perpetual daylight. Unable to say goodbye and thank my new friend, I packed up and headed back through the damp forest and across the road to the café.

Tankavaara far exceeded my expectations. In a way it wasn't a tourist village at all, but more like someone's home that had grown over time into an eclectic collection of buildings and passions. The 'café' turned out to be a fine restaurant with eight dishes on offer, seven of which were reindeer. The eighth was salmon soup, and I had that. It was a thick and creamy chowder and unexpectedly wonderful. The rose-pink wild fish was blended with potato, onion and slivers of the squeaky Lappish cheese, Leipäjuusto – all delicately flavoured with dill.

I discovered that the neat man with the gold watch was the owner, Kauko. He loved trains and had built a railway around his gold claim, while his partner, Inkeri, was fond of teddy bears and had built a museum to house her collection. There were old cabins to rent, real shops and a bar among facades of 19th-century gold rush buildings. A huge gold-pan-shaped construction held a museum of all the world's great gold rushes. Snowmobiles and mining equipment sat side by side, and I couldn't tell if they were parked by the people who lived here or were exhibits on show for the tourists.

It was still early, and the crowds of expected visitors hadn't yet arrived, so Kauko had a little time to talk with me. As a young man, he was a telephone engineer and had been sent to the far north to fix broken lines. He was then supposed to return south, but had met two gold prospectors and that was it. Bewitched by the spell of northern gold, he stayed and together with Inkeri, slowly built this wonderfully bohemian utopia. I have only known two families to create their own world and then move into it – and this was the first of them.

A small booth marked the entrance to the gold-panning area, and I went over to buy a day ticket. Shocked at the price, I quizzed the thin young man at the counter. 'How long do I get in here?'

He pointed with gentle sarcasm at the words printed on the ticket. 'All day.'

'Yes, but when do I have to leave?' I persisted.

'Whenever you like,' he said, clearly already tired of this discussion.

'But how many hours panning do I get?' I continued, anxious to get good value from the expensive ticket.

'There – are – twenty-four – hours – in – a – day,' he said slowly. But, far from feeling snubbed by his petulant summary, I was delighted. Twenty-four hours! This day ticket was an absolute bargain.

The gold-panning area was a large, shallow pond surrounded by a number of rough wooden benches. It had been dug out with a mechanical excavator and the 'overburden' – the soil that contained little or no gold – lay in a huge heap to one side. The rust-coloured sandy clay or 'pay dirt' – the soil that did contain some gold – had been piled up in small mounds around the pond's edge, ready for the tourists. A small stream flowed into the panning pool, refreshing the muddy water.

There were long-handled shovels beside the pay dirt, and I quickly loaded my pan. I was anxious to see if there really was natural gold here, or whether this place was just a tourist-trap fantasy gold claim. But it was real. As I finished washing my very first pan, a few tiny specks of rough gold appeared. *This is fantastic,* I thought, *and I have another twenty-three-and-a-half hours here!*

I worked until my back ached and the panning area became crowded with other visitors. Then I stopped to chat with an effervescent and engaging British geologist called Chris, who turned out to be a fount of information on all things gold, and worked at the Royal School of Mines in London. Wiser and pleased to have met another kindred spirit, I wandered off with my small but satisfying accumulation of gold dust safely stored in my glass medicine bottle. I needed to make camp and get my tent up, and had been told that I could pitch more or less anywhere but with no fires. The sign for toilets pointed to a small log building in the distance and, feeling the need, I wandered over to it.

The only two doors were helpfully marked 'male' and 'female' with Scandinavian earthiness. A penis-shaped stick had been nailed to one door, while on the other a forked branch had been fastened upside down – a crease in the bark perfectly mimicking a woman's parts. And, just in case anybody should take these signs too seriously, both had been dressed with a tuft of fuzzy moss as pubic hair. I paused to consider the uproar that would be caused in prudish England if anybody marked public toilets with graphic stick genitalia. Then I pulled open the penis-stick door and stepped into the gloomy interior.

My mild embarrassment at the door signs turned to horror as I found myself in a small room with no cubicles. Instead, on two sides of the room there was a bench with four large oval holes cut into it. These benches were facing each other, presumably so that people could talk as they used the toilet. This was far too informal for me. How could anybody actually go to the toilet while up to seven other people watched and chatted as they emptied their bowels? I resolved to be very quick and in future to use this place only in the dead of night, and even then, I would bring something to jam the door shut.

Tent pitched, I hurried back to the gold-panning area to extract even more value from my day ticket. When I got there, most of the other tourists had gone and the thin young man closed the booth and wandered off. As if this were the signal to leave, the last of the other panners also packed up and wished me luck as they left. My back was aching, but now I had the whole place to myself.

While scraping yet another few kilos of pay dirt into my pan, I watched the small stream that fed fresh water into the panning area. I could see that when the area was excavated, the natural watercourse had been dug a little deeper and straightened for a few metres before it entered the pool. The clear water now ran quickly through the prepared channel and over a bed of hard yellow clay. Little patches of heavy black sand had formed behind any obstruction and had also filled the small depressions left by the digger bucket's teeth. And it suddenly struck me that this would be the perfect spot to try out 'ground sluicing'.

When panning, the gold pan is itself moved through the water to wash away the lighter sand and gravel. Sluicing is the exact opposite. The long three-sided sluice box is set motionless in the current so that the natural flow of water does the separation work. Within a manufactured sluice, the gold is caught by a series of angled traps called riffles.

The art of panning is to move the gold pan at a perfect angle in the water, just enough to wash away everything but the gold. The art of sluicing is to achieve the same effect through a perfect flow of water across the riffles. Sluicing is usually around six times faster than panning, so traditionally a gold pan was used for exploratory prospecting and, once a deposit of pay dirt was found, a sluice was then made or brought in to speed up the recovery of gold. If the prospector didn't have a sluice box, the streambed itself could be used as a concentrator – and this is called ground sluicing.

Black sand is an important indicator of where gold might be. Many heavy metallic ores that commonly occur with gold are black, and this includes iron, lead, zinc, tungsten and tin. When crushed by the grinding action of a river in flood, these oxides and sulphides form a black sand that is at least twice as heavy as the other paler sand and gravel in streambeds. The dense material left with the gold is generically known as 'the heavies'.

It was now late evening and while there may have been an objection to me setting up a ground sluice during the day, I felt that it would be safe to do so now. I would have the discretion of night-time with the convenience of full daylight. Taking up one of the shovels, I climbed down into the feeder stream and scraped the clay flat. I then dug a series of parallel traps at right angles to the flow of water to create the riffles. To help catch the gold, I pushed narrow flat rocks into the clay, just upstream of the traps. Then I laid a line of large rectangular rocks on either side of my improvised riffles to create a narrow channel in line with the water's flow. Finally, I increased the current's speed a little by creating a Y-shaped entrance to the channel; in the vernacular of sluicing, this final piece of engineering is called a 'wing dam'. The ground sluice that I made was about the length and width of a rectangular coffin – a fantastic gold recovery system and assembled out of nothing. I gazed at my creation with pride and couldn't wait to try it out. My aching muscles were now forgotten, cured by the drug 'hope' and the intoxicating promise of easy gold.

I soon settled on a simple routine. I would fill my pan with pay dirt and carry it over to the sluice. I then gave each load a rough wash to try to free any particles of gold that were stuck to the clay in a process known as 'puddling'. The resulting muddy-brown porridge was then fed slowly into the upper end of my ground sluice. Not having a sieve to remove the larger stones, I had to do this by hand. I took an occasional break to peer expectantly into the improvised sluice to see what gold had been caught. And each time I wasn't disappointed and had the pleasure of glimpsing specks of bright gold on the upper edge of my traps.

The work was very satisfying. I felt that I was now an authentic miner, moiling through the ancient muck as so many had before me. I was sweaty, mud-stained, tired and my fingertips were sore from raking through the ground sluice to remove stones. Naively, I had faith in some form of natural justice, in a universal code of fairness. I was working hard and felt confident that the gold found would be in direct proportion to the effort I made, as if employed on piecework.

Finally exhausted, I stopped and looked at my wristwatch: it was 4.20am. The 'night' was nearly over. I had panned and sluiced for almost seventeen hours, and had just worked the last ten in a very public place without seeing anybody. For me, the wonderful day ticket had now expired. This sunlit night had been another world, so very different from the sunlit day. No rules, no officials, no interruptions – just a quiet island of freedom in an otherwise bustling place.

The only sounds breaking the night's silence had been welcome and appropriate. No grating music had drifted in, nor human voices to remind me that I wasn't alone. My shovel rang with high metallic notes to the rhythm of my digging, while the water flowing through the sluice murmured and chuckled. I found this comforting. And I was pleased to have occasional visits from the resident Siberian jays with their mellow, thrush-like song. I liked these tough birds of the Arctic goldfields. Their rusty and dark-brown feathers are the same colour as pay dirt.

Cleaning up the ground sluice took ages, and while the final show of gold dust was pleasing, it now hardly seemed a fair reward for the huge effort I'd just put in. I moved the rocks that had made up the side walls and scuffed away the large delta of tailings that had built up below the sluice. Finally, the feeder stream looked much as it had before I started. As I wandered back to my tent, I felt that I had just learned an important lesson: keep testing the pay dirt. Never *assume* that the gold is there, *know* it is. While wriggling into my sleeping bag, I cheered myself up with the thought that tomorrow I would head out west – into the vast forest to find the best gold-bearing river in Lapland.

Tomorrow came, but not with the planned journey. I had one of those wonderfully serendipitous meetings that happen while travelling: while wandering around the village in the morning, I met a man called Seppo. He was quiet, with a charming confidence and splendid white beard. He explained that he lived in a railway carriage tucked away on the Tankavaara gold claim, and helped out when the panning site was busy with tourists. The rest of the time he worked on his own claim.

Seppo's tiny home was unique and truly beautiful. The carriage had been heavily insulated, neatly lined with pine boards and divided into four sections. First was his bed – a snug cot heaped with colourful blankets. Then came the carriage's mid-section, a sitting room with a small scrubbed table and walls crammed with books and knick-knacks. The glass carriage window looked out over a patch of verdant bog, as if long ago the train had stopped at a remote station that had now returned to nature. Next, a narrow kitchen was efficiently stocked and seemed unnecessarily small, but this was to make room for the fourth section, his sauna. This too was barely big enough for one person. But judging by his enormous grin as he showed it to me, the sauna was something of which he was particularly proud.

There was a rare gracefulness in this generous man, content to see out the long dark winters alone in his creation. There is a school of thought that happiness is wanting what you have, and here I felt that I had just met the manifestation of such wisdom.

Back at the restaurant, I watched a red squirrel going under the eaves and wondered how they survived the bitter winters up here. Like the squirrel, I was beginning to feel at home in Tankavaara, and I knew that if I didn't set off soon, I would be seduced by the delightful spirit of the place. I seriously considered giving up the hiking adventure and giving in to temptation. I could imagine long, carefree days of eating my way through the fabulous salmon and reindeer menu, at least twice. Of hard but dreamy hours spent cheap day-ticket panning, with some more night work perhaps. Of breaks to enjoy the Siberian jays and make furtive visits to the embarrassing toilets – and all the while, slowly getting to know the people here. But a guilty unease suddenly grabbed me: this hadn't been my original plan or mission. So, I shook off Tankavaara's sweet enchantment, packed up my camp and prepared to leave.

Kauko and Inkeri were going to Ivalo and offered to drop me off by the long dirt road that runs westwards to the Ivalojoki river. Reindeer – or worse, elk – are a major traffic hazard on the Arctic Highway. They can suddenly appear out of the forest and dash across the road. To guard against this danger, Inkeri's small fluffy dog sat in the front with them and watched for trouble with impressive concentration. She barked a warning at any hint of an animal crossing and Inkeri assured me that the little dog's sharp eyes had made their road journeys very much safer.

We arrived at the long dirt road, said our goodbyes and a total silence fell as my new friends drove away towards Ivalo. Finally, I was completely alone. The cold conifer-scented air seemed thin and absolutely pure. Excited, I stretched out my arms in an animistic greeting: 'Hello forest!' I was now a gold prospector, the real thing, heavily laden with all the stores and food I would need and about to hike out into the wilderness. There were butterflies in my stomach. On the one hand, I was already an experienced outdoorsman with a liking for winter camping, and I felt I had the skills to navigate and live out in the immense forest; but on the other, I hadn't been here before and knew that I was a complete innocent.

As I trudged along, labouring under the huge weight of my rucksack, I contemplated what it meant to be off the beaten track up here. I had no way of calling for help should I need it – a sobering thought. For the first time in my life, I was totally responsible for my own welfare. I determined to be extra careful, and would never place a foot casually, nor be careless when using a knife. I would also show additional respect for the fire and my boiling kettle. Unexpectedly, this felt good and strangely empowering. It was now wholly incumbent upon me alone to thrive out here and belong.

I have found all through my life that when my mind is open and I listen, I get nudged in the right direction. I have no idea what this phenomenon is, but I have learned to trust these hunches – they are real and benevolent, and they do not come from within me.

In the middle of the second day, I was tired of plodding along the dirt road and decided to take a shortcut. Instead of continuing as planned until I found the river, I reasoned that I could now head north-west and shorten the journey by several miles. It would also be a more interesting route. I was well aware that once away from the certainty of the road, two things would make navigation quite difficult. Firstly, the usual technique – of taking a compass bearing on a distant feature and then walking to it – doesn't work in a forest where there are no distant features, just a wall of similar-looking trees in every direction. And second, it's not good technique to try to walk a bearing by staring at a compass. Most people tend to favour one leg when walking, and if you don't have a clear point to aim for, or a track to follow, the tendency is to walk in a slight curve, so I would probably end up walking in a large circle.

The method I had been taught was to take an accurate bearing on the most distant tree I could see and walk to it, then repeat this from tree to tree along the chosen route – while also using another important navigational trick. When heading for a linear feature, such as a river, it's best not to aim at the exact point you want to get to, as in most cases you will just miss it. Good technique is to aim off slightly.

This is all challenging enough when you know where north actually is, and that is far more complicated than it seems. There are three 'norths': grid north, shown by the lines that run vertically on a map; true north, the line of axis upon which the Earth spins; and magnetic north, the one shown by a compass. Obviously with no darkness, any thought of using the North Star to help me navigate was out, nor could I use the rising and setting sun. So, there was only my compass to work with – whose needle, unhelpfully, was pointing north-west to the Earth's magnetic North Pole, which hovers over Northern Canada.

Before leaving the Arctic Highway, I had measured how many degrees there were between my map's grid north and my compass's magnetic north; this is the 'grid magnetic angle'. I then knew how many degrees of variation I needed to allow me to navigate accurately. Lastly, a final problem to keep in mind was that in a heavily mineralized area such as this, there was always the chance of a rock called magnetite – the clue is in the name. This ore of iron is highly magnetic and can throw out a compass needle completely.

Once off-road, my progress slowed. It was heavy going with the full pack and frequent stops to take compass bearings. But I was delighted now to be well inside the Arctic Circle and walking through the primal wilderness of northern boreal forest. I did have a plan 'B' if I got lost. The area I was travelling through was vast but boundaried on every side. To the south was the dirt road that I had just left and to the east was the Arctic Highway. The Ivalojoki river flowed to the west and north. If a navigational disaster occurred, I planned to walk in a straight line until one of these boundaries was found. And if I ended up bumping into the Russian border, then I'd got something very wrong!

The forest trees I moved through now were old, slow growing and dwarfed by exposure, with many broken by the winter snows. The upper canopy was a pleasing mixture of evergreen pine and spruce and the deciduous birch, whereas the lower layer, up to about knee-high, was more complicated and made up of vast carpets of blueberry, lingonberry and crowberry. These shrubs were often tangled with tough old junipers and clumps of dwarf birch and the Arctic downy willow – with the pleasingly appropriate botanical name of *Salix lapponum*. There were few birds. Some bramblings quietly flitted past me once, coloured like the Siberian jays but about the size of a house sparrow. I spotted ptarmigan or willow grouse too, but they were always too far away to be seen clearly.

The higher ground was easier walking, being hard, dry and stony, while the hollows and low ground were filled with clumps of cotton grass and sodden sphagnum bog. In Wales only a few of the trees had been hung with usnea, the old man's beard lichen, but here, all of the trees were thick with it. At times the grey-green, sooty-dark threads were so dense on the lower branches that they had matted and hung like ancient cobwebs that I had to push through.

I stopped to brush away a tangled net of the unworldly lichen and had a moment of doubt; should I really be out here alone? It was the most beautiful and pristine forest, but echoes of sinister children's stories suddenly came to mind. In almost all folklore such forests teem with unpleasant things, beasts and people. My confidence wavered. Was I being stupid for pushing on through the scrub like some schoolboy pioneer, with every step taking me further from civilization?

I studied the map and my compass bearings, then carefully plotted where I thought I was and where I expected to be soon. This calming recalculation worked, and the swarm of imagined threats and menace melted away between the trees and back into the shadows.

I had been similarly ambushed by fear in England many years earlier, before gold gripped me, while I was still passionate about collecting minerals. The others in the group had left me alone, gathering chalcopyrite deep in the Coniston copper mine. When I had the pieces I wanted, I started the walk back to the surface along a flooded tunnel and became eerily aware that there were footsteps following me. I was being stalked. Close behind me, in the thick absolute darkness, something dreadful was moving. Twice I span around to catch the thing in the brilliant beam of my head torch. But each time I was too slow, and the long tunnel was empty. I fought to control a rising panic, and it took a quiet minute or two to understand what was happening. The ripples of water created by my own footsteps were bouncing back off the mine tunnel walls, and when the tiny waves collided in mid-channel a little way behind me, they made a slight splash – spookily, but logically, in exactly the same rhythm as my own footsteps.

Perception is so important. We can see the same thing in many different ways, and it's a folly to forget that. Thoreau puts it nicely: 'It's not what you look at that matters, it's what you see.'

Later that day, when out of the usnea-cloaked trees and searching for a place to cross a wide stream, I met two Sámi men who were fishing. The men had laid a net across a pool and were now downstream, beating the water and splashing to drive the fish into it. I watched and waited until they had finished and then moved down to talk to them.

They were both wearing traditional long smocks held at the waist with a broad belt, from which hung a hand axe and sheath knife. I noticed that they also carried a fat roll of iron nails. Each one had been carefully laid head to toe along a length of sticky masking tape and then rolled up. I recalled being taught how to fasten poles together with string, using complicated square and cross lashings, and thought how wonderfully practical the

Sámi technique was. These real outdoorsmen just nailed things together!

One man asked if I would like some food. Expecting to be given a fish and feeling that it would be impolite to refuse, I smiled and said yes. I was then surprised when he opened the front of his smock and reached in to pull out a large chunk of dried reindeer. I was still wondering what else he stored in between the smock and his body, when he unsheathed a beautiful burr-handled knife and cut me off a large slice. Trying to hide the fact that I was squeamish about this morsel, I popped it in whole and started chewing. I frowned knowingly and said how good it was – all the while hoping I was not overdoing it, as I might be given a second slice. As far as I could tell this was simply dried muscle. The meat was chewy and bloody. There was no delicate smoke flavour, nor aromatic herbs to tempt the diner; this was simply food as fuel. *Another lesson,* I thought to myself quietly. *This is the north – here you eat because you need to, food is not an entertainment.*

Moving over a low hill the next morning, I found an abandoned Sámi camp. These indigenous people have lived in Lapland for thousands of years and their bushcraft is real, full-time and in all seasons – and I was fascinated. The long poles that had held up the tepee-like tent, a lavvu, had been left standing; maybe they were coming back soon. The campfire seemed slightly overcomplicated at first. But I soon realized that it was a clever arrangement of sticks that allowed the cook to use any part of the fire, and so get the exact heat needed for whatever food was being prepared.

Most impressive of all was their bed. Whereas the pilot's spruce branches were fairly comfortable, the mattress I saw in the lavvu was bushcraft's deluxe model. Hundreds of tiny sprigs of juniper had been packed tightly at about 45 degrees, giving pocket-sprung

comfort! It was superb and must have taken many hours to make.
I would later meet an army sergeant who held people who were
proud to rough it in great disdain. His succinct observation was,
'Any fool can be uncomfortable.' He too would have appreciated
this field craft excellence, superb in its functional simplicity.
Without good sleep we all soon suffer.

After what had felt like an age of pushing through tangled scrub,
forest and bog, it was a joy to finally find myself up on a ridge
above a long glittering curve of broad water. With the magnificent
Ivalojoki river stretched out before me, I dropped my pack. Then
I sat down to savour success and enjoy my first contact with this
legendary waterway, which gracefully cuts through 110 miles
of rugged gold country. A large pale-coloured bird flew away
upstream, possibly an osprey; if so, this was another first for me.
I scanned the banks as far as I could see for any sign of boats or
other people, and there were none. Once, this was the busy main
highway for the early prospectors, a sparkling ice road in winter
and cool waterway in summer. I chuckled, relieved to see that it
was flowing from left to right, as it should have been according to
my calculations.

I picked my way down the boulder-strewn slope to a large
sandy beach and made camp. I was in very high spirits, uplifted
by the thought that the toughest part of the trek was now over.
As I gazed out across the slow-moving water, I felt the full weight
of the privilege of being here. I was now in the very heart of this
beautiful and remote goldfield.

Standing beside this vast river, I felt at peace. The water had
presence. An ancient spirit seemed to move below the shimmering

glassy surface, as the formidable current herded the mass of tea-coloured water onwards with such animal power – fluid, muscular, immense.

I imagined the immeasurable gold that lay in the river's shadowy depths. The well-guarded riches buried deep by meltwater floods as the last Ice Age ended, the bounty secure, way down in the icy water and locked beneath a rough bed of tightly packed glacial boulders. I could picture nuggets of such rare beauty and ounces, pounds, kilos of sparkling sun-bright-yellow dust. But this gold's layers of protection were too much for me, and I knew that I would see none of it. For me, there were only the crumbs of gold that could be scratched from the river's banks. I sighed and felt the pangs of being human. My insignificance in this vastness, my time measured in days or years – a mere blink of the eye to this river.

I refocused on practical matters to cheer myself up and suddenly had a great idea. I would make a small oven and bake a pizza! My two old-fashioned gold pans were made of thin steel and could be used by putting one upside down on top of the other, and then resting them over a small fire. I knew it was important that the food I made was nourishing, but it also needed to be tasty; otherwise I might start skipping meals. I made dough and baked a large flatbread. I then topped this with tomato purée, flakes of cheese, salami and a dusting of black pepper – then popped my creation back into the oven for the cheese to melt. I know that by city standards my rough pizza was very ordinary, but out in the forest it was haute cuisine.

I was carrying an interesting range of everyday foods, as expedition ready-meals were too expensive for me. My larder for this trip included self-raising flour, rolled oats and dried mashed potato as the basic carbohydrates. Raisins, salami, cheese, dried soup, tomato purée and condensed milk could be added to make imaginatively different meals, while my luxuries were digestive biscuits, coffee, salt, black pepper and chocolate. I was in the habit of making many very simple meals using a cheap trick I'd learned when mid-winter camping. I would boil up a pot of dried soup and then thicken it with instant mash. While in all honesty probably not very nourishing, this savoury gruel was filling and came in a wide variety of flavours. Mindful of the poor chap in Alaska who was eaten by a bear, all of this food was suspended from a tree in a dry bag – some distance from my tent.

The success of my improvised oven lifted my spirits, and I decided to have a wash, as I had been in Lapland for several days now. I stripped off and went to the river's edge with a new bar of soap. The water was peat-stained and still unusually high, with the last of the snowmelt. I inched in and stopped – it was bitterly cold. I had optimistically hoped that the days of endless sunshine would have warmed up the river a little. I decided to push on, thinking that even a very quick wash would be enough to freshen me up. But, by the time I was knee-deep, my feet were in agony with the numbing cold. I stood for a moment, frozen in shock, and wondered what to do. I hardly dared to imagine the pain when the ice-water reached my groin. A full immersion wash was now unthinkable.

While retreating from the river's uninviting bath, I realized I could warm up some of the water in the gold pans over my fire and then wash comfortably. These old steel pans are so versatile – a prospecting tool, an oven, a washbasin and even a fish trap.

*

In fact, everything was going well except the gold panning. The snow that had worried me so much at first had disappeared quickly and was never a problem. But the resulting meltwater was still unhelpfully high, and covered the gold-bearing riverbed cracks and crevices that I wanted to work. Added to that, the high-water riverbank was an unrelenting jumble of large rocks, tough vegetation and flood detritus. What I had learned while gold prospecting in Wales and Scotland simply didn't apply here.

The wildlife continued to be occasional and charming. Once, a pair of tufted waxwings came and drank within 2m of me, and on another occasion, a singularly trusting rose-pink pine grosbeak came so close to me that I could have reached down and touched it.

My earlier worries about the resident carnivores had largely disappeared, until I found a set of very large animal tracks on the edge of a muddy puddle. The find was unnerving, being only a short distance downhill from my tent. But during my time in Lapland, I had already noticed that nobody seemed much bothered about having these predators roaming around them. In fact, for some people it was a source of humour. Vesa, a local prospector, had smiled as he told me, 'I have never yet seen a bear, but I think many bears have seen me!' I was not comforted by the idea that bears might be watching me, but I accepted that any danger was minimal – even though one of them had just walked through my camp.

My panning woes continued as I slowly worked my way downstream. The riverbank was an ongoing obstacle course of huge rounded boulders and thick scrub. The frequent low cliffs had to be climbed over or worked around. Unsettled, I began to wonder if I should have gone up to the north-west instead, to the Lemmenjoki goldfield.

In the September of 1945 three brothers found good gold in the tributaries of the Lemmenjoki river, and started Lapland's second gold rush. By 1948, the whole area had been claimed and was being worked by more than two hundred men. The next year a legend was born. A 26-year-old Dutch adventurer and journalist called Sylvia Petronella van der Moer arrived and immediately fell in love with this northern land. She must have been an amazing woman, strong and incredibly charismatic. While only working in the goldfield for about four months as a cook, she is still remembered with great affection. Petronella, as she is known, is now immortalized with touching sensuality by having two small rounded hills named after her. She was eventually evicted by the Finnish authorities and disappeared into the chaos of post-war Europe. I have read that her daughter brought her ashes over from the USA in 2014 and scattered them here. If so, Petronella is now at peace, and her spirit must be amused: in the end she won over the pedantry of the Finnish officials. It is generally Lapland that enchants its guests, but, just this once, it was the visitor who cast the spell.

Finally, my gold luck changed. I came upon a small ravine with a fast-flowing stream that tumbled over a large plate of fractured bedrock before joining the main river. This was ground I could work. And added to this new good fortune, I noticed an old miner's wooden leat caught in a tangle of willow branches. Once used to bring water to a sluice box, it had been abandoned or washed away from an upstream claim. I was thrilled. The leat was made of three long planks that had been nailed together in a U shape and could be readily adapted for sluicing. Now with rushing water, promising gold ground and the chance to speed up washing the pay dirt with a sluice box, things were suddenly looking good. I have always felt that good luck is largely a matter of foresight and attitude, and it has been said that diligence is the mother of good fortune. But I think the aviator Amelia Earhart had it right when she said that most fears are paper tigers and the key to success is tenacity.

The three old sun-bleached planks had held together well, but needed some minor repairs. I gathered handfuls of moss and crammed this tightly into the few cracks and gaps that had formed. I then needed to make a series of small riffle-traps to catch the gold, and mindful that my ground sluice in Tankavaara had got choked with black sand, I would be more careful this time. I cut short willow sticks, slightly longer than the width of the sluice channel and split them in half. These pieces were bent so that tension would hold them in place. I set the cleft sticks along the box a hand's breadth apart and angled at about 45 degrees. This would create what American prospectors call 'low pressure areas' and the turbulence needed for the gold grains to work their way down through the black sand, and be safe.

Normally a sluice box would have a base layer of carpet or corduroy to catch the fine gold. This stops the thinnest flakes and dust from creeping under the riffles and washing out with the tailings. Having no cloth to do this, I packed yet more moss beneath each riffle – until my improvised sluice looked very odd indeed. The split willow gold traps could hardly be seen through the shaggy green pelt that now lined the entire floor of my sluice. But I was perfectly happy with this. My moss would act like wool.

In ancient times, sheepskins were used in alluvial mining, as even the tiniest gold gets caught in the thick mat of lanolin-sticky fibres. The whole Greek myth about Jason and the Argonauts probably relates to a raid to steal fleeces that had been used to recover gold. And if Jason was off looting 'golden fleeces' almost three thousand years ago, goodness knows how long sheepskins have actually been used by gold miners.

Many pleasant days passed and slowly but steadily, my store of gold grew. I was content; this was what I had come so far to do. In the never-ending daylight, I worked an easy routine and slept, ate my meals and took short breaks as and when I fancied. Every ten hours or so, I cleaned out the sluice, which was always exciting, as I never knew how much gold had been caught and lay hidden in the matted clumps of moss.

Each clean-up was a delicate operation, as to lose any gold now would be tragic. I would lift the upstream end of the sluice and rest it on a boulder. I then sat the downstream end in one of my gold pans, before releasing each willow-stick riffle in turn and sliding the trapped black sand and gold concentrate into the pan. The precious gritty moss was then washed in the other pan to free the gold. I saved all of the moss to be reused, as I knew that some of the very fine gold would remain trapped within the soggy fibres.

I planned to copy the old gold rush miners who burned their corduroy carpet at the end of each season. The ashes were then panned to recover the very last of their gold. It would be a fitting closure to my adventure to finish by drying my moss carpet in a pan over the fire, then totally burning the dry moss in the pan and washing my last precious gold from the white ashes. An extra gram or two of powdery flour-gold would be very welcome, and the tiny pyre would be a pleasingly funereal end to my time here. But none of this happened . . .

Keeping track of time wasn't easy in the perpetual sunlight. I thought I was doing all right until the moment I looked at my wristwatch and, alarmingly, didn't understand it. The watch said it was ten minutes past four, but was that in the late afternoon or early morning? And even worse, I began to wonder if I might have lost track of the days too.

Although I'd carefully steered a course through the sea of trees, I had failed to navigate the ocean of endless daylight. I was lost in time, not in space. The shock of this discovery was like being roughly woken from a pleasant dream, and the distressing reality of my situation gripped me. At some point soon I had a plane to catch. I decided to pack up immediately and set off, to follow the river downstream as it flowed eastwards to the Arctic Highway and the airport. In the end the gold-dusted moss wasn't burned and lived to grow on by the abandoned sluice.

I was now very tired of the midnight sun. The phenomenon that had seemed so wonderful when I first arrived had turned from friend to foe. My casual approach to 'day' and 'night' had probably been the problem, and had thrown out all my natural rhythms and my production of the sleep hormone. I felt muddled and vague, like I was jet-lagged. My troubles were multiplied when I then realized that I hadn't kept a close enough eye on my food stock either.

I do not remember how long I spent moving slowly along the riverbank, but it was long enough to get hungry. This was the first time in my life that I had ever felt real hunger – or at least the beginnings of hunger. I knew that I wasn't in real danger, as most people can live for about three weeks on body fat and muscle alone. But this wasn't supposed to be an endurance test, and accidents are more likely when one is tired. I trudged on for hour after hour through the knee-high willow and birch scrub, every single step an effort. Now totally focused on the determination needed to push forward, I found myself daydreaming about three simple pleasures: food, drink and darkness.

The curious fantasy that dominated my daydream was of going to an English pub and ordering a pint of warm beer with a large bar of fruit and nut chocolate. I would then carry them outside into the velvet darkness of a summer's evening and look up at the stars. At that time my local was the Butley Oyster, a delightful old pub on the edge of Rendlesham Forest in the east of England. It was owned and run by two wonderfully laconic and caring women, Vera and her friend Frieda. As I trudged along in this trance, I talked to them quietly while they refilled my glass with frothy ale and reached up to a chocolate-packed shelf for another bar. I replayed this pleasant and intoxicating dream again and again.

I know that this, of itself, is unremarkable. And I thought it little more than a silly game until I read the book *Castaway*. In the account of her time living on an uninhabited island with her partner, Gerald, Lucy Irvine describes what happened when they ran out of food. She wrote that they yearned for beer and fruit and nut chocolate. How amazing that while worlds apart, we had shared the same cravings.

After the anxious hungry days hurrying to get back to Ivalo, my arrival back among buildings, roads and cars was an unsettling anticlimax. Following my time in a pristine, slow-moving, earth-toned and quiet environment, the return to urban life was a shock. I reeled at the bright, gaudy colours and noise, the smell of exhaust fumes, dust, people, cooking and drains. Yet the southern outskirts of Ivalo were hardly a metropolis.

After checking the date and finding that I had arrived two days early for my flight, I looked for somewhere to eat. I soon found a small café and entered on my very best behaviour, for I knew that I must reek of woodsmoke, at the very least. A glass case on the counter was heaped with fresh salmon and dill scones and the air was filled with the rich scent of roasted coffee. The abundance of good, simple food triggered an emotional response and embarrassingly, I became quite tearful.

The adventure that had so nearly gone wrong was over. I fought back the sniffles as I devoured five of the delicate little buns and sipped a large mug of exquisite coffee. The baffled waitress kept giving me sideways glances, and must have thought that I was her most appreciative customer ever. I decided to forget any more camping and treated myself to a simple room while I waited for my flight home.

As the plane climbed into an azure sky, I gazed down at the olive-green landscape below and reflected upon my time there. At first, all I had wanted was to find some gold in this remote and incredible place. But as I looked out of the tiny window, it felt like I was leaving a friend. I had been enchanted by Lapland's goldfield, its wonderful people and the magic of living for a short while in the land of Christmas. I was pleased to have been visited by some of the far north's most delightful wildlife, yet relieved it wasn't all of them.

I had found abundant 'gold' in Lapland, but mostly not in the form I had expected. The philosopher Arthur Schopenhauer was writing about alchemists when he noted that 'in the search for gold many things of greater value were found'. But he could just as easily have been talking about prospectors, for that is certainly what happened to me.

The aircraft climbed through a thin veil of cloud and a white curtain closed below me. I flopped back into my seat; it was over. But almost at once I knew that this would not be my last visit to this magical region. I would come back to Tankavaara, and rent a little cabin with shutters and darkness, and bring heaps of chocolate. I felt in my pocket for the small glass medicine bottle and its store of Lapland's precious gold. Content, and with an inner smile, I took it out and carefully gave it a little shake. Amid the dull roar of the plane's jet engines there was the faintest jingle, like distant sleigh bells, only heard by those who knew what it was.

5

UNDERSEA GOLD

'The desire for gold is not for gold.
It is for the means of freedom and benefit.'

—Ralph Waldo Emerson, *The Conduct of Life*

Hope's Nose is an unremarkable, narrow peninsula of hard mid-Devonian limestone that juts out into the sea. It lies a little to the east of Torquay, a bustling seaside town in the county of Devon in the south-west of England. But remarkably, it's home to the world's rarest gold.

With a mischievous irony, nature has exposed this most delicate form of crystallized gold at the absolute tip of the peninsula: the very point where its ancient rocks suffer the full force of every violent storm. It is like butterflies emerging into a tornado – and with the same result. The gold crystals are pulverized, which makes them ever rarer. Hope's Nose might also be the world's tiniest gold deposit. During the last hundred years or so, the whole site's total yield is no more than a few ounces. The natural gold found here is unique, a fabulous geological rarity, and it is, therefore, extremely valuable. High-quality and provenanced specimens of natural gold nuggets and ore are sought after by mineral collectors, and command prices well above gold's bullion spot price.

I have seen sublime examples exhibited in both regional and national museums. On a visit to the Smithsonian National Museum of Natural History in Washington DC, I was surprised to see a large, extraordinarily beautiful specimen of Hope's Nose gold prominently displayed. It struck me that with all the huge and wonderful gold discoveries in North America, from California to Alaska and the Yukon, it was a tiny platform of wave-lashed, pale-grey rock in England that had provided the museum's most delicate and enchanting centrepiece.

In most hard rock deposits, the gold occurs in veins of white quartz, as tiny grains, flakes or nuggets. At Hope's Nose, it is very different. Soft veins of biscuit-coloured calcite flow through minor faults and fractures in the fossil-rich limestone. And up to 14 of these veins contain gold. But not as the usual specks, flakes and blobs. Here the natural gold occurs as an unusual alloy with palladium – a lustrous silvery-white platinum group metal. This pale-gold alloy has grown into stunning fractural-patterned crystals – some up to 5cm in length. These fragile crystals are fern-like, intricate dendrites of amazing complexity. The very first ore samples were collected in 1922, and the soft, fawn-coloured calcite was gently dissolved away with weak hydrochloric acid. Arborescent glades of tiny golden ferns were revealed. Such beauty and preternatural craftsmanship – a Midasian miracle.

While in Lapland, I had met an English geologist, Dr Chris Halls. We'd kept in touch over the many years that had passed since then, and I had joined him on various student expeditions to hunt for gold in Cornwall and North Wales and given short lectures at the

Royal School of Mines, where he worked, on the practicalities of prospecting. After one such talk, he wanted me to attend a meeting with him.

Chris led the way through a labyrinthine series of stairs and passages to a small office belonging to an acquaintance, high in the enormous Natural History Museum building next door. I soon found myself part of a fascinating conversation with his associate at the museum, discussing the possibility of the museum doing a 'rescue dig' at Hope's Nose. The museum's concern was that the tiny and precarious deposit of palladium-gold ferns was being rapidly eroded by both mineral collectors and the sea. It was felt that a rescue was urgently needed, or soon there would be no specimens of this extraordinary gold ore left for museums or the geology students of the future.

On the train home, my mind was buzzing. I was excited by everything that had been discussed and the possibility that I would be asked to join the rescue dig. But then my imagination kicked in and I began to wonder if there was something I could do on my own at Hope's Nose. I wanted to keep Chris's trust, and if I were not invited to work with the museum, I would also respect the project that they were planning to do. And then the thought struck me that if I were to find a truly wonderful specimen, I could present it to the Natural History Museum – now that really would be something to write home about!

I knew that the main gold veins that run through the limestone rock come out from the base of a small cliff and across the wave-cut platform before heading straight out to sea. And suddenly I saw that this could be my project: I would look for the gold under the sea. For almost a hundred years, mineral collectors and geology students have hacked away at the gold-bearing calcite by the cliff, and there was probably very little left anyway. However, as far as I knew, nobody before had dived for the gold.

One possible reason why other people had not chosen to look for it under the sea, was that the gold deposit was right beside Torquay's main sewer outfall. But the sewage might actually be an ally and give my crew an advantage over more fastidious prospectors. It was ironic that the last of the most beautiful gold crystals in the world were protected by a thick mat of untreated sewage. In an optimistic mood, I saw this as a real advantage. If I could work out how to keep myself and those diving with me safe from infection, we would have the place all to ourselves!

It helped that I was already familiar with scuba diving. One of the main advantages modern prospectors have over previous generations, is that we can work underwater. Some years earlier I had taken a full course with the meticulous Scottish Sub Aqua Club, and this was my chance to really use what I had learned.

Gazing from the train window as it trundled north, out and away from London, my excitement grew, and I began to form a plan. My mother's observation that I was 'obsessed' with finding gold was probably true. But without this level of passion and drive, dreams will always stay as dreams. And I do nurture mine, as everything good begins with a dream.

After all, there are always so many reasons *not* to do something. It's too difficult, too dangerous, too far, too expensive; we don't have the time, the skills, the experience, the equipment, the permission, the people to help us; or the saddest of them all – the fear of failure. Such excuses are the Angels of Mediocrity, and we must not listen to them.

Over the years I have met so many 'nearly dids' – individuals with dreams and ambitions that they were not able to bring to life. So many times, while out panning for gold, I have encountered the phrase, 'If there was anything there, somebody else would have found it.' Sometimes it's like the very air we breathe is full of negativity. It's said that most regrets are for what we *did not* do in life, a truism, I think.

That day, as the carriage rattled along, and the English countryside flowed past my window almost unnoticed, my resolve hardened: the Hope's Nose dive project was going to happen!

Of all the elements in project planning, the people are the most important. Time, money, equipment, materials and expertise will all come together when you have a good team in place.

Once home, I enthused about the undersea gold project to seven good friends – all those I thought might be interested and who had the ability to take part. They included Mike, who was now retired from a long military career with a tank regiment; my cousin David and his friend Pete, who were both good on the sea; Charlie and Lorna as experienced divers, and John, a diver and work colleague. Lastly, there was Richard, a very capable and tough friend from Tasmania, who by a happy coincidence was in Britain at the time.

I would always choose a team of competent friends over expert strangers. When things get tough, it's their bond, trust and loyalty that will get you through. And the more the team work together, the more efficient they become. Also, working with friends is more fun. A playful sparring soon develops, what the army calls 'squaddie humour'.

The hardest thing for most of us was getting the time off work. At this point in my life, I was employed full-time in an office, and I knew that the three weeks' holiday I needed to take for the dive project was a big ask. A week off was easily arranged, two weeks was normal for a summer holiday, but three weeks would be pushing it. Happily, my boss was a decent and affable man who saw how important this was to me. With a show of weary reluctance, he signed the pale-blue official form that authorized my leave and opened the door to this adventure. Had he said no, my Hope's Nose expedition would have been over before it had even begun.

Only Mike and I would be able to be there the whole time, while the others would come and join us when they could. But this was fantastic: I now had the time I needed and a good crew. And not one of them had been bothered by my mentioning the sewage outfall. We decided to start in early June for the good weather and long days. I cashed in all of my savings and bought a small, flat-bottomed fishing boat and then rented our accommodation, a large, converted barn a few miles inland from Torquay.

June arrived and everything started well. I asked Mike and John to join me a couple of days early as I wanted to get all of the preparatory work done as quickly as possible. The coastline on either side of the Hope's Nose peninsula is mostly cliff. So, the nearest place we could launch our boat was in Torquay harbour.

That early in the season, the harbour was very quiet and we launched easily on the empty slipway. Very soon, we had the boat safely tied up against the massive harbour wall. The 5.2-m (17-ft) cathedral-hull dory, a Pilot 17, was fitted with two small outboard motors, one 40hp as the main drive and an emergency 4hp engine as a backup. Hopefully, we could work with these motors and avoid the expense of having to buy another engine, so I wanted to take the boat out for a quick run to see how it handled. The test run would show, one way or the other, if the main outboard would be enough.

As it was likely to be rough out at sea, John decided to join me, and we both opted to put on our diving suits. While getting into mine, I noticed a stern-faced, bearded man striding towards us. With all the contempt he could muster, he said, 'You're not going out in *that*, are you?' But I had no time to answer before he grunted scornfully, gave us both a withering look and strode away again. We found out later that he was the harbourmaster.

From his manner, I felt that he was probably an ex-military man, and he reminded me of the colour sergeant that had greeted me on my first day at Sandhurst – the British Army's officer training college that I had attended soon after my trip to Lapland many years earlier. I'd run down a long corridor to where the immaculately dressed NCO was waiting. He pushed a form and pen towards me and nodded. When I filled it out quickly and handed it back to him, he lifted the sheet by one corner as if it were dirty and slowly passed it back to me. With practised sarcasm, he explained, 'Sir, *you* are the one with an education – a piece of paper has two sides.' I suspected that the harbourmaster had perfected his haughty disdain somewhere similar.

We discussed the harbourmaster's grunts, the threatening sea and our very small boat, and decided to go out all the same. The wind was now fairly strong and onshore, blowing straight towards a large sandy beach. John and I reasoned that the very worst that could happen to us was to be washed up with a few bruises. Mike, our shore lookout, quietly climbed up onto the seawall to watch.

*

It's often hard to judge the size of waves until you are actually in them. As soon as we left the sheltered waters of the harbour, I realized that this was going to be more of a challenge than I had expected. Once out in the bay, the swell was huge, but the crests were not breaking. The wind was a fresh force 5, brisk but manageable and I had sailed in much bigger seas – this was going to be good!

For many years, my father's business was building powerful speedboats, and I had been out to sea with him often. But never in these conditions. I knew that it was imperative not to be caught broadside by a wave, so tackled each mountain of swell diagonally; then slowed the boat down at the top, to sit comfortably in the water but still have forward movement. Somewhat counterintuitively, we needed to speed up as we left the crest and plunged down into the next trough. This would get the bow up a little and stop us from being swamped by the oncoming wave.

The short voyage was like the most amazing fairground ride – and John was the perfect companion on this menacing roller-coaster! Unflappable, or simply trusting, his cheerfulness built on mine and our spirits were sky-high as we soared and crashed through the threatening grey sea far out into the bay. Finally, we reluctantly agreed that the boat's trial was over, and it had passed.

Once back in the calm waters of the harbour, my adrenalin crashed and I wondered if I had been a complete idiot to go out in those conditions. On the one hand, there was the harbourmaster's good advice and the fact that there were no other yachts or motor cruisers out in the bay that day. On the other, I had just had the ride of my life, and we were now back safely. Mike had a much harder time than us, I think. Up on the seawall, he had watched anxiously as we disappeared down into each trough and were completely out of sight for several seconds. Every time this happened, he wondered if we would reappear.

Years later, this thrilling trip with John still feels like a metaphor for life itself. While I have always been happy to take advice, at the same time, I've found most people to be more cautious than is actually necessary. Risk is an essential part of life, and there is no life without risk. I am not a fatalist, but have sympathy with the view that 'on a long enough timeline, the survival rate for everybody drops to zero'. The timid and the brave will all end up the same, but the timid have done nothing along the way. I have had hundreds of safe, sensible, officially approved boat trips, and I don't remember any of them.

The next day, Charlie and Lorna joined us and the weather was fine, but again the sea was far too rough for us to dive from the boat. Nevertheless, anxious to make a start, we decided to head over to Hope's Nose and try diving from the shore. With two cars fully loaded, we drove to a small road that runs high above the cliffs, parallel to the coast. This road neatly divides two completely opposite worlds, with manicured suburbia on one side and an unkempt wilderness on the other. Here, lopsided, salt-scorched trees and low mounds of tough bramble cling to the rocky peninsula, while rabbits thrive in this meagre shelter and crop small patches of grass into unexpectedly neat lawns.

We parked by the footpath that fishermen use to get down to the point and looked in horror at how far it was. We were going to have to carry our heap of heavy diving equipment all the way down a long, winding path. And then, later that day after an exhausting dive, we would have to haul it all the way back up again. But the desire for a first dive and some gold was strong, so we joked about it and mourned for our idle boat.

This was also the first time that I had seen the sewer outfall – the ally that I hoped had kept other treasure hunters away, while paradoxically not threatening us. The effluent was already clearly visible as it drifted slowly out to sea and formed a vast pale-brown plume. A toxic stain billowed in the slight current, like cheap coal's sulphurous smoke rising from a chimney.

We set up camp on a tiny stone beach in Hope Cove, a sheltered spot behind the main headland. The sea was still too rough for us to dive at the point beside the gold veins, so we decided to go in from the beach and reach the gold site under the waves by moving along the much calmer seabed. Initially, the water was crystal clear, but we soon entered a dun-coloured fog where the discharging sewage had been churned up and mixed with fresh seawater. The visibility quickly fell to barely an arm's length and realizing that it was hopeless, we aborted the dive and turned back. I was frustrated to have got so close to the gold and then have it elude us.

Once back out of the fog and in clear water again, I noticed that there were occasional scallops scattered beneath me on the seabed. As I looked more closely, I spotted dozens of them half-buried in the sand – a seafood bounty stretching as far as I could see. We cheerfully turned our focus to harvesting this unexpected consolation prize. I can only assume that others had left the scallops alone due to their proximity to the sewer. We gathered a large bagful and then hauled our heavy wet kit and the unexpected evening meal back up the rough path to the cars.

Our scallop supper was superb. When seared in butter and splashed with brandy these sweet shellfish are my favourite of all seafood. I was also pleased that there were no ill effects from our risky harvest. However, we decided in future to err on the side of caution, and the Hope Cove scallops once again enjoyed a peaceful life, fed but undisturbed by humans.

A fresh wind blew from the south for the next eleven days, which was a bitter disappointment. We learned on the first and second days that while a southerly blew, we could neither use the boat nor carry our equipment down to the point and dive from the shore. As we waited day after day for the wind to change, boredom became a real problem. Inactivity takes the momentum and energy out of people, lowers morale and wastes that most precious resource: time. It was now clear that the three weeks which had seemed an age when planning this trip, would be barely enough. I began to worry we wouldn't get the chance to find any of the fabulous rare gold.

John ran out of time, wished us well, packed his bags and left, and was soon followed by Charlie and Lorna. Mike and I settled down to wait for my cousin David and his laconic friend Pete to arrive, and Richard from Tasmania was due any time soon.

The days of idleness had spawned a gloomy atmosphere, but to my surprise, this melancholy vanished like morning mist as soon as my good-humoured cousin and Pete walked in. They'd had a long journey and were bursting to hear our news. I had just started to relate the whole sorry tale when I suddenly noticed the time and stopped, as the BBC shipping forecast was about to begin. My heart leapt as the presenter announced that the wind was expected to veer westerly – the one direction that guaranteed us calm water over the dive site. David grinned and punched me on the shoulder. 'There you go,' he said. 'I'm your lucky charm!'

The small outboard motor roared as we approached Hope's Nose across a calm, oily sea. The last of the Atlantic swell was now only a gentle rising and falling of water, like peaceful breathing, as if the ocean were now sleeping. What a difference a day makes. I was elated. From now on, this would be our daily 20-minute commute from Torquay harbour to work, and what a pleasure it was. No traffic, no queues, just racing over long, low mounds of shining water with startled gulls wheeling above, their harsh calls echoing from the ancient cliffs and islands as we sped past.

It was also a great relief, as I had been troubled by a growing sense of having let everybody down. I had encouraged my friends to spend their precious holiday with me, only for us to sit idly waiting for the weather to change. But now here we were, skimming across the sea towards rich pockets of exquisite gold. We dropped anchor just offshore, in the clean water to the north of the outfall and well away from the headland's plunging rocks. Mike was at the helm of our small thin-walled vessel and wanted to keep us safe. He was concerned that if we even brushed against the rocks, the flimsy boat would be holed and the project would be finished, just as things were starting to look good.

As before, I had put on my diving suit before we left the harbour, but still had the boots, fins and bulky lead weights to secure. I settled down on the rocking deck of the boat's cluttered cabin to finish getting ready, which was a mistake. Now far too hot within my insulated clothing, I struggled to reach my feet to put the ankle weights on. But the biggest problem was the foul atmosphere within the hull. Fumes from the idling two-stroke outboard motor were drifting in and mixing with the stench of rotting squid: Mike planned to catch mackerel during our dive and had bought his fish bait a few days earlier. I sat in a growing sweat, while the boat swayed unhelpfully and the rancid air swirled around me. I could sense the awful tightening grip of seasickness and knew that I had to get into the water as fast as possible, or the dive wouldn't happen.

Luckily, David seemed fine, so we climbed over the back of the boat and down the narrow dive ladder. Once in the sea, we held onto a trailing swim-line to get our fins on. Then, when fully prepared, we swam to the boat's bow, ready to go down the anchor chain to the seabed. Dipping below the surface, we entered the sub-aqua diver's underwater world where peripheral vision is lost, as one can only look forward through the face mask's lens. Once below the water, the dominant sound is your own breathing – harsh, distinct and with an eerie similarity to the laboured breathing of the very ill or the *Star Wars* character Darth Vader. There's a long high-pitched hiss as air is breathed in and then a deep, soft roar as a mass of exhaled bubbles leaves your demand valve regulator to rise back to the surface.

The tidal current was still fairly strong and pulled us out sideways so that we hung horizontally from the anchor chain, like two bits of washing flapping on a windy day. As we inched our way down, my nausea became even worse and I gripped the anchor chain with both hands, desperate not to be pulled off. I believed that I was going to be violently sick very soon, and tried to recall from my dive training the correct technique for vomiting underwater.

The air supply demand valve that goes into a diver's mouth is a very clever yet delicate piece of equipment. A thin rubber diaphragm balances the pressure of the air breathed in and the exhaled air then passes through two small exhaust ports. Mindful that I had eaten a large Cornish pasty for breakfast, I wondered how big the pie's lumps of filling still were. Would they be small enough now to pass through the exhaust ports, or would chunks of potato and swede block them? Realizing that my tuition hadn't covered this particular situation, I considered avoiding this risk by taking the demand valve out of my mouth to heave, and then quickly pop it back in again when I needed to draw the next breath. Still feeling utterly wretched, I decided to shut my eyes, keep the air supply firmly in my mouth and fight the impulse to be sick.

It was utter bliss to finally reach the seabed. There was almost no current down on the bottom and I could lie completely still and wait while I quietly recovered. The stinking, wobbling boat was far away now, and nothing to do with me anymore. In a state of mindfulness, I gratefully focused all of my attention on a small heap of rocks and meditatively savoured the cold, clean air that flowed easily through my vomit-free valves. My seasickness slowly eased, and the fight was over.

David was frustrated by my inactivity and wanted to get on with the dive, but I wasn't moving for anyone. While my dive training had covered the need to always work with a partner and I shouldn't have done this, I signalled to him to go away and find something to do without me. Happily, he had a good dive without incident and later mentioned that he had found a large sea cave.

The next day we organized things differently. I had the lightest breakfast, and we arrived at the Hope's Nose peninsula a little later, aiming to reach the dive site as the tidal current fell away to slack water. And this time I wanted us to enter the water right above the gold veins. The waiting boat could then go further out to sea, as it had never been comfortable riding at anchor so close to the shore.

The new system was much better. When ready to dive, we sat on either side of the boat and rolled overboard backwards, exactly above the gold and right in the middle of the discharging sewage. Mike and Pete then took the boat out to fish while they waited for us to complete the dive. After the misery of the first day, this was a massive improvement and felt almost professional.

Once the boat was away, David and I moved close together and joined our gloved hands in a wrist-to-wrist hold, so as not to get separated. We then carefully let air out of our buoyancy jackets to sink slowly through the semi-opaque sewage soup to the clean seawater beneath. We soon learned that the best time to dive was from about an hour before high tide to two hours afterwards. During this time the current was minimal, and the rising salt water had lifted the outfall's discharge.

Once on the seabed, we found ourselves in a strange and gloomy landscape. The raft of effluent hung above us like a vast dull-brown nimbostratus cloud that filtered out all colours. Bathed only in a sepia twilight, the seabed seemed otherworldly. Everything was in shadow and archaic monochrome; it was as though we had just descended into the past, to a scene from the earliest days of photography.

On calm days, the sewage would form a clearly defined layer on the surface of the sea. Whether this was a thermocline, the effluent being warmer than the cool seawater, or a halocline, the filth being less dense than the salt water, I do not know. But the division between the two layers was precise, and each time we sank down through the thick, disgusting slop it ended very suddenly, and we were always pleased to have reached the strange tawny world beneath.

Deep trenches marked where the soft, gold-bearing calcite veins came out from beneath the cliffs, and had been eroded away. The Hope's Nose headland has always been popular with sea anglers and most of the depressions in the bedrock were littered with the lead fishing weights that they had lost. In the shelter behind one large rock, storms had pushed an assortment of these weights into an ankle-high mound. From a gold prospecting point of view, this was really good information. It showed me that the wind and wave action were not random down here, and that heavy things settled in a pattern – and gold is very much heavier than lead.

I suspect that very few people get to experience such a curious environment, and I found it interesting. Strangely, I soon began to feel that it had a charm all its own. Once, while kneeling on the seabed to work, I disturbed a patch of sediment and myriad fragments of pale toilet paper rose up around me. Immersed in this cloud of tiny off-white flakes, it was like being inside a Christmassy globe paperweight that had been shaken up to start a snowstorm. On another day, while carefully scraping out a bedrock pocket, I stopped to watch a group of fawn-coloured tampons drift past. They were travelling silently together across the smooth bedrock, as if they knew where they were heading. All fluffy with their long tails aligned by the current, they looked like small, sleepy mice. In the dun-coloured gloom of this increasingly Lewis Carroll undersea world, I wondered where they were going.

Of all the many things that had made their way down from Torquay's toilets, only the hypodermic needles really troubled us. They lay like disembodied fangs in the very nooks and crannies where we hoped to find gold. And there were dozens of them. I worried that a single jab could lead to the sort of infection that I was so keen for us to avoid.

As part of my early project planning, I had sought medical advice from a cautious doctor. His simple, well-informed opinion regarding the planned dives at Hope's Nose was: 'Don't do it!'

Being naive about medical matters and excrement, I had hoped that the team could take some pills, or have a couple of vaccination jabs, to protect us from the diseases that the sewage might harbour. I was aware that we might encounter nasties such as Weil's disease, salmonella, E. coli, leptospirosis, hepatitis A and so on. The doctor I had met was unsympathetic.

'You're doing what, exactly?' he'd asked, peering at me over his glasses. He listened closely as I ran over the rough plan once more and then gave his verdict. 'It's lunacy,' he said bluntly. 'Don't be a fool, you'll almost certainly catch something.'

He described the many different ways that viruses, bacteria and parasites can enter the body, and assured me that there were no precautionary pills or jabs that we could take. But even after his apocalyptic appraisal, he could see that I was still not convinced. Again, over tilted glasses, he gave me a long stern look and summarized, as a priest might counsel a habitual sinner, 'Just don't do it.'

I left the surgery thoughtful and disappointed. Of course, the raft of human filth was an issue, but surely not enough to cause the trip to be cancelled. That evening, I devised a plan. We would lay a tarpaulin up on the beach and fill it with a strong disinfectant and seawater, to make a sanitizing bath. Then after each dive we would roll about in it for a few minutes to safely decontaminate. Predictably, we made no progress with my ludicrous cleansing-bath idea, but unpredictably, none of us got ill.

Like the scallops, the other marine life in this artificially enriched area was abundant and spectacular. Shoals of small fish darted through the shadowy water, pausing to approach us whenever we disturbed the thick, dark silt and exposed a tangled mass of tiny crimson worms. In the wide, sandy hollows to the side of the effluent plume, enormous well-camouflaged flatfish lay motionless but suddenly exploded from the sand whenever we got too close, as if a part of the seabed had suddenly decided to shift sideways – startling me every time. They were the marine equivalent of a surprised pheasant bursting from the undergrowth during a quiet woodland walk.

I was struck by the intelligence of the mottled and striped cuttlefish that came to watch us. They seemed genuinely curious and would move right in to see what we were doing. Sometimes they even touched my suit or equipment with their tentacles, as if to better understand what it was. I liked these soft, trusting and fearless little beings. Any protected wall of rock was thick with dark-red anemones, often with groups of starfish close by. And it seemed like every species of British crab was scuttling about somewhere around us. The large edible crabs looked delicious, but having survived our scallop meal unscathed, I wasn't prepared to tempt fate further.

Of all the creatures, the hermit crabs were my favourites, as they evoked fond memories. When I was small and my family lived in the caravan above Newgale beach in Pembrokeshire, I had spent many hours on the beach below with my mother, gathering the poor little creatures and filling rock pools with them. I developed a particular fondness for hermit crabs and still find them endearing.

There is a beauty in scuba diving that has no equal. It is often likened to flying, but for me it's much better than that. In most forms of flight, if an engine stops, a parachute fails or a stay breaks, you plunge to the ground – you are not personally 'buoyant' in the air; whereas a good diver aims to have 'neutral buoyancy'. That is, to be able to hang in the water neither rising nor falling, which can be achieved through a careful balance of weights and air pockets. On days when I got this just right, I could swim slowly across the seabed breathing in to rise over an obstacle and then out again to drift back down – sublime moments of zero gravity.

In underwater prospecting, however, weightlessness is mostly a hindrance, as you cannot use most of the normal tools. Picks, spades, rakes, crowbars and even gold pans are useless to the weightless diver. Besides, steel tools rust quickly when used in the sea, so we had brought blue plastic gold pans with us. Struggling to adapt river techniques for working on the seabed, we finally found the Henderson pump to be the most useful. George Alfred Henderson, an expert gold prospector from the English Lake District, had developed these suction pipes to pull gold particles out from cracks in the riverbed. At their most simple, these devices are no more than a tennis ball on a stick in a short length of rainwater gutter downpipe. While clearly a syphon and designed to suck, Alf's invention is mostly known in the prospecting world as a Henderson 'pump'.

We had three of these pumps and soon developed a unique way of using them, whereby our weightlessness became an advantage. Working in pairs, one diver would dump enough air to make himself heavy (negatively buoyant) and lie flat on the seabed while holding the mouth of the pump. His job was to guide the pipe into the hole being worked and wait to feel the other diver pull the tennis ball up. The nozzle was then quickly moved out and over a bucket to catch any heavy debris that fell out. The second diver was simply to act as the pump's 'engine' by moving the tennis ball plunger up and down. When I had this job, I found that the best technique was to put a little air in the feet of my drysuit and then hang completely upside down above the diver below. While comical to look at, this kept my arms and legs out of the way and used my weightlessness to advantage. Obviously, there must be no sea current whatsoever for the technique to work, which meant that the black silt that came out of cracks and holes rapidly engulfed the worksite, reducing our visibility to zero. But by keeping well apart, there was no chance of us bumping into each other or knocking the bucket over.

This acrobatic teamwork was great fun and very different from using a Henderson pump in a river. There was also the element of mystery. With both divers working in a dense cloud of silt, communicating only by tapping on the pipe, we had absolutely no idea what we were finding. This would only be revealed later when the bucket was hauled up to the surface and its enigmatic contents carefully washed in a gold pan.

On the sixteenth day of our expedition, we found our first gold.

With two bucketfuls of heavy, gritty material that had been

sucked out from cracks in the bedrock, we motored around to the little sheltered beach in Hope Cove where we had dived for scallops. When the buckets were taken ashore, the dark muck in them looked really promising, thick with shell fragments, lead fishing weights and bits of copper and iron.

I tipped just enough material from one of the buckets to cover the bottom of my pan and walked out into the sea. It's always important not to overload a gold pan, or some of the gold will be washed over the rim and lost. And it's virtually impossible to use a normal washing technique if the pay dirt is rich with heavy metallic minerals, or the actual metals themselves. When knee-deep, I swirled the pan to make a wave of clear water wash over it. And there, suddenly radiant upon the dark crud, lay a beautiful gold and diamond ring.

This was totally unexpected. I stared at it in astonishment for a few seconds, thinking, *where on earth have you come from?* The whole point of this trip was to hunt for rare ferns of natural gold; I hadn't been expecting to find jewellery. I yelled at the others to come and look. They waded out to see the ring and then watched quietly as I carefully panned the rest of the bucket. The mood was almost sombre; there was no whooping, shouting or punching the air. After over two weeks of failure, we simply felt huge relief at having finally succeeded in finding gold in some form. The panning steadily revealed more gold jewellery: an earring, some broken chain and part of a pendant. Then, as the last of the heavy material was washed away, a bright arc of water-worn fragments of crystallized gold appeared. They formed a neat yellow smile in the blue plastic pan and seemed pleased to see us too.

*

The next day we were understandably eager to clean out more of the bedrock cracks and increase our haul of gold. We arrived on site a little early, and there was still too much current to work with the Henderson pumps. David hadn't forgotten the cave he had found earlier and suggested that I take a look at it with him, rather than sit in the boat wasting time.

I was hesitant. We had spoken to local fishermen the day before and, while they had a moderate interest in our hunt for gold, they mostly wanted to know if we had seen any of the record-breaking conger eels that were said to live in the hollows at the base of the cliff. Nevertheless, not wishing to seem idle or cowardly, I agreed to go exploring, and we were soon making our way down to where the five main calcite veins emerge from the cliff. David led me to one that had been totally eroded to form a long and narrow undersea cave. This was exciting. There was a strong possibility that this vein had been dropping tiny particles of gold onto the floor of this cave for centuries and might even have formed a thin carpet of gold dust!

I am not qualified to cave dive and neither was David, so we agreed to approach the whole undertaking with the utmost caution. We should have laid a line from the outside of the cave, but at that point I hadn't expected it to be so deep. We decided to venture in the first time without any gold recovery equipment just to see what it was like in there. I didn't want to disturb the sediment on the cave floor and lose our visibility, so we crept in using only our fingertips to pull us along, our legs and diving fins trailing behind us, horizontal and perfectly still.

We soon lost all daylight and switched on our underwater torches. As we edged along with fingertip paces, pitch-dark fissures and holes appeared in the cave's walls. I was now plagued by the thought that any one of them could be the lair of a monster eel and imagined the creature, furious at our lights and disturbance, lunging out and grabbing my hand or head. I moved the grip on my torch so that I held it by the very end, as far away from the potentially conger-annoying bulb as possible. While this seemed a reasonable precaution against a giant eel attack, I noticed that David's chosen defence was to drop back a bit and let me go first.

The further in we went, the narrower the sea cave became. The floor was a thin layer of small, rounded rocks and silt, and didn't look promising in terms of finding gold. I imagined that during storms and heavy swell, the water would surge along the full length of the cave. The cobblestones would be heaved back and forth like a quern, grinding any fragile gold crystals into powder.

While still trying to assess the possibility of finding any gold, I moved through a narrow gap where my shoulders brushed both sides of the cave. I had no idea how far in we were at that point, as it had been totally dark for some time. It certainly felt like a long way, but then again, we had been moving very slowly. I stopped and looked up. The air I breathed out was forming large silvery bubbles on the cave roof – mirror bright, like liquid mercury. For some reason this spooked me, and I stopped to consider our position.

My air cylinder contents gauge told me that I still had over 45 minutes of breathing air left. But as I had dismissed the hopeful 'carpet of gold' vision, there was nothing more I wanted to see in here. I considered the narrows that I had just pushed through and what would happen if I were to get stuck. There was plenty of air in my cylinder for the dive, but nowhere near sufficient to keep me alive long enough to be rescued. It was a chilling thought.

I couldn't imagine a scenario where the rescuers would be able to do anything other than recover my dead body. It was time to go home.

I turned to face David and signalled that we were finished. He must have been thinking something similar as he grinned, rolled and shot off back along the cave – finning like mad. The silt rose in thick clouds and all visibility was lost. My torch would be useless now. My scuba training had included a test for this sort of situation, when we'd been asked to dive while wearing blacked-out masks, to see if anyone freaked out. I sank to the cave floor to touch something and think. It was disconcerting to have four of my five senses negated while alone deep in a sea cave. I had experienced a few moments of panic once when caught in a small avalanche at dusk on an Italian mountain. It must not happen here. I have twice seen a diver panicking, and it is a terrible thing.

My hands landed on two breast-shaped cobbles and the idiot in me smiled. The ridiculous moment broke the spell of sensory deprivation, and I relaxed. I knew where I was and, critically, which direction I was facing. I had enough air, so thankfully time was not an issue. The cave probably had no recoverable gold and I was pleased to be leaving it. I took four slow breaths and checked my thoughts again. Once comfortable with being alone in my pitch-black, touch-only world, I began the slow and careful crawl back along the cave floor.

When we were finally out of the cave, up through the sewage and back on the surface, David asked innocently why had I taken so long, but the question was rhetorical. He had a darkly mischievous sense of humour, and it must have amused him hugely to think of me blindly groping my way out, far behind him. Perhaps the fishermen had had a similar sense of humour and were chuckling inwardly when they described the giant eels that lay in wait for us. For the record, the only wildlife I saw while going into the cave were small groups of timid translucent prawns. They glowed in the bright torchlight and, dazzled, flitted about randomly like poor little fairies.

That evening, Tasmanian Richard called and asked me to pick him up from Torquay railway station. At home he specialized in a beautiful red-orange mineral called crocoite, but he was also a good gold prospector. A true bushman, he cut a figure somewhat like Crocodile Dundee's little brother. I found him outside the station, leaning on a stone wall, wearing his customary full-length stockman's coat and a leather hat. A few of the local lads were sniggering at his clothing, which looked completely out of place. Lucky for them he hadn't noticed yet.

I planned a first dive with Richard while the others went off fishing. Some of the gold-bearing cracks that we had worked earlier were not totally cleaned out. The deeper hollows, where the gold was most likely to be, were still partly jammed with a tough iron concretion, formed when pieces of iron lie for a long time on the seabed. Chemical changes cause the iron to corrode and grow into a dark formless mass, gradually encompassing everything that surrounded the original iron object. The lamellar structure of the migrated iron makes it very hard, but not brittle – it easily absorbs hammer blows. A large mass of concretion filled one end of a long narrow fissure and I hoped we could break it up, as it might contain a range of heavy things, from copper nails and seashells, to coins and fragments of gold.

We lay face to face along the fissure, an arm's length apart, and began chipping away with crowbars at where the concretion had grown onto the limestone side walls. At first, I focused on trying to free a shipwreck's large copper deck pin that jutted out of the concretion. It had a square profile and the British government's 'broad arrow' property mark punched into it. The deck pin had probably fallen into this hole centuries ago. If only we could hear it, this poignant length of copper from an old wooden Royal Navy ship could tell the awful story of the wreck. But for now, the pin was silent and stubbornly would not budge. I changed my technique and tried to create a fracture in the limestone. Unexpectedly, the chunk of concretion that held the embedded pin suddenly broke away and, pleased, I lifted it out to examine my prize.

But the moment the lump of iron and copper was clear of the hole, Richard shook his gloved hand urgently and pointed. There was gold glowing down in the shadows. Only a finger's width of the piece was showing, a nugget-shaped, water-worn edge that was very clearly part of something much bigger. Many years earlier I had talked about Hope's Nose gold with the curator of the museum in Truro. And he was very much of the opinion that not all the gold had grown into the signature dendritic ferns. He believed that some of the rare alloy had simply formed into solid blobs. I was ecstatic as this could be one of them, and a truly spectacular find.

With Antipodean indifference, Richard went to give the nugget a bash. I stopped him with frantic signals, trying to emphasise that this piece of gold was delicate and must not be touched. He looked at me scornfully – a soft Pom, treating a nugget like we had just found an unexploded bomb. But he couldn't have known quite how rare a find this was in England, and I didn't want a single scratch on what I hoped was a totally unique and museum-quality specimen.

He humoured me and we switched from using clumsy crowbars to the fine points of our dive knives. Very slowly, we teased away fragments of the dark-grey concretion that still entombed the gleaming nugget. And as we worked the piece got larger and larger, until at last I was able to gently lift it out. It was huge, as long as my middle finger and about half as wide. We took turns to hold the nugget – even in the dull sepia light it gleamed and was magnificent.

It struck me that it was not as heavy as I would have expected. But it was full of holes and still had plenty of iron crud attached to it. Also, the palladium in this natural alloy has a specific gravity of only 12.0 – much lighter than gold's 19.3.

The biggest gold nugget ever recorded in England was found in 1808 in the Carnon valley in Cornwall – a record that I hoped had just been broken.

Our time in Devon now over, we had achieved what we'd set out to do and packing up to go home was a joyous muddle. We were in high spirits, our six successful days having wiped out all memory of the dreadful first two weeks. And we were already fondly remembering the few good times during those idle days: the boat's first thrilling test run in a threatening sea, and the commando-like endurance of carrying all of our diving kit down the long Hope's Nose peninsula and then carrying the whole lot back up again – along with a sack of scallops. The harmless sewage, the abundant wildlife, the cave. I even began to fondly remember the enormous Cornish pasty that had nearly choked me one morning.

Once back home, I looked up the full story of the original Hope's Nose gold find. I had suspected that it was the miners, digging out the new sewer tunnel, who had discovered the dendritic gold. But in fact, these unlucky workers missed the gold veins by a whisker.

Instead, I learned that in April 1922, Professor W T Gordon led a party of geology students from King's College London to Hope's Nose. He was trying to chip off a specimen of calcite, but was surprised to find that it would not come free. Looking more closely, he was astonished to find that the desired sample was being held in place by numerous sprigs of wiry gold. The professor recorded his pleasing discovery with a small report in *Nature* magazine. A few years later, the site was visited by Sir Arthur Russell, an accomplished collector of British minerals. Having more time and some explosives to hand, he recovered fabulous specimens of the crystallized gold from the five main calcite veins. His extensive and remarkable gold collection is now housed in the Natural History Museum in London.

I also discovered that the *Journal of the Royal Sanitary Institute* records a speech made at a public meeting in 1878 by the designer of Torquay's new sewer, Sir Joseph Bazalgette. (This is the engineer who designed London's sewer system after the 'Great Stink' of 1858.) He proudly informed the good townspeople that, 'No seaside waters would be more pure and free from sewage contamination than will henceforth be the waters of Torbay!' I recalled our sepia dives and the lazy arc of thick brown sewage drifting out to sea, and I couldn't help thinking that Sir Joseph had overstated his achievements a little.

I knew that my main priority now was to get the nugget authenticated, and called my friend Dr Chris Halls at the Royal

School of Mines in London. I trusted Chris and knew that he would be discreet. I didn't want the world to know about this wonderful discovery just yet, as there might be even more of these rare nuggets buried under the concretion.

His office was high in the old building and absolutely packed with stacks of books and equipment, with only a narrow path leading to his desk. He squeezed out of the maze to meet me and took the nugget. Like an anxious parent, I hovered in the doorway, watching as he examined the piece with a large magnifying glass. After an age he looked up and called out, 'I don't think it's an artefact.' The tone suggested that this was good news, but I had no idea what he was talking about. His head dropped back down to study the piece more closely with a hand lens. I waited patiently before interrupting him to ask what he'd meant. 'It isn't man-made,' he said. 'I think it's natural.' Delighted and hugely relieved, I relaxed – this was the expert confirmation I had dreamed of.

Chris kept the nugget to do one final test. He wanted to shoot it with a laser and analyse the elements in the vapour produced. 'We'll use laser ablation inductively coupled plasma mass spectrometry,' he told me with a huge smile.

Two weeks later, I was on a train travelling north when Chris phoned me. His voice was unusually calm, and I instantly knew that something was wrong. 'It's not looking good,' he said. 'There are peaks of copper and zinc – the "nugget" is a form of copper alloy, possibly just brass.' I was stunned and utterly deflated. My hope of finding a record-breaking English nugget – and everything that it promised – had just died. All my impassioned 'fortune and glory' dreams were stillborn. I quietly thanked him and flopped back into my seat. Just a piece of molten brass. The bitter irony of the incredible coincidence that the find represented was astounding: with Richard, I had found a gold-nugget-shaped piece of gold-coloured metal, in an actual gold vein – and yet, it was not gold.

I have kept the 'False Hope' nugget and still look at it occasionally – a curious memento of the trip and, while a false dawn, a taste of what success might feel like. No doubt the 'brass nugget' has its own amazing story. Perhaps it is detritus from a terrible fire on the very same ship as the copper deck pin? After all, it lay embedded in the iron concretion just below the pin. But, even so, it wasn't the story that I wanted: 'Divers find England's biggest gold nugget.'

Nevertheless, even after allowing for the nugget's disappointment, overall, the expedition had been a huge success. I had learned so much about working under the sea and adapting river-prospecting techniques for marine weightlessness. This new knowledge would be very useful on future diving projects. Besides, we had had a great adventure and against the odds, nobody had become ill or been injured. And, as the thoughtful Ian Stephen had once advised me, we had made some excellent memories to enjoy in our old age.

The haul of genuine gold that we had recovered in only a few days was pleasing too. We had found a heap of jewellery, which I can only imagine had come down the sewer, along with seven large pieces of rock containing gold-bearing calcite vein and a small phial full of panned fragments of the famous crystallized gold.

*

Some years after our dive, the Hope's Nose sewer was turned off and the sea is now pristine. Sir Joseph's boast has finally come to pass, and the seaside waters of Torbay are indeed pure. It would be good to go back. There must be lots more gold to be had, and it would be much easier to work now, in the better light!

But there was one hard and expensive lesson in particular that I learned from the Hope's Nose diving project. And it was this. If I wanted to do anything more than just skirmishes into the world of gold and treasure hunting, I needed time – and lots of it. More days than any employer would ever allow. The three full weeks that I had planned for this project had turned out to be barely enough.

I promised myself that I would never again be limited by time. The idiosyncrasies of tides, wind and weather would be absorbed and endured as part of any future plan. And when next I went out to find gold, I would double the project's duration to six weeks, or treble it to nine. In fact, I would allow whatever time was needed – because it would be as a free man!

6

ON BEING FREE

'Whatever you can do, or dream you can, begin it.
Boldness has genius, power and magic in it.'

—W H Murray, *The Scottish Himalayan Expedition*

For me, freedom is like sunshine, or love. Dazzling and potent with its promise of unfettered dominion over one's time and self. But it too should be approached with caution.

As a young man, I once asked my mother, 'How will I know when I'm in love?'

She paused, smiled and said, 'You'll just know.'

At the time, her unhelpfully short and mysterious reply annoyed me. But she was right – and being free is just the same. As with love, you can't know where freedom will lead you until you are fully committed to it. And whether spectacular or devastating, you will know when it's the real thing.

After 28 years within employment's comfortable and secure embrace, well accustomed to the voluntary bonds of a civil servant's routines and conformity, I struggled to imagine being free. To leave the familiarity of my tribe and to lose my sense of place, worth and belonging was almost unthinkable. Was it midlife lunacy to abandon my career, which I had so carefully crafted over almost three decades, and with it, the distant candle of a 'gold-plated' Civil Service pension, which, like a desk-bound office moth, I was expected to surrender my life for? After I announced that I was leaving, of all things to go looking for gold, one colleague rushed up and gripped my arm. With all the urgency of a parent stopping a child from carelessly crossing a busy road, he implored, 'For Christ's sake, Vince, think of your pension!' But I already had, and chosen life instead.

I decided to make the transition, and to pursue risk and dreams over safety and comfort. Leaving work was a huge decision and at no point was I flippant or reckless about what I was planning to do. There was always the danger of failing, and I needed to have a resilient plan in place. I was not going through this huge divorce-like wrench, away from a familiar and pleasant job to be lost, poor or lonely. My preparations focused on *why* I was doing this, *what* I was hoping to achieve and *how* I would make it work – especially financially. I had dreams, but was not some hippy dreamer who thought that I could live on thin air. For the first time in my adult life, I would be without a regular salary and wholly self-sufficient. My freedom had to be thrilling, exciting and full of life, or the cost of achieving it would be too high. If you don't know where you are going, you're unlikely to get there – and I *did* know!

My 40th birthday lit the slow fuse for everything else that followed. In the event it was nothing like a midlife crisis, but rather a spectacular awakening. And all from a few moments spent pondering about what being 40 years old actually meant. The maths was simple and a total shock. At the time, life expectancy for men of my generation in the United Kingdom was 77 years. So even if I had average luck, I realized that I was now more than halfway through. This singular birthday, my 40th, a fulcrum hardly noticed by many, forced me to face a harsh reality: that I had just passed my life's tipping point.

And then my awakening became even harsher. I began to recollect all the people I'd known who had not been lucky enough to reach the age of 77. After all, the number was an average, not a threshold. Now aware that the Grim Reaper might soon notice me too, further maudlin thoughts added to the pressure to get a grip on my life. I recalled conversations with elderly people who cheerfully related how time had speeded up as they got older. This was another factor that I needed to consider: that on top of the unwelcome life-expectancy mathematics, there was also our *perception* of time to consider. Even Albert Einstein considered time a 'stubbornly persistent illusion'. Could I slow down my own perception of time by filling each day with wonder and new experiences?

Until that moment, I had been happily drifting through life as if I were immortal. I still felt young, with a hazy, overconfident expectation of an unlimited and healthy amount of time ahead of me – easily enough to do anything and everything I wanted to. And comforted by this illusion, I had been perfectly content within a conventional working person's framework – my days each year being divided unequally, with my employer having the lion's share of them, and structured as a long ribbon of fives and twos. I was, of course, grateful for the few precious extra holidays granted at Christmas and during the summer.

As at school, each one of my five working days was ruthlessly governed by the clock. My punctual arrival, use of breaks and timely departure were routinely monitored and recorded. My diary set a course through each cluttered week, and my wristwatch was the compass with which to navigate safe passage through the sandbanks and shoals of meetings, deadlines, appointments and the never-ending flow of incoming mail. Every week, the voyage was slightly different, yet almost the same . . .

I discussed all of this with my father, who added yet another woeful thought to the growing list. He said that he had known many people who had made wonderful plans for their retirement, but upon reaching their sunlit uplands, he had watched their passion wane as they lost interest and gave up. The life-affirming vision that they had nurtured all through their working lives was simply abandoned, ultimately ripped to shreds by the merciless shrapnel of illness, accident, apathy, their partner's death, or the most disappointing of all – simply discarded for the siren call of comfort, television and slippers.

The startling revelation of what it really meant to be 40 years old was life-changing, as powerful as when I'd met the gold prospector in that old tungsten mine 20 years earlier. As a convert to the cult of *carpe diem*, I evangelized to all those who would listen. More recently some have asked me, 'So what about your fiftieth and sixtieth birthdays?' Well, they meant nothing to me in comparison, as I had already accepted the transience of my own existence and had taken my life up a gear. And now, every day, I am just delighted to still be above ground!

If my 40th birthday lit the slow fuse to freedom, the Hope's Nose project blew on the smouldering cord and it glowed a little brighter. The scuba diving adventure to find crystallized gold had almost failed through a lack of time. I learned that if I wanted to throw myself into big gold-hunting projects, it had to be as a free man.

In the years before this, I had accepted that my time was limited, so I fed my prospector yearnings with rushed weekend trips to rivers in Scotland and Wales. My family's summer holidays were, by careful coincidence, always taken in the gold-bearing areas of the country that we were visiting. And these were truly halcyon days – of rushing water, summer sunshine, fresh sparkling gold and my trusting and tough little children, completely at home in these wild places. It's fair to say that I was obsessed with finding gold all through my parenting years. But I kept my ambitions in check, as I knew that I needed the security of employment to support the family – at least until my children were raised. And now they were.

Another important point to make is that I wasn't unhappy at work. In fact, I had a lovely office with a huge antique desk, a big comfy ergonomic chair and two windows that actually opened – as good as it could possibly get. And the people I worked with were great too. I had known some of them since my college days – many were more like friends than work colleagues. My leaving was not about running away from something bad, but running towards something better.

I was interviewed recently on a windswept clifftop. We looked down into the wide rocky bay and talked about the fortune in gold that was lost on a shipwreck just below us. The presenter paused, then suddenly said, 'I suppose we could call this your office.' What a lovely thing to say. My office now has no doors, infinite windows and can be anywhere in the world that I choose . . .

*

While it's important not to ignore money as a base resource, I believe that money is choice and nothing more. A curious illusory lubricant, promissory notes and numbers that smooth life's path. A bit like religion, money works as long as everybody believes in it. And God help anyone without enough of these 'choice tokens'. So yes, money is choice and nothing more, but choice is freedom – and that is everything.

I wasn't rich nor due to inherit any time soon, and I didn't suffer from a gambler's treacherous sense of feeling lucky. The odds of winning the UK National Lottery were about 45 million to one. Apparently, and tragically, hopeful ticket holders were far more likely to die while watching the draw than to win it. These were not odds that I was comfortable with. The chances of me finding enough gold to live on were very much better, but still far too slim to be relied upon. So I needed to create just enough money to exist in my new life.

I have met many people living an alternative lifestyle who've been disparaging about money. I do not trust these people. It often turns out that their family have wealth, a trust fund or a large manor house hidden away in the background somewhere. As the old saying goes, 'Scratch a hippy and find a Porsche.' I had to fund my freedom with work and ideas, not wishful thinking.

Twenty years earlier, I had felt the desperate, sickening grip of hardship; of a hopeless despair that had burned right through me. It had been when I'd mortgaged myself to the limit to buy and renovate a derelict house in Scotland, but badly underestimated the effort and money needed to do this – and then the mortgage interest rate soared to a home-wrecking 14 per cent. First to go were our luxuries – no more holidays, meals out, cinema, treats, new clothes or new toys – but it still wasn't enough. Next went the comfort of heating, but again, it wasn't enough. Lastly, our food was rationed and basic. As the breadwinner for a family of five, I felt a total failure and couldn't think how to tighten our belts any further.

One evening our dinner was a curried cabbage. I sat staring at the steaming pile of spiced pale-green leaves and thought, *we cannot live like this*. Overwhelmed by the melancholy of knowing that we had hit rock bottom, an inspiration suddenly flashed into my mind. The answer was obvious. In focusing totally on how to *save* money, I had missed the other option: to *earn* more. It was as if an angel had just murmured to me, 'Work harder, dimwit!' There are 24 hours in each day, and only about 8 are needed for sleep. I would work through the wakeful 16. Very soon we ate well, were warm and had holidays again. I can only say that this is what got results for me: when things get tough, don't sink into belt-tightening misery; look up, get a grip and work harder.

Scarred by the misery of the lesson learned, I swore that I would never let it happen again. In the years since the curried cabbage misery, I nurtured a portfolio of new skills and knowledge, and I now planned to fund my freedom with short bursts of intense and lucrative activity – until I struck gold. I would reverse the work–life balance of my old employment by selling Christmas trees in December and running a few gold-panning courses during the summer. All other time would be mine.

In preparation, I had already rented a field from a local farmer and planted a thousand little spruce and fir seedlings. It would be a couple of years before they could be harvested and I would buy in trees to sell in the meantime and build a market. Alongside this, I arranged a handful of weekend gold courses with the entrepreneurial owners of a small country hotel in Scotland. This simple 'sausages and ice cream' business model worked, and I had a safety net to underwrite the uncertainties of my new life as a gold prospector. My wealth lay not in having money, but knowing that I could make some whenever I needed to. Besides which, I was single again now and knew that I could live very modestly if necessary. I drank little, had no sense of fashion and wore my clothes until threadbare. Also, if unexpectedly things got really tough, I could forage for some of my food and heat my tiny cottage with sticks gleaned from the local woodlands.

I am dwelling upon the finances out of honesty: it was a worrying time. During 28 years of being employed by a government department, it was as if a paternal benevolence had always walked beside me in life, holding my hand. I was accustomed to this kindly benefactor generously paying me whether I worked hard, or barely at all – as if it were my birthright. For 336 months, my wages effortlessly appeared in my bank account, as regular as clockwork, even when I was off sick, injured or scuffing about on holiday. But now the ticking had stopped. I had chosen independence and nobody would be there to hold my hand anymore.

There was a brief time when I thought that I might be able to boost my new life's income with television fees. A production company had got in touch, as they were making a series about people who were radically changing their lives. My story seemed to fit the bill perfectly: 'civil servant with gold fever absconds to go prospecting'. A crew came to my home and interviewed me, then visited the office and filmed several of my colleagues. It all seemed to be going really well, and I was excited. How wonderful to have a programme made that captured my dream and recorded the transition and how it all panned out.

But a telephone call from the director brought me back down to earth: my story had been rejected. I was so disappointed.

Vainly, I could not imagine what other stories had bettered my plans for gold-hunting adventures. The frustration must have been apparent in my voice. He paused, and in the way that people speak their truth quietly, he lowered his voice. 'Look, you should be pleased,' he whispered. 'Don't you realize that people are selected to fail, and we don't think that you will.' I put the phone down and sat back, bewildered. I had just been dropped from something that I really wanted to do, and apparently, this was a curiously back-handed compliment. The production company wanted heartache for a *schadenfreude* audience and had decided that I wouldn't provide any!

In the sombre community of large organizations, if somebody resigns unexpectedly there is always the suspicion of wrongdoing. But mine was a joyous exit entirely of my own choosing, and I wanted everybody to know that. I decided to address this institutional prejudice with a grand valedictory statement, and blew my last two months' salary on a spectacular farewell party. The merrymaking was to mark my crossing a Rubicon. For whether I succeeded or failed, I would not be coming back, tail between my legs, begging to be reinstated.

I resent money being wasted, leaking away on such things as unnecessary insurance and over-filled kettles. But I am completely happy to splash out all that I have on celebrating any of life's great milestones: births, marriages and resignations. I was once chastised for overdoing everything and maybe I do, but I have never yet found this trait to be a disadvantage. So now I styled my goodbye celebration on the one J R R Tolkien wrote for the hobbit Bilbo Baggins when he was leaving the safety of the Shire. It felt appropriate and metaphorical.

A large neat lawn stretched away from my office, and passed beneath a copse of graceful silver birch. Three picnic benches tucked among these trees offered workers dappled shade for a break in the fresh air, or a quiet lunch. It would be the perfect private setting for my farewell. Soon, before the morning's dew had even dried, excited chatter filled the airy space. On this day alone, tranquillity withdrew, and the forest garden bustled with eager preparations. Had Tolkien been there with us and his books as yet unwritten, he may have made some notes! Four dozen golden straw bales were scattered on the verdant turf – scratchy rustic seating for the many guests. A huge white marquee, my canvas cavern feasting hall, billowed as four strong men heaved it into shape and scattered yet more bales within. Later, weary dancers soaked in wine and sweat would rest on them, grateful for the straw's soft warmth. And later still, these simple benches could be pushed together as they made their beds.

I overdid everything – too much wine, two stout barrels filled with frothy hoppy beer and two-score bottles of champagne. And food spread across five tables, a feast piled high in hog-roast scented air. Then morris dancers came and leapt and kicked and cracked their short sticks hard. A cheer went up, we all enjoyed their show and shepherded the ragged troupe towards some well-earned beer.

Still sober, I wandered through this merry medieval fair to greet and thank all those who had travelled from far and wide to join me. I was humbled by the abundance of goodwill. And then, the strangest thing . . .

Three friends grabbed me and roughly stripped me of my office shirt and tie. Podgy and confused, I stood lily-white and naked to the waist. Then worse, the self-appointed captain of the farce commanded that my clothes be burned – and so they were. First splashed with an incendiary oil and held up high on a long pole for all to see, and then a match was struck. To whistles, whoops and clapping from a most appreciative crowd, the curling yellow flames soon engulfed my neat attire. Charred fragments fell and scorched the grass, and like a man condemned I was ushered centre stage.

The plot continued to unfold, but its purpose was not yet clear: was this to be a baptism or another rite? From within the grinning throng, my three grown children stepped forward. I looked on, helpless but enthralled. Each held a scarlet cushion, bearing the essentials for my new career: a long stockman's coat, a thick bushy beard and battered wide-brimmed hat. Once clothed again and my modesty restored, and having sprouted an unlikely set of whiskers, the old leather hat was slowly placed upon my head as if to crown me. Yet in place of mace and orb, I was handed the symbols of a gold prospector's rough office: a traditional steel pan and fine, long-handled shovel – one for each hand.

I posed silently for a flurry of photographs, feeling silly but overwhelmed. These were my friends, and their playful generosity in constructing this performance had left me speechless. To support me so well on this day, and rejoice in my metamorphosis, my rite of passage from two windows to the world. I stood and smiled, choked with emotion, and knew that I had already gathered my first treasure. The gold and gems were scattered all around me, big-hearted and still grinning as they wandered off to find fresh drinks.

As dusk fell, figures moved between the slender birch to set up pyrotechnics. Two long belts of dark-red Chinese firecrackers were hung like banners, each holding five hundred shots. Once lit, the fuses smouldered for a moment, and then as in a fearful ambush, the very air was shocked and ripped apart. One thousand detonations flashed and boomed and echoed from the empty office wall. Then sudden silence fell, the deafening barrage over. A thin white smoke hung like eerie mist and drifted through the watchful crowd, who waited, not sure they wanted any more.

Across the lawn from deep within the marquee, a fiddle sprang to life and called us in. The folk band, coiled and ready to explode, sprang into life. Our admiration fed them through the hours, and tirelessly they stayed and played with jigs and reels well past their hired time. Still clad as a clichéd prospector, with whiskers, hat and long brown coat, I grabbed the last two bottles of champagne and thrust one into each side pocket. I felt a stockman would approve, in principle at least. Through the dark hours, I drank and danced and laughed, and revelled in this joyous night.

When voices hushed, and more people had made beds of bales than were still awake, I left the marquee and headed back to the birch trees. Above, the stars were fading now, and the damp grass was thick with shattered scraps of firecracker paper, like autumn leaves that rustled as I walked. Wrapped tightly in my tough new coat against the pre-dawn chill, I lay on a picnic bench and looked up. Through the tracery of myriad twigs and tiny leaves I watched the new day's birth. Content to my very soul, I sighed, it was done – my office life was over.

7

THE SUMMER OF DREAMS

'Never in my life had I felt so fat with time.'

—Laurie Lee, *As I Walked Out One Midsummer Morning*

On the Friday, I had been middle-management, employed and office furnished. On Monday, I was nobody – and it felt good. I had been reborn, reincarnated, with a second chance at life. My eternity was now stretching out before me, an unfettered freedom in this undiscovered country. I woke up just before eight o'clock on Monday, 9 May 2005, sat up in bed and deliriously happy, I chuckled to myself, 'Now Vince, don't mess it up!'

The rest of May passed with an unfamiliar grace in my new world. There was no pressure to do anything, and each day was mine and mine alone. After so many years of being employed, I surprised myself at how quickly I adapted to this feral existence. Time flowed measured only by dawn, dusk and whether it would rain, and I relaxed and drifted with the current. My wristwatch was ceremonially put away, an object of control from my past and of no use in my present. And I decided to stop shaving, not so much from wanting to look like a gold prospector, as simply out of idleness. Shaving was an office routine, and my electric razor followed my wristwatch and alarm clock into a cluttered drawer that was seldom opened. I took to having long baths instead of showers, relaxing in the water's warm embrace until finally, the hot water tank drained and, crinkled as a newborn, I had to get out. The pace of life dropped to a languorous mindfulness, and I wallowed in the unfamiliar luxury. It felt like I had just won a 'time lottery' and was now a millionaire, all of a sudden immensely rich in days.

Yet I was not idle. I made the time to stand and stare and filled each waking hour. At first light, I got up to hear the dawn chorus. Like the sunrise itself, each day was wonderful yet different. Long before the sun appeared, a wood pigeon's soft notes might rouse the other birds. Or a tuneful blackbird would start the day with virtuoso confidence, a soloist sublime, head held high and yellow beak wide to let its rich and fluid melody cut through the twilit air. Others followed, each joyful voice unique, but lost in the cacophony of springtime's morning concert.

At midday, drowsy from each busy morning, I retreated to a hammock hung deep in the shadow of an ancient hawthorn. A short lunch, and when replete I would doze. Clusters of the tiny pink-white flowers above me, sun-warmed and ripe, poured their heady scent down through the spiny boughs, their curiously pleasing perfume washing over me. Somewhere above, an unseen yellowhammer called for bread and cheese. This blessed May with no rough winds, in perfect peace and welcome vernal warmth – the darling buds and I unfolded.

But the beloved month was ending. The apple blossom, perfumed bluebell, grassland's sweet cowslip and long lacy ribbons of roadside cow parsley wilted and left the stage. Wild roses rushed on to drape the hedgerows with fresh sprays of delicate pink and herald full summer's approach. I wondered, was I wasting my time? I had taken the bold leap from the security of employment to be free, not to dally about as a dreamy idler. My new world was full of possibilities, and now refreshed, I made a sweeping plan to go prospecting for the whole summer – until, with gold fever sated, the chill of winter sent me home again.

June broke like a rolling wave and tumbled towards summer's shore, washing aside the fragile spring. Ebullient life bustled beneath aquamarine skies and foaming cumulus, unrestrained, awakened and nurtured by sudden warmth and endless days. The sentient earth knew this time of ease and celebration, and relaxed. I felt it too, and telephoned Alf.

George Alfred Henderson was the bundle of energy who had developed the gold-finding suction pump. His lovely but stern wife, Jean, answered the phone, and as she held the purse strings, I phrased my question carefully: 'Can Alf come out to go panning?' I was in luck; she had been wanting him out of the house and my timing was opportune. Seventeen hours later, Alf and I arrived in Helmsdale in the far north of Scotland.

We planned to visit the site of one of Britain's very few genuine gold rushes. Short and sweet, it was all over in barely a year. The find is generally credited to a man returning from the Australian goldfields in 1868, one Robert Nelson Gilchrist. And this may be true, for he certainly prospected the area thoroughly and the widely publicised results of his work started the 1869 gold rush. However, the seminal work *The Gold Rocks of Great Britain and Ireland* by John Calvert, published in 1853, mentions a large gold nugget being found 'in the bed of the Kildonan, a mountain stream in 1840'. It also records the find of a nugget of about 15g in the River Helmsdale in 1818. So it is possible that this gold location was known to a few people much earlier. And drifting even further back into Scotland's ancient past, this area is said to have far more of the Pictish defensive stone tower 'brochs' than most of the far north – so, perhaps they knew too.

There were three reasons why the rush was over so quickly. The easy gold was soon worked out and, while widespread, the gold found by the miners rapidly diminished and did not pay. Of more concern to the Duke of Sutherland, who owned the estate, was that the diggings were taking place on the best sheep pasture and upsetting his tenant farmers. And lastly, the presence of a few hundred men digging in and around the waterways was damaging the estate's deerstalking and salmon fishing interests.

Once Alf and I had pitched our tents at Baile an Or, a hallowed place, where a shanty town of wooden huts had sprung up during the rush of 1869, we hurried off to the estate office to get our gold prospecting licences. I wanted to work by a small shepherd's bridge that crossed the Suisgill burn next to a large bun-shaped outcrop of bedrock.

Many years earlier, during a heatwave, I had met two men working hard beside this mound of water-worn schist. They'd seemed incongruous prospectors, dressed for the beach in colourful T-shirts and tiny shorts and sweating as they laboured with a rusty pick, shovel and long crowbar. The thin one, Bob from the Isle of Man, took a break and told me the story of his wonderful gold find – well, it was his wife's, really.

At the time, he had been obeying the laws of gold deposition and working some gravel on the inside of a long bend in the river. His wife didn't pan, so she was sunning herself on a warm rock across from him while giving herself a manicure with a small metal nail file. She idly began to scratch at the rock with the file and poked it into a long fissure that ran across the top of it. The file suddenly slipped from her hand and fell into the crack; annoyed, she implored Bob to help her retrieve it. He admitted he was not best pleased at his work being interrupted for such a menial task. But, to keep the domestic peace, he waded over with his gold pan and a large crowbar.

He told me that as soon as he opened the crack, he could see glints of gold in the dark peaty clay that had accumulated inside. Excited, he scooped out the promising muck with a sharpened spoon and loaded it into his old metal pan. His voice hushed as he told me it was the *sound* of the gold, not the sight of it, which told him just how rich the find was. As he dipped his pan into the river and swirled the dirt to free the gold from the thick clay, he heard the thrilling high notes of metal upon metal – of gold nuggets tumbling upon the pan's thin steel. He said it was enchanting, transcendent, and sounded like 'the ghosts of carthorses on a cobbled road'. I have forgotten just how many ounces of gold Bob said that he found that day, but he did show me one of the nuggets that he now carried with him for luck.

Crouching on the very rock where the jackpot discovery was made, Bob told his amazing story so well – impassioned, animated and all true. And I would have enjoyed it even more, if I had not been distracted the whole time by one of his testicles hanging out.

Trevor, the man working with Bob, was huge and had straight white hair in a sort of pageboy cut and an endearing chuckle.

He became a lifelong friend and constantly impressed me with his encyclopaedic knowledge of precious metal antiques. He was also close to brilliant at finding traces of natural gold in the most unlikely places. He once cautiously confided in me how he had helped some divers to extract gold coins from a chunk of concreted shipwreck, but the anecdote passed over my head, as at the time, I had no interest in that sort of treasure.

My friend Alf also knew Bob's story and told me that all the ground by the shepherd's bridge had been worked out, and he had a better place in mind, upstream and unknown. In a popular location there is little point in working the obvious gold traps, as every prospector worth their salt will have been there before you. The best you could hope for is to find a tiny piece or two that they've missed. In such rivers the trick is to find the second-best traps, or even better, those that lie hidden under gravel or beneath rushing white water.

I followed Alf upstream for about 20 minutes, when he stopped at a long straight stretch of unremarkable river. 'This is it!' he whispered, as if not wanting to be overheard.

There were no bends to predict a 'gold line', nor any tantalizing outcrops of cracked bedrock to tempt us – just a seemingly barren expanse of shallow water flowing smoothly over a level bed of coarse gravel. The 'gold line' is the theoretical path that gold takes as it moves downstream while a river is in full spate. When present, it's fairly predictable, as the gold flows along the shortest possible path. A motorcycle champion once told me that they call this a 'racing line'. While not all prospectors believe in the formation of gold lines, having found them more than once,

I do. The confusion may be caused by some gold-bearing rivers not having one. Past events, such as glaciation, landslips, fallen trees or the river changing its course will all confuse the 'gold line' phenomenon – or even create more than one line.

Alf could see what I was thinking and winked. 'Nobody else comes here,' he said with a grin.

We had each brought simple equipment – a gold pan, small crowbar, garden rake and 4-foot-long Henderson pump. Alf explained that he wanted us to move along each side of the riverbank, hunting for clues in this second-best, inconspicuous location. If we could find little cracks or weaknesses in the riverbank's bedrock, which then ran out across the river, we might be onto rich pickings. Any little pockets of bright gold should have been hidden from other hopefuls by the even carpet of cobbles and gravel.

We soon found a 'quartz stringer' – a narrow, fractured vein that crossed the river under the gravel at a slight diagonal. The more at right angles to the river's flow, the better the trap is, and this one would do fine.

Something not often talked about in gold prospecting, is just how much sunlight helps. A shallow river soon warms up and this allows for easier working and longer days. The panner isn't constricted by the mass of clothing needed to keep warm, nor grows so cold that shivering becomes a problem. (One February, I was so cold in a river that I couldn't even open my flask to pour a hot drink – and my panning was hopeless.) There is also the light. The sun shining over your shoulder brilliantly illuminates every murky nook and cranny, and even the most timid grains of gold shine out. The Suisgill is like this. The shallow water flows through sheep country with few trees, and everywhere the tough grasses are grazed down to little more than a green stubble that lines the banks and casts no shade. On stony slopes, clumps of heather provide shelter for the cackling grouse – and unimpeded, the sun warms the clear water and reveals all.

Working from each end of our quartz vein find, we set about clearing away the knee-deep layer of gravel that had hidden this gold trap. When I first started gold panning, I hadn't believed that a garden rake was a bona fide piece of prospecting equipment. I had never seen a rake being used by the gold-crazed old-timers in Hollywood films. But they are an excellent tool for pulling stony overburden away and quickly uncovering the bedrock.

Alf and I had settled on a good way of working – together, but separate. Just close enough to be of help if needed, but far enough apart not to crowd each other. And we would keep the gold we individually found. Partnerships nearly always end up with one person begrudging the other their share of the gold – a common theme in films! We worked so as not to tempt fate, or our friendship.

Besides which, Alf worked harder than me, which was perhaps surprising as he was 20 years my senior and half my size. Slim, whiskered and wiry, he was so smitten by gold fever that once he was on a river, he hardly ever stopped working. He was a decent and genial man with many idiosyncrasies, but he was not soft. There was also a streak of ruthlessness beneath the smiles and chatter – which is a good thing in the gold world. His main weakness was a fondness for very thin hand-rolled cigarettes. On sunny days, with playful carelessness, he would light these with a strong magnifying glass. And feign injury with a yelp if the searing point of focused sunlight missed and scorched his beard instead.

Unlike Alf, I liked to pace myself and took a short break of five to ten minutes every hour or so, when I would snack on a little chocolate, cheese and salami, or a small tin of fish. I wanted energy without feeling full, as panners spend much of their time hunched over and a full belly doesn't help. Out of a genuine concern, I sometimes suggested to Alf that he slow down a bit and join me in eating something. But he would scoff at my idleness and mutter that he didn't have the time. This was always followed by the phrase that seemed to be his life's guiding principle: 'We're a long time dead!'

We used his pumps to recover about 6g of gold each from that stringer of fractured quartz – an excellent start. The days that followed blurred into a similar pattern. We stayed on that same stretch of river, hunting out the small pockets of gold hidden beneath the shallow gravel. The natural gold in the Suisgill burn has a surprisingly high silver content, making it close to the alloy electrum. But when looking at the butter-coloured golden grains and tiny nuggets, it seems almost pure. Deep in the rock joint and fault crevices, the gold lies like ground black pepper scattered on top of white clay. This kaolin clay was formed *in situ* over millennia as aluminium silicate minerals, such as feldspar, were altered by chemical weathering. I have heard panners ask how the clay gets under the gold, as the gold is clearly so much heavier. But it works the other way round – the clay forms *under* the gold – so goodness knows how long the gold had actually lain there. The Suisgill also has plentiful almandine garnets, which pan out with the gold. We collected the best of them, lovely port-wine-coloured, ruby-like souvenirs.

Alf was indefatigable and I was soon exhausted. In June this far north in Scotland, the night is short – barely four hours. We had originally agreed to drive down into Helmsdale village each evening to get a meal and have a beer, but Alf resisted leaving the worksite until it was too late to do this, so we lived on our stores. I have worked with many people over the years, but none with his drive and gold-fevered passion. One morning, after working until almost nine o'clock the evening before, I heard him banging on my tent at seven in the morning and saying, 'Are you ever going to get up!' Not, 'Would you like a coffee?' or 'It's time to make a start.' It was clear that he had already been up for some time and was already exasperated by his slovenly workmate.

Before leaving, I walked up onto the hillside above the Suisgill to say goodbye to this generous stream. The permit only allows working in the present waterway; the banks and benches above it are not to be touched. Looking down at the mounds and hollows created by the miners in 1869, I was struck by how little of the gold-bearing alluvium in the valley had yet been worked. It felt good to know there was a vast amount of wonderful Scottish gold preserved for the people of the future. With all that our heirs will have to face in this changing world, here at least was a fine treasure laid up in store for them. Alf called out to me to get ready to go, anxious to set off and baffled by my apparent daydreaming. 'I know,' I said. 'We may well be a long time dead, but it's good to stop sometimes and fully appreciate being alive.'

After dropping Alf back home in England's Lake District, I returned north and pitched my large bell tent in a field on the shores of Loch Tay, the tent's thick white canvas a welcome shield from the heady glare of July's scorching sun. The ravine in which I had come to work was bliss in the summer heat. Beech trees, grown tall in the sheltered glen, cast a deep shade and the air stayed cool and fresh. The only sounds echoing through the trees above me were of willow warblers calling high in the branches, shrill bursts of rich notes – like when a child first learns to whistle. And beside me, the calm voice of moving water. The small river's banks were thick with huge, ragged ferns, grown large in the shelter and leaf-filtered sunlight. And it seemed to me that the place was blessed and had the slight scent of apples.

As far as I knew, this gold find was very recent and had been totally unknown to earlier peoples. River gossip said that a fireman, local to this part of Scotland, had first found the gold here only a few years earlier. But word of the discovery was out now, and many panners had been here, hoping to gather some of the pale rounded nuggets that are the signature of this river's gold.

It is one of Britain's most beautiful gold locations. During my visit, the statuesque trees were serene and gave the place a reverential presence that demanded respect. In this natural cathedral, I planned to use the most benign of all gold recovery techniques, known as 'sniping'. I had noticed over the 27 years that panning had been my hobby, that people with a huge heap of gold hunting equipment *might* be good prospectors, but those with almost no equipment usually *were* good! I once watched a man slip quietly into a Welsh river in a grey wetsuit with nothing more than a small iron bar, barely longer than a pencil. He lay still in the water for almost an hour before emerging with three small nuggets. I was very impressed. Here was a prospecting master, using his skill and knowledge rather than the conventional collection of rough tools to find the gold. In time I learned to do this myself, using only an old table knife and small pair of tweezers, and sniping became my favourite technique.

I had invited Tim to join me on this trip. He was a friend from Norfolk who wanted to make the rings for his forthcoming wedding from the natural gold that he had found. Of all the many ways that wild gold can be used, I delight most in it being used for love.

For both the sake of my own pride and as an intended kindness, I wanted Tim to succeed. So I quickly set about testing the river from far downstream to right up to where the ravine walls became cliffs and formed an impossible canyon. A few well-spent days of preparation, checking for a gold line and identifying promising traps, would help enormously; it's a truism that 'time spent in reconnaissance is never wasted'.

Tim arrived, opened the flaps of my tent and had a fit of the giggles. He had expected me to be living rough and was shocked by my domesticity. In my tent's shady interior, neat as a doll's house, I had carefully furnished my single canvas room with all the comforts of home. A futon-bed complete with large royal-blue duvet and white pillow dominated the space, and beside this extravagance lay a fluffy bedside rug. My food stores were arranged within a pyramidal stack of six tough cardboard boxes, with a stove safely away to one side. A bean bag served as my armchair and the floor was my table.

I believe that when you're travelling by car, there is no need to travel light. I defended my temporary home while Tim, still scoffing at my self-indulgent pampering, moved in. He quickly unpacked a very thin airbed and army sleeping bag, and then crowned his austere preparations with three military 24-hour ration packs.

That first night, I was surprised to be woken up just after midnight by the energetic sound of puffing and heavy breathing.

I was shocked and a little disgusted. After all, the randy little devil had only been away from home for one day. Not wishing to interrupt and cause us both considerable embarrassment, I drifted back into my own celibate sleep. The next morning, I was still wondering how to raise the matter diplomatically – just in case this was to be a nightly occurrence – when, to my surprise, Tim brought up the subject. Apparently, his wretched airbed had gone down during the night and no amount of blowing it up again had helped. I feigned ignorance of the whole thing, not wishing to confess how quickly I had jumped to the wrong conclusion.

My earlier scouting of the valley had identified a very promising gold trap. The river had cut a sharp bend, on the inside of which nestled a pile of huge boulders – a testament to just how powerful this small river was when in furious spate. A fault line in the bedrock had formed a large crack that came out from beneath the heaped boulders. This perfect natural riffle then headed straight across the river and passed under a chute of fast-moving water. The trap was a beauty, and I felt sure that other prospectors would also have seen it. But just in case I was wrong, we put on our diving suits to give it a try. Sniping is a slow technique and it is important to identify barren ground quickly. We started in the calmer, waist-deep water beside the boulders, but as suspected, we quickly found that this obvious gold trap had already been worked.

Over the years, the many small and heavy things that are moved downstream during floods also get caught in the traps. And this mixture of dense materials is then stratified by vibration. Each river varies, but in this trap there was only light sand and no evidence of any of the naturally occurring heavy minerals, such as garnet or the oxide of tin, cassiterite, nor any iron, copper or arsenic pyrites, lead or zinc sulphides or creamy baryte pebbles. The usual human detritus was also missing – rusted iron nails, fragments of corroding copper and the white lead pellets and bullets from centuries of shoots and hunting up on the moors above the ravine.

With all signs of virgin ground absent by the boulders, we waded out into the faster water and began work on the most difficult section of the crack. My hope was that the river's flow through the chute would have been too strong for those before us, and they would have given up and moved on. Besides which, this spot needed to be worked by two people – one to hunt for the gold, while the other held them and stood firm to deflect at least some of the current. Moving water is extremely powerful and even though this was barely waist-deep, we struggled. A passer-by would have been puzzled to watch these two wetsuited men rolling about like a pair of otters as they laboured away in this unremarkable stretch of river – and all for no apparent reason.

We resorted to using a short length of knotted rope to anchor ourselves. All the while, my excitement was building, as this was indeed a difficult spot and promised handsome rewards. While clinging one-handed to the rope, we took turns to duck under the water and chip away at the stones lodged in the top of the crack. It was slow and exhausting work, but soon, to my bitter astonishment, it became obvious that this place had also been cleaned out.

We decided to press on in the forlorn hope that at least one little nugget had been missed. And then, as so often happens in gold prospecting, our perseverance paid off. We found that although the people before us had cleaned out both the easiest part of the gold trap and the most difficult, amazingly, a short section of the margin between these two workings was untouched. For almost a metre's length, the fissure was still tightly packed with spirit-lifting, rust-choked, heavy sand – and hope.

Tim and I lay calmly side by side with face mask and snorkel to unpick this wonderful find, and it was glorious. Almost immediately the pristine ground began to yield nuggets. These were small, but after the massive effort of our fruitless earlier work, it was heavenly – such stuff as sniping dreams are made of. We used a small pair of tweezers to tease each darling nugget from its timeless bed. And sometimes, as one came free, the iron sand would slip to reveal the next. This was joyous work, the Holy Grail in the art of sniping. There was a moment when it was so overwhelmingly good, we stopped working just to take it all in. We had uncovered a row of the tiny, rounded nuggets, sitting like golden peas in a gritty pod. They lay so neatly in a line that it seemed this couldn't simply be random chance; more like some ancient hand had lovingly hidden them there. Prospecting is so often a roller-coaster of hope, disappointment and joy. And this day was a perfect example.

Tim was great company, with bags of enthusiasm and energy, and I was sorry when it was time for him to leave. Alone the next day, I went back to our spot to follow the crack where it disappeared under the pile of boulders. I had brought an underwater torch with me, a piece of equipment not usually carried by gold panners, although I always do. It is such a bonus to be able to see right into the depths and dark corners of gold traps and search the places beyond the reach of sunlight and more casual prospectors.

I took a deep breath and ducked under the water to look below the first boulder. It was massive, the size of a flattened armchair – like the capping stone for an ancient tomb. The torch beam immediately lit up a curious bottle-top-sized 'white stone' on the far side. It was jammed where the crack narrowed and, in the brilliant glare of the torchlight, I couldn't make out for sure what it was. Excited, I ducked under again and struggled to work it free with my sniping knife. I was getting cold before it finally came loose. From the first moment I saw the piece, I had tried to check my rising excitement – after all, it might only be a chunk of white lead, or just a white stone . . .

Once prised free, it fell sideways to lie flat against the smooth bedrock. I was wearing neoprene diving gloves against the cold and struggled to grasp it. Finally, I felt its hardness in my palm and gripping it carefully, I stood up out of the water. I pulled off my face mask and looked down at my tightly clenched fist. What was I holding? It meant so much to me that I needed a few moments to compose myself and prepare for the triumph, or bitter disappointment. It was like holding the envelope that told the result of an important examination or decision of a promotion board.

I took a deep breath and uncurled my fingers. And there, bright as a tiny goldfish, lay a gleaming nugget. The pale wet gold seemed almost alive as it sparkled in the morning sunlight. It was by far the biggest piece of gold that I ever found in that river, and my only regret is that Tim wasn't there to celebrate the extraordinary find with me.

Unsociably, as August began, I fled from the traffic, crowds and high prices to the quiet of Lewis – an Outer Hebridean island in the west of Scotland. I had recently read a newspaper report of a fist-sized rock that had been picked up beside a track and found to contain sapphires. Some were the size of small grapes, and this extraordinary rock had apparently been sold for a fortune. I liked the idea of trying something new and hoped my gold-prospecting skills might also work in the search to find a source of these cherished gemstones. The site where the sapphire-studded rock had been found was now officially protected, but I felt it couldn't be an isolated occurrence – that there must be more sapphires somewhere on this wild island.

I pitched my tent on a flat sand machair that faced north-west out across the Atlantic. My plan was to camp on this remote beach and use a prospector's basic exploratory techniques to find a new outcrop of sapphires. I would work my way along the shoreline, systematically sampling the gravels of every stream that flowed out into the sea, while also carefully watching for any concentration of heavy black sands that had accumulated on the beaches. Of course, most streams would be barren. But by testing at the mouth of each one, I hoped eventually to pick up the tiniest fragments of shattered gems that had been washed downstream from a vein outcrop. And once even the slightest trace of a sapphire had been panned, I would work my way up that stream, frequently testing the gravel, until the vein was located.

Sapphires are almost twice as heavy as most stream sediments, but far lighter than gold. I knew that I would have to use my pan with the utmost care to be sure of success. And I did feel sure that I would succeed. Although my plan was simple, I hoped that sooner or later my perseverance would lead to me locating gem material buried in a stream's gravel.

How quickly I was disabused of my initial confidence. Swarms of the infamous biting midges plagued me as I scrambled along the rough coastline, where there were few beaches. The shore offered little more than an ongoing jumble of large erratic boulders, dropped as the ice finally retreated around 11,500 years ago when the Late Devensian glaciation ended, and the present Holocene began. Atlantic grey seals basked on the warm boulders and taunted me before slipping away into the clear water. It was easy to imagine that nothing much had changed up here since the first hunter-gatherers followed their playful prey north.

And the rocks that make up this island are unimaginably old. The predominant type is a Lewisian gneiss, thought to be around three *billion* years old – making these rocks the oldest in Britain. The sapphires were found in an ancient vein that reached deep into the earth and had cooled very slowly, allowing the large crystals the time they needed to form. The exact process is very technical to describe, as geologists have their own language for these things, but I think it would be right to say that 'the corundum megacrysts occurred in a xenolithic camptonite dyke'. And I felt sure there must be some more of those about!

Even though I did not know the island's full geological history, the place felt old and raw. Domes of ice-striated rock rose through the mantle of deep peat and glacial till that covered much of the central area. The tough grasses were olive green and thousands of tiny dark pools, sweetly known as 'lochans', made walking in a straight line impossible. The mournful cry of the curlew and lapwing and the deep croak of the raven hung in the air. This haunting song of the north suited the landscape perfectly. There were corncrake, red-throated divers and more duck species than I had ever seen before. I particularly liked the rafts of eider ducks, which rose and fell as the Atlantic swell passed under them; they reminded me of my time mineral hunting in Iceland. And all of this wild island felt at peace, its treasures secure, hidden beneath the rolling tundra-like bog and huge skies, resiliently moated by the surf-pounded shore and a crystal-clear ocean.

After another fruitless day of rambling along more of the beautiful but impossibly rock-strewn beaches, I came back early and was surprised to find a group of archaeology students busy in the dunes behind my tent. They confided in me that they were excavating a small Late Iron Age settlement. As evening fell, they left, but enchanted, I stayed by the diggings. I hadn't expected to be introduced to the home of one of the ancient peoples – not the seal hunters that I had imagined earlier, but nonetheless venerable. Out of respect I touched nothing, but in the falling dusk I wanted to call up their ghosts. To try to feel, even for a few moments, what life here was like back then.

The most striking feature of the tiny hamlet was a huge midden the size of a small room and strewn with all the clues needed to glimpse how these people once lived. Fish bones the size of my thumb, small tusks and mussels lay scattered amid an absolutely vast mass of limpet shells. Like a giant fruit cake, the pale midden was a mound of these small pyramids, sparingly enriched with the other scraps of discarded life. I was astonished. In Britain limpets are seen as little more than a survival food, being tough but easily gathered. These villagers, however, had enjoyed them as a staple part of their diet. The midden showed just how abundantly rich the sea was back then, before over-fishing and pollution caused the collapse of many marine populations.

*

Having found the coast beautiful but thoroughly unhelpful, I turned my focus to the many streams that flowed across the island. But I soon found that they were no more promising than the beaches. They weaved their way across the vast layer of peat and cut into the stony clay, but rarely reached the ancient rocks below. Coated in midge-repelling DEET, I trudged about hopefully with a pack full of prospecting equipment for two days, but my gold pan, rake, shovel and pump all stayed dry, never once coming out to be used.

I decided to try the southern edge of Loch Roag, and work my way towards the low hills in the west. I was scuffing along a narrow road, absent-mindedly scanning the verge and hoping to find another sapphire-studded rock, when a woman called out to me. She was sweeping the front path that led up to her low, corrugated-iron-clad home and suggested I join her for tea.

I agreed to this welcome break and wondered if it might be a chance to gain some local knowledge. Her home was threadbare but spotlessly clean, and she chattered cheerfully as the kettle boiled. I soon found that our pleasant conversation was going around in circles; she noticed and paused, embarrassed by her Alzheimer's. I told her that I had been alone for several days and was loving our chat, another human voice was pleasure enough and I didn't care if we repeated everything a dozen times! She relaxed, and brought out a small plate of heavily iced cupcakes, then told me all about her home in Glasgow, again.

I seized a chance to lead our discussion and asked if geology students ever came digging around here. She smiled and my heart leapt. 'Oh, yes!' she said conspiratorially. This was what I should have done over a week ago – simply ask a local person where the sapphires are.

As calmly as possible, so as not to alarm her, I asked the next logical question, 'And do you know where they go digging?'

Again, the excited reply, 'Oh, yes!' I was on the brink of discovering in a few minutes over a cup of tea what several days of hard prospecting had failed to achieve. I nodded at her to continue and, with eyes bright, she took a sip of her tea before letting out the secret: 'All over the island!'

In the course of just a few minutes, I had been lifted to the profound heights of almost gaining privileged information, and then dashed on the rocks by her staggeringly unhelpful answer. And the lovely thing is, I really didn't mind that or my lack of success. I didn't find a Lewisian sapphire, but as I packed my car to head back south, I reflected on just how wonderfully different this fascinating island had been. It is so important when prospecting to be accepting of triumph or disaster – as both will happen.

A few years later, I was sitting around a campfire with a small group of lively Welsh gold prospectors. Beside me was a Scottish friend, George. Mid-evening he pulled a small chunk of creamy rock from his pocket before whispering, 'What do you think of this?' It was exactly what I had failed to find on my visit to Lewis, and I was a little jealous.

'It looks like a fragment of camptonite,' I said, showing off. 'Probably from somewhere near Loch Roag on the Isle of—'

He hissed at me to shut up, and only when assured of my discretion did he pass me the precious piece. As I turned it over, reverently admiring the scatter of small dark sapphires embedded within the rock, he told me of a bend in a stream that had cut into the bank. A grassy turf hung from above shielding and shaded the outcrop; it was so well hidden that he had almost missed it.

I wondered if George would invite me to go there with him next summer, but we never got the chance, as he died that winter.

September arrived and settled in, a lovely month, the late afternoon of the year. And having found no gemstones to deflect my gold fever, I hungered again to find nuggets. Keen to fill my first summer's freedom cup to the brim, I called Mike – the man who was with me at Hope's Nose and had ordered my office clothes to be burned back in May. The rivers are often quite low in late summer, before the autumn rains begin. I had built a syphon-dredge, an unusual piece of gold recovery equipment, and I was keen to try it out. We chose a gold-rich stream to the north-west of Edinburgh in the Ochil Hills.

I knew that the sheep-farming family who owned the land would welcome us, because I had been taken to this place some years earlier, as part of an expedition with Leeds University. A group of geologists and gold prospectors had been assembled for the challenging task of finding at least 15 pieces of gold in a set of predetermined locations, all within the general Glen Devon area. In some of the target streams, we struggled to find the statistically significant number of gold grains required. But in one fabulous stream it was easy. The gold was so plentiful that we had recovered ten times the university's target before some people had even unpacked their pans.

The valley was wide and open with almost no trees. Two hundred years of sheep grazing on this land had reduced the vegetation to a blanket of tough upland grasses, with patches of bracken marking the drier ground and clumps of soft rush sitting in the damp hollows. The area had been heavily glaciated and the stream that traversed it had cut a narrow channel through the thick layer of boulder clay. Small coarse grains of gold could be found throughout the valley, but one place in particular was outstandingly good. A band of hard rock crosses the valley here and the stream tumbles over it in a small mossy waterfall. This was perfect and gave us the drop in height that the syphon-dredge needed to work. Even better, the wonderful bench concentration of alluvial gold was only just above these falls.

It was hard to see why such a rich gold deposit had formed here, and I had discussed this helpful anomaly with Rob, a geologist friend with an unusually good understanding of gold deposition. His best guess was that as our warmer inter-glacial Holocene period began, and millions of tons of melting ice broke up and tumbled down the valley, some of the ice blocks got caught on the rock bar and formed a dam. Like one giant riffle across the whole valley, this barrier then halted the muddy torrent of meltwater just long enough for the gold to settle out. Coincidentally, an unusual heavy mineral, the brick-red sulphide of mercury called cinnabar, had also collected here with the gold.

The syphon-dredge is a wonderfully straightforward and delicately balanced piece of equipment that is not often used by gold prospectors. It works by creating a fall of water within a section of pipe that literally 'syphons' an upper section of river a few metres downstream to a lower section of the river. In doing so, it must generate enough flow to suck the heavy sediment and gold out from within cracks and pockets in the bedrock. The heavy material sucked into the pipe then flows along it and finally out of the tail end and across a sluice box.

What I particularly like about gold recovery using this dredging technique, is that there is no engine. So no motor roars away all day, drowning out the pleasing sounds of the river. Besides this, there is no pollution, no tool kit or heavy fuel to carry, nor are there any moving parts to go wrong. The dredge works on gravity alone and is simplicity itself. The sole limiting factor is that there must be enough fall in the chosen stretch of river to create the necessary suction. My syphon-dredge was built to have two 10-m lengths of 100mm-diameter pipes feeding the sluice, so that Mike and I could work in different parts of the stream at the same time, hopefully doubling production.

As with many things in life, we soon found that there was a considerable difference between the theory of running a syphon-dredge and the practice. There were many idiosyncrasies to master before this apparently simple piece of equipment would work. We set the sluice box firmly in place below the rock bar and piled small boulders over it to keep it stable. Next, we had to prime the two 10-m pipes by filling them with water. In a relatively small stream this proved far more difficult than it sounds.

Mike and I wrestled with the first writhing anaconda-like pipe, trying to keep one end under the water while purging all of the air out from the rest of it. But the air would move and suddenly lift great arcs of pipe above the water's surface – alive and playfully frustrating our best efforts. We persevered, knowing that we would never generate the suction we needed if even the smallest pocket of air remained. Finally full of water, the pipe gave up and lay still – sullen but sentient, latently mischievous, knowing that we now faced the next challenge.

While holding the pipe firmly underwater, Mike and I discussed how we could get one end over the waterfall and down to the sluice box without air racing back up into the pipe. At first we tried speed, thinking we could throw the pipe over the rock bar quickly enough for the water flow to start before the air got in. We could then attach each gushing pipe at leisure to the input end of the sluice box. This never worked. Even our relatively small pipes were too heavy to move quickly or throw anywhere.

The farmer arrived on a quad bike to see how we were getting on, and tried to stifle his amusement at the two sodden figures and tangle of pipes before him. He suggested we create a 'boot' for the downstream end to give us a seal while we hauled the pipe down to the sluice box. It was a great idea at just the right moment. We improvised by cutting the arm off an old coat – the cuff pulled tightly closed with cable ties and then held in place with a strong bungee cord. And this worked perfectly. The coat sleeve prevented both the water flowing out and the air getting in just long enough for us to haul the tail end over the rock bar and down to the sluice.

It is a fine thing to take joy in simple pleasures, and we beamed like schoolboys as a glassy column of water now gushed out and across the nine gold-trapping riffles. We were keen to find some gold and once the first pipe was lashed securely in place, we gave up on the idea of fitting the second pipe. Aware of the fragility of our mining technique, Mike stayed to manage the sluice box, while I moved upstream to the input nozzle and started hoovering out promising crevices. This was all new to me, and I had expected more teething problems. But now, immersed in the calm of this lovely place and warmed by the glow of the myriad gold grains hidden all around me, I relaxed. I watched the sand and small stones swirl effortlessly into the pipe and disappear. Our unique gravity-driven gold dredge was finally working – and silently, as if by magic.

After what seemed like only a few minutes, Mike came up and tapped my shoulder: 'You need to see this!'

I lodged the pipe in a deep hole, weighed down with two rocks, and followed him. While a sluice box is working, the heavy material caught in the riffles is never still. Tiny eddies and changes in the current's sinuous flow keep the dark sands constantly moving – rolling, swirling, then suddenly parting like clouds to reveal sun-bright specks of the gold beneath. There was not that much to see, really, but I was pleased that Mike wanted to share this early success. I leant forward and watched as the dark sands caught in the first riffles shifted. Like tiny curtains waving in the current's breeze, they coyly allowed me to glimpse a scatter of fine gold and lentil-sized pieces of cinnabar. I didn't need an incentive to work harder, but had just got one anyway, which had perhaps been Mike's plan.

As I walked back up to resume work, I looked out across the vast expanse of rolling grassland – just sheep country, as far as I could see. The primal forest that had once cloaked this land was long gone, as were its wolves. I knew the wolf was once such a problem here that bounties and cub hunts were organized. At college we were told that the last wolf in Scotland was killed in the late 17th century, somewhere just north of where we were. But that was only in the official records, so it's likely that there would have been more.

It's interesting how the wolf became our nemesis in folklore, attacking travellers and digging up fresh graves, a devil in canine form. But they are elemental, the true spirits of wilderness.

I have a very short bucket list of things I still want to do – and listening to wild wolves howl at the moon is at the top.

My geologist friend Chris Halls, who tested the Hope's Nose 'nugget' for me, said that he was bathing in a hot spring in Canada once, when the wolves started calling. He said it was unearthly and the melancholy howls sent a shiver right through him. Alone and vulnerable, all rational thought deserted him, and the ancient fears awoke and crowded in. He said he experienced what it felt like to be a prey species again.

I kneeled down to pick up the dredge hose nozzle, pleased for now that the forests had been cleared and decided that wolves are probably best enjoyed from a distance. Back at work, I soon noticed that in shallow water, or if the pipe was left still for any length of time, a vortex formed – as in a bathtub when the plug is pulled. If unchecked, these would pull in a thin spiral of system-crashing air bubbles. We called these 'air devils' and they were enough of a threat that we stopped working and again sought to improvise a solution. We found that a piece of thin plywood could be used to partially blank off the input nozzle and reduce the water's flow, which stopped the air devils from forming. This 'blanking plate' allowed us to work successfully in the shallows and park the nozzle safely. The plate was attached to a short length of rope so that it was always available. With a boot to help start the water flow and a plate to keep the unwanted air out, we finally had our syphon-dredge working comfortably.

There was one further subtlety that should have been obvious to us. A sluice box works by having a perfect flow of water across the riffles, and most people achieve this with a slope of 5–7 degrees. Our problem was that whenever the blanking plate was used, the force of water across the sluice box also changed, upsetting the riffles. We never solved this particular problem, and at the end of each day we panned the tailings closest to the sluice. Being optimists, we regarded anything found as 'bonus' gold, rather than 'almost lost' gold. There were no big pieces in the tailings, but as each day passed an extra few grains of bright gold were added helpfully to our store.

Looking back, it's often easy to smile at foolishness, but it is rarely amusing at the time. We needed to move some of the boulders that were sitting on the bedrock, and had brought a small hand-winch to help. But there was one rock that would not shift, and we wasted almost an hour struggling to pull it out of a hole. The more it refused to budge, the more gold we imagined lay trapped beneath it. Exasperated, we finally made a more thorough examination of the stubborn boulder, only to find that it was actually bedrock.

During that first week, we fine-tuned our skill at controlling the flow of water through the equipment, and to some degree, learned to vary the depth of the stream's water to expand our working area. Once the deeper easy ground had been worked, we made small dams to raise the water level in shallow areas, which then allowed us to deploy the syphon-dredge. We used a simple trick to make effective dams, without needing to cut turf and possibly cause damage to the banks. I had brought along a roll of thick hessian sacking. We simply made a wall of rocks and stones and then lined the upstream side with the hessian. This was quick and effective, and once we were finished with the dam, the area could easily be put back as it was.

During our time working the dredge, my number one fear was of getting a 'plug-up'. That is when a single large stone, or a group of small stones, suddenly jams somewhere within the pipe and stops the flow. As our pipe was an opaque grey, a plug-up would have been a nightmare, as we would have had no idea where in the pipe it was. We would then have had to beat the whole length of the pipe to free the stones, before the tiresome job of purging all of the air from the system again. But rather wonderfully there was never a blockage. I had fitted a bar of strong wire across the inlet end of the pipe, to stop the large stones. And the second trick was simply not to be greedy. I would suck material into the pipe for about five seconds and then lift it slightly for a few moments to pull in clean water. This let the sand and stones run freely along the pipe without ever overloading it, or choking the sluice box. While it did feel inefficient to be doing almost nothing for roughly half of the time, it was well worth being patient, avoiding the effort and staggering waste of time involved in unplugging the pipe.

We finally ran out of workable ground, and days. After dropping a couple of bottles of whisky off at the farm as a thank you, we headed south. It had been great working with Mike; big, strong and endlessly cheerful, he had honed his organizing skills over many years serving with the military, and I was now the beneficiary of his accumulated talents. There are relatively few places on most gold streams where the conditions are right for a syphon-dredge to work. But when they are, it's a delightful way to find gold – especially in the company of a kindred spirit.

My summer was almost over now, but there was just time for one more trip. I repacked my car and headed west towards the mountains of North Wales.

Nipped by the chill of October mountain air, the first leaves of autumn fell, swirling like huge dark snowflakes – the fragile heralds of approaching winter – as my car bumped along the rough dirt road towards the East Cwm Heisian gold mine. I was glad to have planned one more trip away before my gold prospecting season was over. And now I hoped that I had remembered Ken Williamson's instructions, and that I wasn't now lost in the huge Welsh forest. He had said to look out for a 'false gate'. The gate itself was real enough, and it was ostentatiously secured with three turns of stout chain and a huge padlock to keep uninvited visitors at bay. But, cunningly, the gate could be opened at the other end. It had been hung so that it could be lifted off its hinges and easily pulled wide – saving time and the worry of lost keys.

Around a bend, an impressive five-barred gate came into view. Conspicuously locked and chained, and totally blocking the track with such a daunting show of theatrical strength, it virtually commanded, 'You shall not pass!' I smiled, relieved; I was not lost, and I knew this barrier's secret. It still felt odd to open it at the wrong end, yet appropriate to be entering this remarkable man's world in such an artful way – and I murmured gratefully, 'Thanks, Ken.'

I parked where the track ended in a large turning circle and looked down to the river, where Ken was working on a large flat plate of bedrock, using a long-handled shovel to clear away heaps of shattered mining spill. A mass of quartz comes out of the hillside and crosses the Mawddach river here. Thought to be the junction of 14 veins, the quartz band is up to 12m wide in places. While highly mineralized with sulphides, gold was also found here in the 1840s – 20 years before the great gold rush to this area in the 1860s. But it wasn't the history of East Cwm Heisian that had first attracted Ken to work here; it was a nugget. He told me that while casually exploring the area after a great flood, he was astonished to find a 9g, water-worn nugget lying on the surface beside the vein. And, as he believed that nuggets come in 'families', he knew that where there was one, others were sure to be close by.

Ken was one of the most extraordinary men I have ever met. Clearly at times his life had been tough; his hands were self-tattooed, and he was of necessity endlessly resourceful. For all of his tales of opals, white lions and providing a safe house for distressed aristocracy, as far as I know, he never lied to me. No matter how tall or unlikely the story seemed at first, it always turned out to be true.

Once, when sat in his kitchen, he casually remarked that he had recently had dinner with an African president. I considered Ken, wiry, tattooed, unshaven and nursing a dirty mug of sweet tea, and thought, *I'll let that one go.* Then his wife, Denise, drifted past in a dressing gown, searching for matches to light her cigarette, and said that she had seen the photos somewhere. She rooted through the drawers of a wooden dresser and finally pulled out a large envelope. And there was Ken, seated at a long, beautifully laid table, looking cool, calm and very much the same in the photograph as the man sat facing me now. To his right was a very different figure – a large, confident man flamboyantly dressed in a uniform of state, the jacket of which was embroidered with such a triumphant mass of intertwined gold filigree that he positively glowed. I glanced back across the table at Ken, still quietly sipping his tea, and wondered – *who on earth are you?*

Parked now in the track's turning circle, high above him, I closed my car door very quietly. We had played a childish game for many years of creeping up on each other – fun, but with menacing overtones. Time after time, while quietly absorbed in carefully washing the dirt in my gold pan, I would suddenly catch the slightest whiff of tobacco smoke in the air – and know that I had lost again. Ken considered it a clear win if he could move through the riverbank's tangle of branches, bilberry and sedges unseen, and then, when just behind me, roll a cigarette and light it. And given his shady background, I was always glad that it was just a game that we were playing.

But this time I had a good chance. He knew that I was coming today, but his head was down, totally focused on digging and he should be deafened by the roar of water pouring over the enormous quartz vein. I recalled the basics of concealment from my army training – colour, movement, shape, shine, shadow, silhouette, sound and smell – and moved carefully down the edge of the scree of old mining waste. I was excited to have the advantage this time and crept down the slope with an assassin's stealth. When crouched five paces behind him I paused and prepared to declare I'd won this time. But before I could step forward and claim the victory, he suddenly turned and swung the shovel in a wide arc. I leapt backwards to avoid the blade, and he laughed – and again I wondered, *who are you?*

With the current round of our game now over, he took a break to outline what he was doing and showed me a small plastic pot that was already half-full of beautiful water-worn nuggets.

The modern gold prospector has two clear advantages over the miners of the past. We have metal detectors and can easily work in and under water. Historically, the big money was in finding a rich, hard-rock mother-lode. And so the early miners at Cwm Heisian seem to have ignored the exposed bench and put all of their efforts into digging the hillside. Ken was clearing the stony spoil off deep fissures and cracks that crossed the bench and then using a Fisher Gold Bug metal detector to hunt for nuggets. The machine was an old but classic gold-hunting design and still easily good enough to find them.

I picked up a short-handled mattock and started to scrape dark muck from out of the deeper holes; it was filthy and stank, sour and anaerobic – perfect! We worked together to fill one bucketful at a time with the promising dirt, and then spread it out on a slab of clean rock so that Ken could go over it with his detector. The nuggets were few and far between and I wondered how long it had taken Ken to half-fill the little pot.

The next day, I suggested that it might be best if we split our efforts, with Ken continuing to work the cracks up on the rocky bench with the detector, and for me to enter the river and snipe for nuggets. As with other aspects of human relationships, and as I had with Alf, I thought it best to work together but apart. I put on my drysuit and slipped into the flow, delighted to be in the clean, fresh water and away from the pyritic sulphurous holes above me. The current was too strong for me to hold a position and concentrate, so we rolled a couple of large boulders just upstream of where I wanted to start. The rocks deflected the rushing water like the bow of a ship, and I settled down to work in the small, sheltered pool that we had created.

I poked and scraped at the cracks and hollows that time had worn into the quartz, and then noticed that a small pebble that I had just pulled out of a hole moved strangely. It was almost cubic, like a slightly rounded gaming dice, and rust-stained to a patchy ochre brown. I had put it to one side when, quick as a tiny mouse, it suddenly shot back into the hole with an unnatural speed. Curious at what had just happened, I fished it out again with my tweezers and rubbed it against my drysuit. And there it was, the brassy glow of gold – hunted for, yet somehow unexpected.

Gripping it tightly, I proudly climbed out of the river and went up to show Ken.

The nugget weighed in at 11g and was the biggest I have ever found in that river. And it also felt like I had just won my spurs, and was now worthy of working with this extraordinary man. It had been found on his claim, and he needed the gold, so I was happy to part with it and watched contentedly as it dropped into the little plastic pot and joined the rest of its family. As a footnote, I should add that there is a large boulder-filled hole just below the quartz vein that must have some really good gold nuggets – but I doubt that I will ever try to get permission to move all the boulders and work it.

That evening, while sitting with Ken and Denise by their living-room fire, the conversation flowed more freely than before. We talked about diving and Ken told me all about a shipwreck that he had worked on many years earlier. The salvage team he was with craved big nuggets, bars of bullion and boxes full of gold sovereigns, and he had watched as the unloved gold dust fell through their steel-mesh screen back into the sea. He advised me to set up a diving project to recover gold dust from the wreck of a famous ship, the *Royal Charter*, and I would be rich! Such are the very best fireside chats, where easy talk of gold and treasure drifts in the flickering light and fastens on the open mind, and there is absolute trust between friends.

The dark days of November finally arrived and found me working back among my Christmas trees; the longest summer of my life had just ended. Much of that which I'd experienced had been expected, such as how good it feels to be free and have total sovereignty over each day. And then, the delicious anticipation of knowing that for the rest of my able life, each summer could be similarly filled to the brim with adventures and friendship. I had just enjoyed the equivalent of several years' worth of office-job holidays. And unbelievably, over the next four years I would be blessed with more 'annual leave' than I had been granted during my entire working life.

That first summer's lessons were surprising. Firstly, I noticed that time had slowed down for me. Often in the office I had heard things like, 'Is it Friday already – where did the week go?' Each unremarkable day merged into the next. Now, each carefree week felt longer than a month of shuffling paperwork. Paradoxically, I also began to realize just how expensive it was to go to work, and I still struggle to understand this irony. I think that the money saved must have been from an accumulation of small things, like my propensity to buy coffee and snacks at work, the need for a wardrobe of good clothes, the cost of daily commuting, buying ready-made meals or eating out, paying someone else to make and mend things for my home, and the incremental nature of taxation – and there must be many more.

Earlier, I shared some words by the author Laurie Lee, as I particularly like the way he draws attention to the importance of having time in life, as I did when leaving my office job. Most tellingly, during this first summer there hadn't been a single moment of any day when I'd wished I was back at my desk. Like so many before me, I had already learned that happiness lies not in material possessions, but in the relationships we nurture and the experiences we have.

8

SOUTH FOR THE WINTER

'A good traveller has no fixed plans.'

—Lao Tzu, *Tao Te Ching*

In late November of my first year of freedom, I took a break from Christmas tree work and headed to London for a meeting. The mid-morning train, still littered with rush-hour detritus but now almost empty, trundled south. Rivulets of rain flowed sideways across my window, partly obscuring the cheerless view. I peered out at the dormant countryside, sodden fields bordered by leafless, sleeping trees beneath a leaden sky – England in winter. My grandfather disliked this season, often referring to 'the dark days before Christmas' with a melancholy resolve, and it was hard to disagree with him.

I had been trying to ignore the suntanned man sat opposite me, who fidgeted constantly and clearly wanted to talk. But the dreary view was relentless, and it would be impossible to feign interest in it for the whole journey. Finally, I gave up on the landscape and gave in to conversation – and thank goodness I did. It is so often the people we meet unexpectedly who enrich our lives.

Finally released from the shackles of my ill-mannered indifference, the man leant forward and gushed his story. With the evangelical enthusiasm of a young salesman, he explained that he was just back from the Philippines. I listened and grew to like this man. He was the completely wrong fit for a wet train in sombre November; his tan, colourful clothing and cheerfulness were totally out of place. He told me that he lived on a beach in a small house, where his daily rent was less than the price of a pint of beer. A warm blue ocean lapped the steps of his modest home, and behind it, up in the bustling streets, every food and fruit could be found that he could possibly wish for.

An hour passed quickly in his lively company, and as we approached the capital, the miserable rural landscape gave way to urban sprawl. We both fell silent and looked out. The brooding sky hung so low, it touched the distant rows of slate-grey roofs. As if at dusk, the wet roads sparkled as lunchtime traffic, headlights on, crawled somewhere slowly. He turned to me, incredulous that so many people tolerated months of this dour existence. Then, as if to himself, he mumbled that he simply couldn't understand why they didn't just head south for the winter. I am a bit slow on the uptake at times, but this inspirational spark landed in the ready tinder of my imagination and caught fire. The train juddered into King's Cross station and with a smile and a wave, the man was gone – before I had the chance to thank him.

Heeding the train passenger's muttered advice, I left England on a dark day just after Christmas and arrived in dazzlingly bright Melbourne three days later. I had been starting to wonder if the man on the train had exaggerated to make his point, my only other reference to life in Australia being a misleading diet of neighbourly television soaps and disturbing films, but I was immediately overwhelmed by the country's glorious energy, variety and quality. And there was not a post-apocalyptic motorcycle gang or cheerful knife-wielding bushman to be seen. I was expecting Australia to be different, and so it was. From first contact, this blessed land swept me off my feet and then it just kept getting better.

My friend Beth met me at the airport and upon finding that I had neither a place to stay nor any transport, offered me the use of her flat and car for a few days – just while I got sorted out. She assured me it would be fine, as she could stay with her boyfriend and get a lift into work with colleagues. I had only met this level of big-hearted generosity before in Ireland, another country where long years of shared hardship have forged a culture of kindness.

The first morning, I woke up to the unexpected sounds of home: a blackbird's rich song, chattering house sparrows and in the distance a lone chaffinch stuttered its short tumbling call. The still air and deep-blue sky told of the coming heat – and I lay in Beth's neat, narrow bed feeling jet-lagged and totally confused. I had leapt from a silent, dull-grey English winter to vibrant midsummer, and an unexpectedly lively and English dawn chorus. But that too was disorientating, as among the familiar host of English songbirds were the disjointed but melodious notes of the exotic Australian magpie. As if in eager greeting, a riot of birdsong from two hemispheres heralded my first full day in this unfamiliar country – and it seemed prescient, an omen of all good things to come.

I needed a hat and headed into the city to find one. But before I reached the shops, I was sidetracked by a group of magnificent English elms in a large park. Such trees had become just a childhood memory for me, as in England they were all dead.

I could recall looking out across a bleak lowland landscape during a summer train journey in the 1970s: the crops and hedgerows were all that they should be, but, as far as the eye could see, the trees had died. In those moments I understood the true level of devastation that Dutch elm disease had caused; and today, my need for a hat was temporarily forgotten. As if in a bucolic Constable painting, I dawdled in the elms' cool shade and gazed up into the vast canopy of these unexpected behemoths – survivors of a plague that I thought had rendered them extinct.

When I eventually turned away from the wonderful trees, I had another surprise: across a wide road stood a line of elegant Victorian buildings. For no obvious reason, I had expected the city to be a modern, soulless conglomeration of glassy prefabricated structures and for the streets to be littered with fast-food outlets. I could not have been more wrong.

I left the park, swapping the elms' welcome shade for that of the old stone buildings, and wondered if there might be an outdoors shop somewhere nearby. I eventually found one in a side street and self-consciously started to try on a range of expensive wide-brimmed leather hats. An assistant drifted over to help me.

The small man with a wide smile was busy explaining the effects of sweat and flies and how to counter them, when he suddenly stopped, and, as if he had only just noticed, asked, 'Are you from the old country?'

I acknowledged being English and waited for some light ribbing. Instead, he rolled up his sleeves and pushed his wrists out towards me in a triumphant gesture. 'Look, the marks have gone!'

I replied that I thought we weren't supposed to talk about Australia's convict past, and my stuffy reaction triggered a machine-gun torrent of staccato laughter – I had made his day.

He said that it was cool now if you could trace a prisoner of Her Majesty in your family tree.

It's claimed that we more readily buy things from people we like, and I left the shop with an excellent hat that I still have and use.

Three days later, I was able to give back Beth's car and flat as, by great good fortune, Peter, an English geologist friend, had called me to ask if I fancied finding some rubies. This wasn't a question I'd been asked before and having failed to find sapphires on the Isle of Lewis, I jumped at the offer. I was in Victoria to find gold, but hunting for rubies would be an exciting diversion.

Peter lived in a pleasant suburb of Melbourne, where the large houses were graced with mature and colourful gardens. He was already loading his car with prospecting gear when I arrived and he asked me to fetch a couple of Henderson pumps from the garage. There were four leaning against the wall in one corner, and I gathered them up to check the seals and suction and choose the best two. I picked up the first pipe and innocently looked inside.

And there, glaring straight back at me was a monstrous spider, bigger than any I had ever seen, a huge grey-brown brute lodged diagonally across the inside of the tube. I dropped the pump and called out to Peter that we had a problem. He laughed, coaxed the hand-sized hairy creature out and chastised me for being frightened of a simple huntsman. I considered pointing out that it had fangs the size of a baby's fingers, but decided not to embarrass myself further. Apparently the spiders liked hiding in his pumps and were always going in them.

So this was normal life in Australia, living cheek by jowl with its unique and often murderous wildlife. I would have to learn very quickly which creepy-crawlies were deadly, and which, like the huntsman spider, simply looked deadly. Calm once more, it occurred to me that Peter had specifically sent me to fetch the pumps, knowing what might be lurking within. It made me wonder: *was it an oversight, or a glimpse of his wry sense of humour?*

With no responsibility to drive or navigate as we headed west, I gazed out of the side window, revelling in this exciting land – where the bizarre was normal. Grass paddocks that would not have looked out of place in rural England slipped past. But time and again I was jolted from a proprietorial sense of ease by wallabies hopping out of the shadows. A distant flock of small greyish-pink animals seemed to be grazing peacefully on an undulating meadow, then suddenly all took to the air. 'Galahs,' Peter said. I learned that these large, grass-seed-eating parrots often play the fool, and are a favourite out here.

In the mix of my love-at-first-sight infatuation with this bright and promise-filled land was something I hadn't experienced before: 'season-lag'. Leaping from the overcast skies and darkness of Christmas Britain to a sparkling high summer, filled with cheerful tanned people, was pleasing but strange. The rhythm of the seasons had been dishonoured somehow. It was as if spring's welcome arrival had been thwarted, simply cancelled and brushed roughly aside by this bold premature summer, brazen in all its aestival glory.

The patchwork of neat fields ended as we left the low-lying pastoral land and moved into dry hills thick with grey-green eucalyptus. The baked red ochre clay that is so definitively Australian was now evident in the ruts of every side track and cutting. Looking back at the road behind us, I could see dust rise up in swirling clouds to mark our passing. I strained to see more; this was the outback, unfamiliar, exotic and utterly thrilling.

The creek that Peter wanted us to work for gemstones was small and almost dry. It had cut a deep channel into the soil and patches of slatey bedrock were exposed between a string of shallow, stagnant pools. He was prepared for this and knew that there wouldn't be enough water to work a sluice, so he had brought along a 'high banker'. This neat piece of equipment is a combination of a small sluice and motor-driven pump to create the water flow needed to recover gold – or rubies! The high banker is also really useful when it's easier to move water to the pay dirt, rather than carry the pay dirt to the water.

We set up the equipment on the gravel beach beside a long pool. The water pumped across the high banker's riffles could then drain back into the pool and be recycled all day. Peter set about digging heavy material from within bedrock crevices and asked me to prospect up and down the stream to identify any other good traps that we could work later.

This was my first time out in the bush, and I loved it. The warm, scented air buzzed with the sound of a million busy insects high in the eucalyptus – a deep monophonic drone, but somehow pleasing, like the clamour of a distant schoolyard at playtime, with such commotion and energy. A kookaburra called through the trees from somewhere far away. And the ravens laughed at us. They had a strange call, like a drunk old man who found something funny, but could hardly be bothered to laugh.

Peter pointed out a koala. The scruffy, grey-brown animal was wedged unconvincingly in a fork – like somebody had propped a stuffed toy high in the tree as a joke. Maybe it actually was one, as it didn't move once in all the time we were there.

The rubies wouldn't find themselves, so I decided to crack on with prospecting before Peter got fed up with his idle companion. A short way downstream, a small tree had fallen across the creek and a mass of branches and leaves had formed a small dam. During the last heavy rains, water pouring over this dam had washed away the stream gravels and exposed a large plate of the slatey bedrock. It looked good and I crouched down to make a start when Peter spotted me and hollered, 'Not there! I saw a tiger there a few days ago.' This triggered a momentary confusion. Of the many species of Australian wildlife that I was minded to give a wide berth, tigers hadn't been on my list. He saw my 'innocent abroad' puzzlement and yelled again, 'The snake – a tiger snake lives in that brush.' I moved away sharply; this land was going to take some getting used to. The huge arachnid in the Henderson pump was nothing, apparently, but this seemingly empty pile of sticks and leaves might just be deadly.

We worked steadily for only a few hours, but that was long enough. The tiny water-worn rubies were hard to see among the heavy rust-brown iron sands, yet they were there. When we cleaned out the sluice and washed the concentrate in a gold pan, they became obvious. Too small to be of any real value or use, they were nevertheless delightful. I picked out a few and laid them in the palm of my hand to examine more closely with a pocket lens. Rounded with a glassy opalescent sheen, the petite gems glowed reddish-purple in the sunlight – like faded drops of petrified blood. Even when magnified ten times, the precious stones were still small – but we were satisfied that we had found treasure.

Well pleased with the day, I dozed contentedly on the drive back to Melbourne. We had found rubies and a few grains of rich-yellow gold. Working with this quiet man had been a pleasure. As had the dried-up creek bed – with its shaggy trees and spiny bushes, warm medically scented air humming with insect life, home to one soporific koala. Cats snore, dogs dream-fidget and whine, but the koala had been catatonic; I wondered again if it was real. But if Peter had put it up there as a joke, he kept his amusement very private. Happily, the 'tiger' had not been at home – or my southern winter adventure might have been very short-lived.

Two days later, I travelled to Ballarat, where I was met by Gerry, a wise and wonderful prospector with such a full beard that only his eyes and nose were visible. When he spoke you couldn't see his mouth move; words came out of the thicket as if a ventriloquist were at work. He was so full of energy and blessed with such a lively sense of humour, that there was never a dull moment in his company. He was working at the town's gold mining museum and had invited me to help out at an inter-schools' gold panning championship.

Sovereign Hill is a vast open-air museum that skilfully captures what life was like during the 1850s gold rush. Opened in 1970, it rapidly became a mecca for all those with gold fever – and it's my favourite museum in the world. Gold was first found here in August 1851 by two men working on the misleadingly named Poverty Point. But for many, Ballarat is more famous for the shocking 1854 rebellion by miners against the colonial government's administration of the goldfields. The fees for mining licences were unfair and their implementation was often corrupt. Tensions built until there was a pitched battle at the Eureka Stockade between the governor's forces and the gold miners. It was all over very quickly, with around 30 deaths. But the legacy lives on and some say that Australian democracy was born at Eureka.

Today, the museum has more than 60 recreated historical buildings and many staff and volunteers, all of whom dress in period clothing. As I already favoured a rough woollen shirt, dark-green corduroy trousers and brown leather boots, I fitted right in and felt very much at home.

Gerry led me down to the winding creek where the schools' competition was to take place, and the children greeted him as if he were their favourite uncle. I was invited to entertain the waiting youngsters by telling them about England. Suddenly thrust before the expectant multitude, I struggled to think what on earth to say that would interest them all. And then I remembered Ken's story of shipwrecked Australian gold.

In October 1859 the steam clipper *Royal Charter* was carrying at least two hundred successful miners and their families from Melbourne to England. But when almost home in Liverpool dock, a severe gale blew up with winds reaching hurricane force 12; it was the storm of the century and wrecked the ship on Anglesey's rocky shore. Many that perished would have come from the area around Ballarat, and I hoped the children would feel a connection to the tragedy. The story is grim, with the terrible loss of human life and an absolute fortune in Australian gold that vanished beneath the sea. I unfolded the tale of storm, treasure and death and they listened politely – but I never knew if they actually enjoyed it.

In mid-afternoon the groups of schoolchildren left, and the panning area was once again open for tourists. Watching their efforts while resting in the shade, I began to wonder just how much gold was being lost by these beginners. The creek was concrete-bottomed and the gold flakes that were washed out as they learned to pan couldn't go far. Small steel gold pans lay scattered along the banks for the visitors to use. I chose one and knelt to scoop up some of the roughly washed gravel. The quick test revealed a few colours of gold, certainly enough to be of interest.

It was awkward leaning over the creek to dig out the gravel, so I took off my boots, rolled up my corduroy trousers and stepped in. I had barely started when a young man in full colonial police uniform rushed down and told me to get out again. I guessed that they didn't want people taking gold from the stream and would rather they buy the little sacks of pay dirt that were on sale for tourists. Fortunately, I decided to check with him. To my surprise, he wasn't in the least concerned about the gold, just that I was barefoot and there was broken glass in the stream. I said I would be careful, and to my relief, he shrugged and agreed to let me continue. It felt good to be in a country where individuals are allowed to take calculated risks; in England, I think I would have been escorted off-site.

Now with tacit permission, I tried pans all along the stream, attempting to work out where the most gold had been lost. But the results showed that losses were fairly even, and I would have to pan a mass of the gravel to get a decent sample of gold. It was then that I noticed the museum had placed three wooden replica 'rocker boxes' on one bank.

This piece of traditional equipment was widely used during the 1850s gold rush and was extremely important in all the early goldfields when water was scarce. It works a bit like the high banker that I'd used with Peter, in that gold-bearing gravel is fed into a hopper on the top and then washed through a sieve to take out the bigger stones. The graded material passes next over a rough cloth to catch any fine gold, before flowing over a sloping plate of gold-catching riffles. And all the while the box is rocked side to side as if trying to get a baby to sleep, its other name being a 'cradle'. Unlike a high banker, when using a rocker, the miner doesn't have a motor-driven pump to bring water and has to carry it in with buckets to feed the machine. The digging, fetching water and rocking is best done with two or three people. But even though I was working alone, a rocker would speed up my gold production enormously.

The young policeman seemed content to allow heaped pans of gravel to be poured into the exhibit, and watched as I clumsily tried to rock and feed it water at the same time – a trick not unlike rubbing your belly while patting your head. The box was beautifully made and swayed easily on its curved base, similar to a rocking chair. I soon mastered the technique and thoroughly enjoyed the work. This was the first time I had 'cradled for gold' and there was the exciting prospect of finding much more gold than I would have done with just a pan. But my luck got even better with some unexpected help.

Three Japanese tourists obviously thought that I was a museum employee demonstrating how to work a rocker. They asked permission to pose for photographs with me, but I stepped aside and invited them to have a go. They were quickly organized into the three principal roles of feeding gravel, sloshing in water and rocking vigorously, while I stayed in the creek and scooped up pay dirt for them as fast as I could. This was fantastic; I had leapt from being one man with a small gold pan to being part of an energetic four-man rocker-box team.

The tourists' families and friends came over to take more photographs and I pushed the men to work harder and faster, knowing my luck wouldn't hold out for much longer. I could see that they were confused, and I should have felt guilty at such flagrant exploitation of their good-humoured interest. But I wanted the gold, and they were finding it for me.

At first it must have been fun for them to join in with the scruffy man in Victorian clothes. But there was no end to it. Soon they were splashed, clay-smeared and sweating heavily. They worked for almost 20 minutes, and I thanked them profusely as they left – happy but none the wiser. For what it's worth, I do feel guilty about it now. That said, if they ever look at their photographs in a quiet moment and wonder precisely what happened, they might just realize that for those few minutes they were the real thing: gold miners.

The rocker box was back to being worked by one man, but not for long. I too was tired and itching to see how much gold we had got. I'd glimpsed the odd speck of colour while the water poured through the swaying machine. But even at my most optimistic, I wasn't expecting the 4-g heap that appeared in the clean-up. It felt a little like cheating – that my best prospecting day in Australia so far had come from a concrete river in a museum with a bunch of tourists. But then again, as the oft quoted maxim has it: 'Gold is where you find it.' And I had just found lots.

*

Fortunately, Gerry was pleased for me and said that there was someone he wanted me to meet. We drove to a small house where we were greeted by a tall, thin man. He was charming, with an old-fashioned politeness, like a true gentleman. We talked of family and gold over tea for a while, and it was enough just to have met this interesting man. But then, with some ceremony, they revealed why Gerry had brought me here.

A neat parcel of white cloth was carefully placed on the kitchen table, and I was invited to take a closer look. The clean cotton was folded around a long, angular lump the size of a small carrot. To show respect, I unwrapped it slowly. From the weight alone I knew it must be gold. Even so, I gasped when a beautiful nugget of several ounces rolled free onto the table. The natural gold in Victoria is almost pure, and in the dimly lit kitchen the piece positively glowed, radiant in its glorious virtue, as if a light shone from within.

It was then that I noticed a flat patch of parallel scratches at one end. This wonderful specimen had been truncated, its integrity lost to a small hacksaw. I had fought to prevent even a single scratch blemishing the much smaller Hope's Nose nugget, and I didn't understand. With homely indifference, the tall man explained that the nugget was simply his bank account, and whenever he was short of money he simply sawed a bit off!

It felt like I had just stepped back 150 years, to days of the gold rush mentality where the precious metal was merely money. The miners paid for their goods with the dust, and exchanged nuggets for coin. Very few genuine gold rush nuggets have survived, as they were almost all melted down. Even the biggest nugget ever found, the 109.59-kg Welcome Stranger, was only seen as money. In 1869 two Cornish miners uncovered the massive lump of gold in Bulldog Gully near Moliagul in central Victoria. It was hidden in a fireplace, then taken to a blacksmith to be cut into three pieces before being weighed, as no scales were big enough. The chunks were then taken to a bank in the small town of Dunolly before being melted down and shipped to England. All of the current models are replicas based on drawings that were made from the memories of those who had seen it.

Now, the tall man's bullion nugget was rewrapped in the white cloth and put back into its hiding place, and we left for a local bar. I had expected to spend a jolly evening swapping gold stories and drinking. But a big man with an outrageous mullet haircut came in and Gerry attacked him with a torrent of historical abuse. The big man seemed ready for the assault and ably defended himself. My knowledge of history is fairly poor, but even so, I neither wanted to join in, nor could I. These two extraordinary men locked horns, energetically arguing about the Battle of Agincourt in October 1415. The most heated point of the expletive-laden disagreement was the length of the arrows that were used to such terrible effect on the French nobility. Their surreal combat raged on, shattering the small bar's peaceful ambience, and I slowly realized that this was a game. And that these two were actually good friends. And your mates and friendship is everything in Australia.

Early the next morning, Gerry took me to the coach station. We were both unusually quiet. I was sad to be leaving my lively and good-natured friend, but it was time for me to head back to Melbourne. As the bus pulled away, I turned to wave goodbye to this remarkable man, but it was already too late. His leather hat was pulled down and only a mass of whiskers showed between its brim and his red flannel shirt.

*

My old friend Mike staggered out of the airport under the weight of a massive rucksack, muttered, 'Welcome Stranger' and gave me a huge hug. I think he had been working on that greeting for some time. I grinned; this hearty man bursting with questions was just the tonic I needed. He had no interest in seeing Melbourne itself, so we hired a car and headed straight for the hills. After his long and dreary flight from the UK, Mike was impossibly cheerful and itching to find gold. And it was great to be with him again. This was the man who had so ably managed the boat during our time diving at Hope's Nose, and who was now managing our car. Hurtling along with the side windows fully open, we sang 'Waltzing Matilda'. As both of us knew the tune but few of the words, it was a tragic though agreeably boisterous rendition of this fine song. Mike was buzzing, revelling in the joy of sudden summer after bleak England.

While he drove, I could again gaze out at the scrubby bushland and look deeply into this four-layered landscape. The ground, a honey-coloured rusty earth, was thick with spiny Chinese scrub and wattle, above which the graceful silvery grey-green eucalypts ruled – and all below the immaculate sky. It was such a sky as I had never seen at home, of the purest blue, and so intense, it was as if nature displayed the true colour here, with no wisps of cloud to flaw the cerulean intensity, and all other hues of blue were only this one tarnished. Far ahead, a big kangaroo hopped lazily out of the scrub and stopped at the edge of the road, and Mike's uproarious singing leapt to a new discordant level. At joyous times like this I feel cleansed; the perfect moment washes through me until I feel refreshed to my very bones. I settled back to bask in the euphoria and attend to the task of navigating us to Bendigo – where we would buy two of the best metal detectors in the world.

The enormity of the central goldfields surprised me. It is one thing to see the area marked out on a map, but quite another to drive past mile after staggering mile of cratered hummocky ground. And to know that this vast broken landscape was created only 150 years ago, by people with nothing more than picks, shovels, courage and sweat.

The gold found here was exceptional too. There was so much, and it was almost pure. Most natural gold is a metallic alloy that commonly contains a significant proportion of silver and traces of many other metals. But in Victoria's Golden Triangle the nuggets generally average 94 to 98 per cent gold with few impurities, making it one of the purest natural gold deposits in the world. And the quantity found was phenomenal. People flocked here after reading newspaper reports of gold nuggets lying on the surface of the ground – which was true. During the 1850s and 1860s it is recorded that 1,100 tons of gold were recovered. But, as in Lapland, it can be safely assumed that a significant amount was smuggled out and the true total weight of gold found was probably much nearer to 2,000 tons. (For some perspective, Lapland's goldfield has yielded barely a ton.)

Not only was the gold in Victoria unusually pure, the nuggets were extraordinarily big. There were 1,300 lumps of gold over 20oz recorded, with 400 of these giants weighing over 100oz. Again, assuming some level of smuggling, the true haul of large nuggets must have been staggering. Certainly enough to drive six thousand people a week here, all gripped by gold fever and wanting to take part in the world's latest great adventure. And now there were two more hopeful panners arriving.

The Minelab SD 2200 professional-grade metal detectors that we bought, and later shipped home, were enormous. They

were too heavy to hold and were powered by a motorcycle battery
housed in a backpack. These state-of-the-art monsters hung
from a shoulder strap on an elastic shock cord and felt great to
use – our electronic companions, as hungry for gold as we were.
These 'pulse induction' machines were the very best for working
in this highly mineralized, iron-rich ground and could sense a
large nugget with ease – or even a small one. We purchased our
'miners rights' gold prospecting licences and two strong pickaxes,
because there was going to be a lot of hard digging – as there had
been here ever since the 1850s.

Fred, a friend from Maryborough, gave us a quick tour of the
area, and pointed out several good locations where we could make
a start. We decided on Daisy Hill because we liked the name. Once
there, we got straight down to business. Inappropriately dressed
in a bright Hawaiian shirt and shorts, Mike cut an incongruous
figure for a gold prospector. I was still mindful of Australia's
menacing wildlife, so rather timidly stayed in my thick corduroy
trousers, which were tucked into my socks.

Our new metal detectors turned out to be almost uncannily
sensitive. Unhelpfully, being so wonderfully powerful, they
could find every scrap of metal that had ever been discarded.
The shop told us that the rubbish to gold ratio was about 50:1,
but nevertheless, to dig every signal. We soon discovered
that everyday things like the microwaves from mobile phone
networks, or the magnetic field from overhead transmission
wires, could also distract and upset them. It was like taking a
pedigree bloodhound out to track someone down, but then
finding that the dog couldn't concentrate due to an abundance
of rabbits, other dogs wandering past or the wafting scent of a
distant barbecue.

The detectors had to be disciplined and trained to focus on the task at hand – and the procedure was almost comical. The big flat head that housed the sensing coils had to be held high in the air, then moved slowly in a full circle to locate any and all confusing interferences. These were then tuned out, one by one, until the detector found a clean frequency with which it could work.

As I strapped myself in with all the necessary paraphernalia of belts, backpack, water bottles and headphones, and gathered up the heavy detector, pick and shovel, I was reminded of scuba diving. The situation could not have been more different, and yet, here I was again, enclosed within and burdened down by a mass of heavy equipment. Maybe nothing worth doing is easy, especially with gold.

Mike set about trying to get his detector to hang correctly, perfectly balanced on the shock cord. The search head was supposed to hover just above the ground, with the control box acting as a counterweight. I turned my attention to the tricky job of tuning in my own detector. Up on a low mound, I held the search head high and patiently scanned the airwaves looking for a quiet channel. A distant car approaching caught my eye and I called out to Mike that we would soon have company. He looked up at me, impressed. 'You're getting really good with that!' he said. I smiled, flattered that he thought I already had such mastery of my new machine, and to my shame I considered accepting the compliment. But I would never be able to live up to it, so admitted that I could see the car.

Soon, the air crackled with the crisp sound of Mike energetically sweeping through the bone-dry carpet of dead leaves and sticks, and I thought that at any moment he would find our first nugget. Anxious that he should not find too much gold before me, I pulled on my headphones and joined in with the hunt. But I need not have worried. That first day we dug lots but found nothing, nor the next. My optimism was tamed with the reality that this gold was going to be much more difficult to find than I had expected. We were in one of the richest goldfields in the world – so where was it?

We gave up on Daisy Hill and moved to Blacksmith's Gully, thank goodness. The pulse induction detectors were hard work, but we were slowly getting to know them. The most wearing thing was not their weight, but the constant whining. The headphones are set so that a 'threshold signal' is just heard – all the time. It oscillates in an endless stream of fluctuating 'oooh' noises – like a small nervous child with a high voice who cannot quite decide on something. Periodically, the dithering child was interrupted as the detector passed over a scrap of metal, and a clear 'Yoo-hoo!' greeting call broke through the warbling threshold. There are only so many scraps of lead, nails and assorted rubbish that one can dig up before this cheerfully promising salutation loses its magic. But we persevered and finally our eureka moment came. The first nugget was about the size and shape of a child's milk tooth, and curiously, so was the second.

This prospecting was so different from anything I had done before. The heat and dryness, the ground and tree trunks crawling with so many ants that sitting down, or even leaning against a stem to rest, was denied us. But even though I discovered two scorpions hiding in the dead leaves beside a hole I was digging, I relaxed a little and started wearing shorts.

However, my corduroy trousers nearly went back on again after meeting another big spider. Being very dark, it stood out against the pale ground as it tiptoed past. I was curious about the wildlife, so I snapped off a stick about as long as my arm and went over to take a closer look at it. I had no intention of harming it. The spider, however, had no such sensitivities. To my astonishment, it stopped, turned to face me and reared up with its front legs in the air and fangs exposed. I was awestruck by its bravery. Here was I, at least ten thousand times bigger than the furious mouse-sized ball of legs and spite – and yet it was fearless, the honey badger of the arachnid world. This funnel-web spider had full confidence in its lethal venom, and chastened, I stepped back to let it pass.

Richard, another of the Hope's Nose diving team, came over from Tasmania to join us, as he put it, to visit the 'north island'. We worked through an area riddled with shallow mining shafts – relics of the early prospectors digging down to the bedrock. Richard explained that if the holes were round, they were made by Chinese workers, who were superstitious and wary of the rectangular 'coffin-shaped' excavations made by the Europeans. At the bottom of each pit the sides had been hacked away to form an inverted mushroom shape. I began to wonder if we would do better detecting down on the bedrock in these old workings, and voiced my idea. Richard agreed and said that he would help to lower me down into a shaft. Suddenly struck by the thought that every snake and venomous creature that had fallen into the hole might still be down there, I declined. He scoffed, unclipped his detector and made ready to climb down into one.

'Well, what will you do if you meet a taipan or something down there?' I asked, genuinely concerned.

'Step on it!' he replied and still grinning, he cut a large stick and began his descent. Watching him clamber down the rough side walls, I also found myself smiling. It seemed that cheerful, knife-wielding backwoodsmen were still alive and well in Australia.

In the wonderfully named Mad Dog Gulch, I found my smallest piece of gold – a mere 0.1g and a devil to find. It was half the size of an apple pip, rounded and stained rust brown – like all the little stones that lay with it. The crumb of gold played with me, whispering 'yoo-hoo' on the very faintest of signals every time I was about to give up. And with perverse irony, the biggest piece of gold that I found started as an irritation.

The easy ground had been very well worked, and I had taken to concentrating on the more awkward places. This time, I was crouched down and pushing the detector's sensing head up under a clump of tough spiny bushes, when a signal called out from a small heap of stones. I groaned, thinking I was going to have to fight through the tangle to retrieve yet another piece of junk. But it soon became clear that it was actually one of the clay-coated pebbles that was giving the signal, and I hooked it out with my pick. Even when holding the rough, muddy, walnut-sized lump, I still felt that it was probably rubbish. As when forced to open an unwanted present, I reluctantly took out my water bottle, splashed a little onto the piece and rubbed off the clay. Slowly the orange-brown ochreous coating washed away and revealed a water-worn nugget of vein-quartz – an absolute beauty, riddled through with Victoria's purest butter-yellow gold. Similar to clouds, every nugget is a unique shape and like pets, the finders name them with a touching fondness on seeing a face, a hand, little pig, or dog tooth in the gold's form. Mine had a curved band of gold running through the milky-white quartz, and so became 'the Smile'.

As with many things in life, a dogged resolve was key, and my friends enjoyed similar success. By the time they headed home, we had all been rewarded with a wonderful range of small nuggets. While we'd found none of the huge chunks that Victoria is famous for, there was always next time. It was also very satisfying to have glimpsed the early pioneer's life with its picks, shovels, courage and sweat. They would surely have felt blessed if pulse induction electronics had been around to make their hard lives easier.

Alone again, I was grateful for the invitation to stay with a family and detect on their vast area of open grazing land. I repaid their kindness by making stacks of thin breakfast pancakes and teaching the children how to toss them. The house was a single-storey building with thick bluestone walls, which helped to keep it cool. Gerry hadn't minded that his house was like an oven, and Mike and I had rented a portable cabin, which was even worse. This traditionally built home was cleverly arranged as a hollow square, so there was always shade in the neat central courtyard. One whole room housed nothing more than a battered pale-green chair and large central shower. Such delightful and practical minimalism. As each day's fruitless detecting ended, my reward was to stand in the cool of this wet room, on the large stone flags beneath the shower's drenching waterfall, and slowly wash away the day's dust and disappointment.

I found no gold, but was surprised to uncover one small, thought-provoking coin. It was mid-afternoon and I was working my way along a ridge, up into a grove of old eucalyptus trees. The detector sang out and I resigned myself to yet another lead bullet. But this time, as the find came free of the soil and grass roots, it was an old silver shilling. This surprised me and I was at once struck by a sense of connection with the person who had lost it. Minted in 1860, it had Queen Victoria's young head on one side and the words 'one shilling' on the other. I considered the date. This coin was lost at the height of the gold rush, but it felt like I was holding something that a miner had only just dropped. The intuition was palpable – something detectorists talk about, but I hadn't experienced it before. I was the first person in 150 years to hold this coin, yet inexplicably I wanted to give it back to the owner. Somehow, I felt their loss. Perhaps, like me, they weren't having much success, only for them it really mattered. And the sadness of the coin's beautiful young queen herself, who lost the love of her life only a year later. Detecting is like beachcombing, but where history's metal flotsam and losses have washed through the rigours of time – finally to appear right under your feet.

The family sympathized with my modest haul of a single shilling and suggested I take a break. A visiting friend of the family offered to take me out fishing for yabbies – something I had never done before, as I had no idea what they were. I watched, somewhat puzzled, as she borrowed two old saucepans, some string and four rashers of bacon. She led the way across a dry paddock, to a large patch of woodland that shaded the small pool of murky water within. Here she nodded towards the muddy billabong: 'There'll be yabbies in here.' Notwithstanding their unappealing habitat, apparently these small freshwater crayfish eat really well. The quiet, competent woman then taught me to keep still and feel when the yabbies were feeding on the bacon, before gently bringing them up to the surface and scooping them into a saucepan.

Shortly after our outing, with my bright hard-earned nuggets and melancholy silver shilling, I headed back to Melbourne, hoping to spend the last of England's winter in New Zealand's summer. Whether the ancient Chinese sage Lao Tzu was an actual person or not, I liked the advice attributed to him that 'good travellers have no fixed plans'. For that had been my serendipitous approach to Australia, and I loved how it had all worked out. The thrilling land and its warm people had been an absolute delight.

Several years earlier, Britt, a work friend, had left Britain for Los Angeles. She kept in touch for a while, saying that life was good there, after which her correspondence stopped. Then, out of the blue, an enigmatic postcard arrived from Sydney, urging one simple imperative: 'Vince, sell everything and get out here!' At the time I didn't understand the urgency and passion in her one line of simple advice – but now I did.

Gold had been found in New Zealand since the 1830s, when whalers, ship deserters and convicts washed a little colour around the Coromandel Peninsula. A modest find in 1852 sparked a small rush, but it petered out after only three months. In 1856 another small alluvial goldfield was discovered in Nelson Province near Golden Bay. There were many of these 'duffers' rushes' where the place failed to live up to expectations. But as the easily won gold in Australia began to be worked out, excitement grew about the possibilities in New Zealand. Experienced prospectors arrived and, often together with Māori guides, fanned out across the country in their search for a new Bonanza.

If the 1850s had been a slow burn for gold discoveries in New Zealand, the 1860s saw the country catch fire. The first flame was in 1861 at Gabriel's Gully in Otago Province, where nuggets 'shining like the stars in Orion on a dark frosty night' were found beneath knee-deep gravel. The gully yielded 12 tons of gold. In 1862 two men working the Shotover river found 31kg in only two months and declared it 'the richest river in the world'. Upstream, two fortunate prospectors found a beach paved with gold nuggets and quickly picked up 12kg.

In 1866 a record 22 tons of gold were recovered, and New Zealand was firmly on the map of the world's great rushes. The South Island's sodden, mountainous and thickly forested west coast had not attracted European settlers, and was home to very few Māori. But now people flocked there. As the Reverend James Buller, a weary clergyman who had hoped to bring God to the miners, observed, 'Nothing populates a waste, howling wilderness like gold.'

I headed down from Christchurch to Cromwell and into the heart of South Island, to the proven Otago region, the ground where fortunes had been made. Unwittingly, I was following the well-trodden path taken in the gold rush days by those prospectors who were finished with Australia. Like them, I was bright-eyed, full of hope and had great expectations of this new land. I had no friends in New Zealand to guide and advise me, so following careful research, I had created a long list of promising locations.

The land was surprisingly different from Victoria's scorched rust-coloured earth, eucalyptus scrub and the dazzling skies that I had grown used to. I should have known, but I think that we in Europe tend to roll these nations together casually and wrongly as Australasia. Or maybe that is just me. I was still slightly disorientated by the sun being in the north, the unfamiliar stars and the disconcerting fact that it was mid-February and autumnal.

Also, if Australia was lightly peppered with the descendants of plants that the settlers had brought with them, New Zealand was full of these relics. The land felt so familiar at times that I struggled to believe that I really was on the other side of the world.

My first stop to pan the gravels of a once-famous stream was such a moment. Stiff from the long drive, I stretched and relaxed as I took out my panning gear. And then I noticed that all around me, in verdant repose, was my England. Growing beside the tussocks of an unfamiliar grass were red and white clover, and all along the roadside verge were the wild plants once common at home, before our farming became so intensive. They seemed content in their new home, this eclectic mix of immigrants. Yarrow, St John's wort, thistles and docks sat in easy close company with ragwort, weld, great mullein and foxglove. I pushed through a thicket of slender broom and dodged the claws of a dog rose to get down to the stream. And as I crouched to begin panning, a yellowhammer called – evoking a flashback to my May-time hammock almost a year earlier. This meeting with the rural familiar should have been a comfort, but it was not, and I felt the first pangs of longing for my distant home and family.

Each promise-filled location on my list was tried and ticked off, and my unsuccessful days soon grew into frustrating weeks. Like the ball in an arcade pinball game, I bounced between the legendary rush sites – Dip Creek, Lindis Pass, Cardrona, Arrowtown, Queenstown and Wānaka. Places that had once yielded kilos, with nugget-studded beaches that had made some men rich in a day, gave me at best a few grains of gold. Mine was a duffer's rush and being alone made it so much harder. The mountainous land with its lakes and fjords was sensational, but there was nobody to share the joy of the landscape with me. And as each hopeful spot proved almost barren, there was nobody either to commiserate with, find a bar and laugh at our misfortune. My spirits sank, my money diminished and prudently, I rented only the most basic and threadbare of rooms.

One in particular stands out. It was so awful that I sort of enjoyed it – a penance perhaps, as if I deserved nothing better. That it was thought reasonable to let out as 'accommodation' still astounds me. The clue was in the price, but I missed that, thinking I had simply found a bargain.

There must have been a time when it was a pleasing room. When the door had a lock and the lower half was still there, when leaves had not blown in and the neighbouring 24-hour sawmill only worked a day-shift. Woodworm had enjoyed a life so untroubled by any human interference, that their frass had formed neat cones on the floor beneath the table, chair and wooden bed. I wondered what wildlife might have made its home within the bed itself, and if my weight might collapse it. Very gingerly, I unrolled my sleeping bag on top of the moth-eaten covers, thought of the money I had saved and drifted off to the rising and falling whine of a band saw.

With my 'promising locations' list now exhausted, I asked anyone I met for advice on where I should try next. They were quiet, honest, decent people and keen to help. But each time I was told of a great new place, and believed them, it came to nothing. The generous up-to-date local knowledge proved no better than my own research. The last of my optimism began to wane and increasingly downhearted, I felt an affinity with the miners of the 1860s. In all gold rushes, only a tiny proportion of the prospectors actually became rich – usually around 5 per cent. I had realistically never expected to uncover a fortune, but had fondly imagined having a few good finds. There was a delicate subtlety in my disappointment. I was not sad for the gold I hadn't found, but for the growing realization that I wasn't going to find any. That I was another duffer, alone on the far side of the world and one of the forlorn 95 per cent.

But this handsome land, the setting for the *Lord of the Rings* film trilogy, was exquisite. And wandering through Lothlórien, touching the ancient trees of Fangorn and spending time sat on moss-cushioned rocks beside sparkling rivers was healing, and my mood lifted. The distant Southern Alps, aptly cast as the Misty Mountains, beckoned me to cross them. But once more letting hope triumph over experience, I set off for another 'great spot' that I had been told about by a woman selling ice cream.

There was a small man sitting beneath a large tree when I arrived. He looked a bit ragged and nothing like a tourist, so I parked up and went over to talk with him. I was delighted to find that he too was there for the gold – and had been for some time. For two weeks he had waited for his prospecting mate to turn up, and now, instead, there was me, a kindred spirit – scruffy, bearded and eager to learn. I discovered that he had worked in gold all his life, and talked constantly. But I missed much of what he said, as he kept talking no matter which direction he faced, which was a pity, as he obviously had real expertise in gold prospecting. Unable to join in, I soon found that if I listened carefully, all the information was repeated. After a while the peculiar monologue stopped, and he surprised me by apologizing for his poor conversation. He said that it was hard to keep up with two discussions at once – the one with me, and the other with the voices in his head.

Down in the creek, he led me to a long bed of gravel and flat rocks that had nestled together like a line of toppled dominoes. The closely packed chunks of slate were aligned as perfect natural riffles. He explained that this unusual pattern was great for trapping the very fine gold that washed down whenever the river was in spate. In the unimaginative world of prospecting, this is known as 'flood gold'. And the great thing about a flood gold deposit is that the precious metal is replenished in the deluge that follows every storm or snow melt. The gold found in deep bedrock cracks and deserts may have taken thousands, even millions, of years to collect.

We started work on the upstream end of the domino rocks, lifting each one carefully and washing the gritty silt off its upper side into a pan. He then used a trowel to scrape a little of the stony alluvium from beneath each rock, saying that there was no point in digging down any further. This form of gold deposit is a surface enrichment, and the earlier miners would have found all the deeper gold.

An odd couple, we worked all afternoon with me saying little and him struggling at times with the unhelpful voices in his head. However, the gold we found was pretty – a lovely sample of powdery bright-yellow dust, although still not enough to buy a sandwich and coffee. As the shadows lengthened, we packed up and he settled back under his tree – hunched patiently, as he had been when I first arrived. And I felt for him, wondering if the mate he was waiting for was even real. I left him with a packet of biscuits and my water.

I have always believed that while most people quit too early, there is a time to give up. After bouncing about in Otago for a month, it was clear that the commercial gold dredging of the waterways, and high-pressure hydraulic washing of the gravel hillsides, had made it difficult for someone like me to succeed, equipped with only a pan and shovel. Failure keeps us humble, a good thing, but I'd had a full ration of being chastened by let-downs. I now needed a change and the pleasure of good company. So I contacted Peter in Melbourne, as I knew that he had once done very well in New Zealand. His advice was to cross the mountains and head north through the thick forest that cloaks the western slopes, up along the coast to Greymouth. He had been thinking about coming over to New Zealand for a while, and said that he would join me there.

The drive passed through some of the most outstanding scenery in the world. The dry east, with its tussock grass and familiar plants, changed very suddenly – as if Nature herself had created a border. In what seemed like the blink of an eye, I found myself driving in rainforest, with trees and shrubs I'd never seen before, tangled with creepers and elegant tree ferns. It was a totally different world, and I revelled in a thousand shades of green. The fire of hope rekindled as the hours passed – with each one bringing me closer to a genuinely 'good spot'.

Having chosen not to be alone anymore, I booked into the Empire Hotel in Ross. My guidebook said that it was 'threadbare' and that suited me fine – so was I. Here, the showers had locks but not the toilet; there was a rock you could wedge against the door instead.

My readmission into society, like the vegetation's abrupt change, was sudden and lavish. I sang Irish folk songs in the bar with an itinerant, banjo-playing Scotsman and, when out of breath, the locals told me about the 'Honourable Roddy'. Perhaps foolishly, it had never occurred to me to research the biggest gold nugget ever found in New Zealand. This 3.1-kg, hand-sized and rose-shaped lump of gold was discovered in Ross in 1909. My informant's voiced hushed as he told me of the nugget's awful fate. This spectacular and singular piece of the nation's history was named after the Minister of Mines. It toured the country in a jubilant fund-raising raffle, before being presented to King George V at his coronation – and then, the nugget just disappeared. It seems likely that it was melted down to make a tea service, to the embarrassment of the British royal family and the dismay of New Zealanders. As an afterthought, I was told that the country's second-largest nugget, the 2.7-kg 'Victory', was found not far from Ross in the evocatively named Moonlight Creek.

On the move again and sorry to leave behind the lively Empire Hotel, I booked myself into another venue about which my guidebook urged caution. The rebelliously named 'Formerly the Blackball Hilton' was situated a little way inland from Greymouth and I thought it would suit me fine while I waited for Peter to join me. But if the Empire shook me cheerfully out of my spell of loneliness, this amazing place was almost too much.

Arriving late in the day, I was perturbed to find 17 Harley-Davidson motorcycles and a pale-blue Corvette Stingray parked outside. Bass guitar and saxophone music boomed out through the half-open doors, the decibels enhanced by the riotous hubbub from the bikers themselves. My courage almost failed me, and I hesitated, as this place was well beyond the boundary of my experience. Ex-civil servants didn't usually come to places like this. But then again, I had fully embraced the freedom to be scruffy; I was a prospector now and the dishevelled and unshaven new me might just fit right in.

Oh, my goodness, nothing about this wonderful old wooden hotel disappointed! An island of mirth drenched in laughter, from the saloon swing doors to the huge nude portrait above the bar, it was like the set of an old western. As I went in, four men were vigorously playing table football, another was juggling bottles, and a live fiddle player and guitarist were battling with the owner's sound system while a woman stood on a chair, shrieking that she'd just seen a mouse. Unlikely, I thought, as the three barking dogs and the cat would have caught it. Numbed by the sheer force of this sensory overload, I ambled across the room and ordered a beer. 'All prospectors welcome,' said the grinning barman and made me a Bloody Mary instead.

At around 10.30, the bikers started drifting off to bed. I chided them gently, saying that they would give Harley-Davidson riders a *good* name! They replied, almost apologetically, that it had been a long day, and they needed their sleep. Now the only bar customer, I was joined by the owner and the cook until about 3am, when we too ran out of steam. The 7am dawn chorus was the roar of Harleys revving up and the deep tones of the Stingray, driven by a lone woman with a sweet but unnerving smile.

This is the very best of serendipitous travel and a little courage – when a new world unfolds and sweeps you up and away from your comfort zone. And to think, I almost turned away from the best night of my life.

Clad in full waterproofs, Peter was sitting on the veranda of a small café when I arrived. Rain drummed hard on the overhanging corrugated-iron roof, which felt appropriate. This was the Wild West coast – a land of snow-capped mountains, earthquakes and flash floods. I walked over slowly to join him, savouring the reunion: the welcome moment when two prospector friends met again, and particularly exciting, as only one of them knew where they were going.

We headed inland following the Grey river for a while, before turning north and bouncing along a rough track that squeezed its way through the thick bush. Huge tree ferns lined the route, their regular woody columns forming a neat avenue that seemed strangely at odds with the chaotic tangle of all the other vegetation. Finally, we pulled into a cleared area, and I could just see a small river rushing over shallow bedrock – it looked good.

Peter's face lit up as he turned to me. 'Welcome to Moonlight Creek!'

I couldn't believe it: this was where the 'Victory' nugget had been found. Such fame, yet clearly the river was still giving gold, or we wouldn't be there.

I had bought a simple two-piece drysuit in Queenstown and quickly put it on. When I got down to the river, Peter was already digging away the gravel overburden to get at a deep bedrock trap that had yielded over an ounce of gold the last time he was there. But it was empty, and so was the next trap. And this was more of a disappointment than it should have been. He had just travelled over from Australia to join me, and I had pinned all of my hopes on this one last chance, the favourite location of my knowledgeable friend.

However, only a fool expects finding gold to be easy. We absorbed the bad news and set about hunting for somewhere new. It need only be the tiniest patch of ground, missed by the dredges and sharp eyes of those before us. Equipped with a face mask and snorkel, I lay in the shallow river and set about teasing stones from the numerous cracks in the slatey bedrock. But understandably for such a famous river, they were all cleaned out: any day of brilliant sunlight would have illuminated every speck of gold to even the clumsiest of prospectors. And then, perhaps a nudge or just my experience kicked in. I remembered the small underwater torch buried deep in my pack. It had seemed obsolete, given the intense sun beaming through the clear, shallow water. But there were still shadows, overhangs by the bank, which might have been too small or dark to be noticed by brash, bustling gold seekers.

And there, finally, I discovered the joy of Moonlight Creek: slim, rounded nuggets, like tiny gold coins, were packed in the narrowest of cracks, with darkness cloaking the treasure a mere hand's breadth from the sunlit barren ground that had been worked by all for decades. These shimmering pieces had lain hidden since long before humans came looking for gold. Again and again, I ducked and shone the tiny beam sideways, deep into joints where the fractured grey schist met a conglomerate rock. And like small, tired children playing hide and seek, one by one the nuggets gave up their hushed places and came out – the game was over.

New Zealand is wonderfully free of poisonous critters. No spiders rear up at you or sneak into your panning equipment, and you can lean back against a tree without bull-ants raining down on your head. Piles of leaves are scorpion-free, and heaps of brushwood sticks will never conceal a tiger or any of the other deadliest snakes in the world. But there are sandflies. I have been bitten by mosquitoes, midges, ticks, flower bugs, harvest mites, horseflies, and once, when panning in southern France, I had so many leeches sucking my ankles dry that when I looked down, I honestly thought that they were clumps of matted pondweed caught against my legs. Sandflies are small, quiet and, like leeches, you don't feel them bite, so I chose to ignore them – a big mistake!

They were thick along the western coast, including at Moonlight Creek. During much of my first innocent day, when testing the gravels with a gold pan, I had rolled up my sleeves and was vaguely aware that I was getting bitten. That night I couldn't sleep for the pain, having taken about 60 bites on each arm. I had to get up and lay my hands in cool water to ease them. After that, I covered up and used copious amounts of insect repellent.

Not long after Peter went home, I too gave up the search for gold. And of all the things that might have decided this for me, it was the sandflies. I had taken to wearing gloves to protect my hands, but one day, while working in Buller Gorge, I looked down at my left wrist and saw a neat line of eight sandflies happily feeding. How had they found that tiny strip of cold, pale skin, no wider than a pencil? It was time to go, I decided; I had prospected New Zealand for almost six weeks and enjoyed this splendidly natural and unspoiled land, and I had a small bag of 'Victory nuggets'. Now I needed a holiday.

With no intention of prospecting, I headed north to where gold was first found at Coromandel. I was told of sandfly-free beaches with springs oozing hot water through the fine yellow sand; it sounded absolute bliss, and it was. After the quiet of South Island, North Island seemed crowded and busy, but I had missed people and enjoyed the lively throng. I shouldered my way into the nervous raft of giggling tourists paddling on Hahei's Hot Water Beach – where the springs were a lot hotter than any of us had expected. I sipped a civilized morning coffee from a cheerful café on the beach, chatted with a lovesick poet and befriended two joyfully energetic semi-itinerant Argentinian surfers. The beach had palm trees and a swing, and the swing was instructive.

A young couple who were clearly very much in love spent hours on it. The pointless act of swinging to and fro on a long rope delighted them, and the sight of such happiness delighted me. They seemed carefree, living in the moment as their pendulum swung between sunlight and shade. A metaphor of their life to come, I hoped. The essence of freedom, to have time and few cares. To be content with simple pleasures, to want what you have, to live in the now. I thought back over my first desk-free year and wondered: *am I free now?* Barefoot, I decided to paddle and let the small aquamarine waves break over my feet. *I think I am*, I decided.

9

THE CALL OF THE YUKON

'The proper function of man is to live, not just exist.'

—Jack London, *To Build a Fire*

When I was a boy, our fragile clifftop caravan home in Pembrokeshire was held in place with guy ropes, as gales were common in the west of Wales. I had such freedom, and it was a paradise.

My mother sent me out to hide whenever the school inspector was due to call. In her view, my inspiring home schooling was not to be doused by the wet blanket of well-meaning authority. When my Royal Navy helicopter engineer father was home, we studied mathematics. And when alone, my mother poured her love of literature into me, so that soon my head swirled with the power of words. New worlds opened for me with each thumbed page in her small collection of well-worn books. But of all the treasure islands, diamond mines, giant whales and journeys to the centre of the Earth, it was the world of Jack London, writing about Dawson City in Canada's Yukon territory during the Klondike gold rush, that called out to me the most.

I have made two pilgrimages to the venerable city, both times coming home with a little gold and a huge sense of fulfilment.

My journeys may have been ten thousand times easier than the hellish, life-threatening slog made by the toughest of prospectors in the late 1890s, but they were, nevertheless, almost spiritually pleasing. Dawson City is hallowed ground to all those who have even the mildest touch of gold fever. It is the scene of the world's last great gold rush – and perhaps, the cruellest of them all.

In October 1897 Jack London, a tough and very capable 21-year-old, was one of the first to arrive. But it was already too late: all of the good ground had been claimed. With his companions, he had just spent two months hauling a ton of food, and all the necessary clothing and mining supplies, over 600 miles of glacier, canyon and bog to arrive as the northern winter began. Many he passed on the Chilkoot Trail didn't make it at all. The incredible cold was unrelenting. Living in a tiny log cabin with his three friends, he said that even with their stove going constantly, the meat stayed frozen and 'it was like living in a fridge'.

They suffered terribly, and Jack worked his passage back home to California the next summer. Although his body was starved and wrecked by scurvy during his short Yukon adventure, his mind was filled with wonder and a zest for life that never left him. He had found 'gold' in the Yukon, in the fabulous stories that were soon to bring him fame and fortune. But there is a sad irony to his words, 'I shall not waste my days in trying to prolong them.' He died at 40, a superstar author after publishing many works, including the books my mother read to me.

Of my four rules when travelling, 'talk to people' is the most important. The other three – travel light, arrive early and expect things to go wrong – are sensible, stress-relieving and healthy, like having porridge oats for breakfast, but open no new doors.

I had met a small group of lively Canadians at the World Goldpanning Championships when they were held in Europe the year before, who had invited me to visit them in Dawson City. It was such stuff as prospectors' dreams are made of, so I readily accepted their kind offer and was on my way. The flight from London to Vancouver had gone well, as had the next onward stage up to Whitehorse, the capital of the Yukon. But now I had a problem.

I was in Whitehorse airport, which was about to close for the night. I had neither the money nor the inclination to travel through the driving rain into town and find somewhere to stay. Besides which, the early hour of my flight out the next morning might make getting back to the airport tricky. Wondering what to do, I noticed a huge, cheerful-looking security guard and went to talk to him. He was sympathetic and offered me a deal. He said that the only room with the comfort of a carpet to lie on was the upstairs restaurant and, if I promised to be gone before the catering staff arrived, he would let me sleep there. And then came my side of the bargain: the guard explained that he was of Scottish descent and yearned for news of his ancestral land; he wanted a copy of the *Glasgow Herald*. When I swore I would send him two copies once back home again, he unlocked the carpeted room. I do hope the newspapers I sent got to him and reaffirmed his much-appreciated trust in human nature.

So as not to embarrass my helper, I was up at first light and sheepishly peered out at the ragged grey dawn that still cloaked the airport. It was then that I noticed a museum-piece aircraft parked below the restaurant window, with *Yukon Sourdough* and a gold prospector painted on its tail fin. It was a fabulous Douglas Dakota DC-3 – real *Indiana Jones* transport, the workhorse of wild places and Land Rover of the skies. I packed up quickly, hoping that there might be time to visit this historical attraction before I had to board my plane. It was a complete surprise, then, and slightly alarming, to be led out to the antique and invited to climb on board.

This was far beyond all of my previous experience of air travel and, excited, I soaked it all up. When we were airborne, my window rattled as if it were loose and I watched oil seep out and flow down the side of the left wing's roaring engine. The right-hand side of the plane was loaded with stores. Bulging sacks were heaped from floor to ceiling along with stacks of cardboard boxes, all securely held in place by a curtain of black cargo netting. And of all possible foods, what were the odds – the boxes nearest to me held tins of faggots, a Welsh savoury meatball and my childhood favourite. As we rose up into the thick cloud, the stewardess started preparing the in-flight meals: a cheese sandwich, toasted in a small oven. Three of my few fellow passengers were First Nation women with newborn babies, which suggested that Whitehorse probably had the best maternity unit in the area. I could see the pilots chatting through the open cockpit door, and wondered what instruments the old plane had to help them fly through fog and over forested mountains. Given that the aircraft had obviously survived for so long, I flopped back, relaxed and smiled to myself – welcome to the Yukon!

With a swirl of dust, the DC-3 landed on Dawson City's dirt runway, where a polite young man in an Air North uniform greeted me and directed me to the bus. In the town that afternoon, this time dressed in casual clothes, the same man served me an ice cream. And then, later that evening, now formally dressed, he took my bets at the roulette wheel in Diamond Tooth Gerties Saloon. Impressed, I asked him how many jobs he actually had.

'There's only work here in the summer,' he said, suddenly serious. 'And that's barely two months long.'

I am constantly humbled by the generosity of people who live in faraway, off-the-beaten-track places. No sooner had I arrived in their huge powder-blue home, where I would be staying for a month, for free, than my host family lent me a car and whisked me off to a salmon barbecue party. The spawning run had started, and huge fish were being hauled straight out of the Yukon river. Skilfully gutted, filleted and splashed with a teriyaki-style dressing, the great chunks of dark-pink meat sizzled over hot coals. I have never tasted better.

That evening, I asked about the practicalities of living there through the winter months. Many things had changed over the last one hundred years, but not the bitter weather. This simple question triggered a fascinating northern fashion parade. Items of clothing that are neither seen nor needed in England, and which had been put away for the summer, were hauled out and demonstrated. While the base layers were comical and seemed unchanged since the Victorian age – with silk or woollen button-up vests, baggy long johns with the necessary flap for when nature called – the outer layers were new to me, and sobering. The massive elbow-length, thick-felted mittens, insulated boots and one-piece padded boiler suits looked like parts of a giant baby's romper suit. But it was the arctic parkas that stood out. Long-sleeved, double-flapped, with fur-trimmed hoods that pulled out into a long tube to save the face and eyes from freezing, these huge cover-all coats seemed to define life here in winter. This was apex clothing – such stuff as London wrote about, and I loved it! Yet I was surprised to learn that even this was not enough for the really bitterly cold days: nobody went out then. This family would set an alarm clock every four hours, day and night, to feed their stove, or else the terrible cold would reach in and freeze everything. As it always had in the past.

The next morning, my hosts set off for work and I headed out – up the Bonanza Creek to find Jim, one of the Canadians I'd met at the World Goldpanning Championships, who had invited me to visit his claim. A remarkable man who combined the rare talents of being a top international competitive gold panner with an exceptionally long and successful mining career, he had worked his claim since the early 1960s.

I travelled south-east from Dawson, across the Klondike river to find the world-famous creek. The seats in my borrowed car were coated in a thin film of road dust, and the windscreen had so many cracks that I was amazed it stayed in place. When I swung right onto a rough dirt road and found the legendary waterway, little more than a large stream, weaving beside the track to the left of me, I pulled over to let the magnitude of the place sink in. So, this was it, Bonanza. A small brook, strewn with white quartz pebbles and flowing through an unremarkable valley, its low hills now quiet and sparsely wooded with thin arctic spruce, pine, young birch and willow. Already I felt at home.

Somewhere in the terrain before me, George Carmack with his wife Kate, her brother Skookum Jim and nephew Tagish

Charlie found the gold that started the Yukon rush. Which of them actually made the discovery in mid-August 1896 is contested. George claimed the find, but the others were adamant that he was asleep under a birch at the time. Some versions have it that Kate first saw the gold while rinsing dishes in the creek, but most say that Jim found the gold while cleaning up after shooting a moose. Whatever the truth, the find was incredible, being rich and easy to reach. Apparently, the gold was trapped in a thick layer between flaky slabs of schist bedrock, like cheese in a sandwich. No fools, they measured out and staked four claims, then rushed to a police post at the mouth of the Fortymile river to register them. According to the Canadian historian Pierre Berton, George later said of the moment: 'I felt as if I had just dealt myself a royal flush in the game of life, and the whole world was a jackpot.'

The only loser in all of this was the prospector Robert Henderson, who had first advised them to try the area after finding gold in a nearby creek. He had given them the information on the understanding that they would let him know of any gold they found. It's possible that his racist views had rankled the three, so they decided not to share their news and to cut him out of the fortune they had just discovered. Within a few weeks, the once innocuous and peaceful Rabbit Creek was renamed Bonanza, and became the epicentre of perhaps the most brutal of all the world's great gold rushes.

The bitter cold was this rush's signature hardship. Disease, starvation, injury, animal attacks and robbery were normal for most new goldfields. The poet Robert Service weaves dreadful images of how 'the frost fiend stalks to kill'. Looking up along the sun-kissed summer valley, I found it impossible to imagine how hard it must have been to live and work here. To be trapped for several months of winter in a tent or cabin hardly bigger than a garden shed, where anything further than two paces from the stove would freeze. And all the while sustained by the customary 'three Bs' diet of bread, beans and bacon – simple, monotonous meals that seemed enough, until the lack of vitamin C caused scurvy and your teeth fell out.

I set off again and shortly Jim's long, low house came into view, up on a ridge to my right. I had been wondering how his season was going, when I noticed a light aircraft parked on a short strip of cleared land behind the building – obviously not too badly, it seemed.

Jim greeted me, took two cold beers from a large fridge, then sat me down for a lesson in goldfield etiquette. Firstly, never enter a claim, unless invited. Secondly, stay away from the owner's sluice box, unless invited. And even then, do not touch it, unless invited to do so. Clean-ups take time, so the harvest of wealth can accumulate over many days, and how much gold is trapped in the riffles is nobody's business but the owner's.

It was sobering to hear this quiet and capable man calmly tell me that if a stranger wandered onto his land, he would be annoyed. If the stranger headed for his workings, he would fetch his rifle. And if this trespassing miscreant put a hand in the sluice box, he would fire a warning shot. Apparently, in peaceful, law-abiding Canada, this was a perfectly reasonable thing to do.

For the first day or two, Jim sent me out to test areas of freshly uncovered ground. If I routinely panned up more than two colours, I was to tell him, as that patch of dirt was good enough to put through the sluice. I was never sure if this apparently important work was just him being kind – making me feel useful, but keeping me out of the way. Then, having been tested perhaps, I was promoted to helping him with the actual sluicing.

Back home in England, my own sluice box was tiny, smaller than an infant's cot. In comparison, Jim's was huge and the toughest I have ever seen, roughly the length and width of the lane in a bowling alley. It was noisy too, with a torrent of rushing white water tumbling the pay dirt over its riffles, made from thick iron bars of old railway track to catch the chunky gold and frequent nuggets that this claim produced. An 85-oz nugget, the biggest yet uncovered in the Yukon, had been found hereabouts. Jim was reworking one of the original claims that had once yielded tons of gold during the first years of the rush, unimaginable wealth from such a tiny area. A ton of gold today is worth roughly a hundred million US dollars – and they had found several tons.

Unusually, the pay dirt material wasn't screened and classified before entering the sluice, so my job was simple: to use a long bar to free any rocks that became lodged. Once loose, the boulders rolled along in the current, rumbling as they bumped across the riffles, and all the while being chased by Jim's dog, barking furiously. Whether he thought he was herding the rocks away to their rest, or seeing these nuisances off the premises, he never tired of the job.

Finally, the big moment arrived and the water was turned off so that the sluice box could be checked. This wasn't for a total clean-up, just a quick look to make sure that everything was OK and to recover any 'pickers' – the larger pieces of gold. Mindful of my etiquette lesson, I put both hands in my pockets before stepping down onto the glistening wet ladder of polished railway track. Trapped behind each iron rung, large patches of promising heavy black sand had concentrated and crunched under my boots as I slowly made my way up along the sluice. No gold was visible.

Disappointed, I wondered what riches were hidden a mere finger's breadth beneath my boots. And then I saw the nugget; it was the size of a slim cigarette packet. With my heart racing, I tried to be 'Yukon cool' and nonchalantly called out to Jim, 'There's a good piece here.' When invited to do so, I took my hands from my pockets and crouched down to pick up the precious beauty, as careful as taking a sleeping baby from its mother. As he walked down the sluice to examine the find, I had time to rest the nugget across the palm of my hand, my fingers glowing in its soft golden light, and feel its potency seep into me. It was like a primal energy was entering my veins – powerful, and the only known cure for gold fever.

Clearly pleased, Jim smiled and quickly slipped the nugget into his jacket, saying, 'I thought we would find something good. We're washing old boulder ground.' As this explanation obviously meant nothing to me, he paused, then beckoned me to follow him up to an area of the claim I hadn't yet been to, where he pointed at an old shaft amid his recent excavations. I was fascinated and approached the water-filled square hole cautiously. It was shuttered with rough planks and had a vertical ladder on one side, which disappeared down into dark, icy shadow. This was real history, a genuine fragment of the original gold rush, still *in situ*.

I tried to imagine the last miner who had climbed up these rungs, and hoped he had been happy. Working on one of the richest claims in the Yukon, he had probably succeeded where so many had not. Maybe it was his gold being unloaded in San Francisco from the steamboat *Excelsior* in mid-July 1897 that had confirmed the rumours of a big strike in the Yukon. A vast crowd had watched in astonishment as wheelbarrows were used to bring some of the gold ashore, and the Klondike frenzy that gripped the world had begun.

I recalled one of the lines in Robert Service's poem 'The Ballad of Blasphemous Bill', which lists some causes of gold miners' deaths: 'By battle, murder or sudden wealth, by pestilence, hooch or lead'. I find the idea of being killed by 'sudden wealth' particularly haunting: to have succeeded against all the odds and staggering hardships, and then be felled by the very wealth that you had fought so hard to find. I wondered what this claim's first owners' wealth had bought them, and whether they'd had the wisdom to deal with it.

Jim interrupted my daydreaming to explain that the early prospectors soon found that the best gold lay deep underground in the ancient riverbed. They dug shafts down through the permafrost until they hit bedrock, and then tunnelled along through the frozen ground, bringing the rich pay dirt up to the surface to be washed. But they faced a problem whenever they hit a big boulder. As they were using hand tools in very limited space in a frozen gravel tunnel, they couldn't move the biggest rocks, so had to go around them. This now meant that whenever Jim uncovered a group of large boulders, or even a huge one on its own, he had a chance to work a tiny patch of virgin ground. And for a day or two, he got to experience the gold rush heyday thrill of knowing that anything was possible.

'Find the boulders, find the nuggets,' Jim said quietly, as if to himself. He was still holding our find, his hand moving slightly within his jacket pocket as he judged the nugget's weight and felt its water-worn contours.

This man has gold fever worse than me, I thought, *and is absolutely in his element here.* How wonderful to know where you belong, and to be there.

I too was loving the Yukon. The enormity of this land was almost overwhelming, and it smouldered with the promise of all the gold yet to be found. And here I was, revelling in the moment, scuffing about with a battered steel gold pan, in the excellent company of competent miners – including fourth-generation descendants of the original Klondikers. For some reason, the big mining conglomerates hadn't moved in and taken over. Most of the claims still seemed to be owned by individuals and families.

And then there was Dawson City itself, bustling yet curiously serene, an island of civilization in an ocean of pristine wilderness. In some respects the word 'city' might seem misleading, as Dawson is only slightly bigger than the small English village where I live. Yet the breadth of opportunity in this cosmopolitan hamlet was staggering. Most strikingly of all, people could be themselves here. The tough and the lonely and the dreamers all belonged. What other small, self-sufficient community in the world embraced dusty, oil-stained miners who were still pulling gold from the creeks? Or had saloons and dance hall girls, artists and poets, a casino and an airport? This tangle of exuberant individuality worked smoothly in Dawson. The structures of law and orderly local governance were firmly in place, while bears and wolves still prowled its borders. Dawson was a place of extremes, with sweet warm summers, ice-bound bitter winters and a joyous kaleidoscope of possible careers. If a key to happiness is to live and not just exist, that lesson was well understood here.

If they would have me, I could live here too, I decided, with the fresh chill of each morning, the air softly scented by the first touch of warm sunlight on the old wooden buildings and heavy with the ominous call of ravens. And all the while, lapped by the vast and icy waters of Mother Yukon herself. The third-longest river on the North American continent passed by slowly, an immense and unstoppable migration of water moving west, timeless and indifferent to humans and their tiny outpost city on the northern shore.

I hadn't come to get rich; just to be in this legendary land, breathe its air, meet its people and get a smudge of its pale clayey dust under my fingernails was enough for me. But I did know that riches were still possible for a visitor.

My English friend Alf Henderson had left the area with a glorious heap of gold dust only the summer before. This was a wonderful win–win situation for Alf and the claim's owner, who had thought the place barren. The owner had taken over the new claim and cut away the overburden gravels to get down to bedrock, but found no gold there. So, fortuitously, he gave Alf and his two companions permission to prospect the quarry-like open-cast hole.

At first, their panning simply confirmed the owner's findings – the odd speck of colour, but nowhere near enough to be commercially interesting. They were close to giving up, when Alf noticed a narrow band of rusted gravel. It ran the full length of the quarry's side wall, about halfway up – like the jam layer in a slice of sponge cake. He stretched up, used his pick to carefully chip out a sample and took the panful of red-ochreous dirt over to the muddy pool they were using. He told me that he was simply curious, and held out no particular hopes for the rusty dirt. But as he panned it down, he was stunned to see a wide arc of gold appear.

Against the odds and the normal rules of deposition, the gold had been deposited within a thin band of pyritic material high above the bedrock. The agreement with the claim owner was they could keep all the gold they found, as long as they shared the knowledge with him.

As soon as he was home, I visited Alf to see the Yukon gold that he had found. Beaming with pride, he lifted down a heavy glass bottle and poured out a glittering stream of bright gold that filled my cupped hands – the first and only time that this has happened to me.

The owner, now wise to where the gold was on his claim, reworked the discarded overburden and then focused his efforts on the rusty layer. Alf never told me what he, or the owner, earned from the discovery. It's an unspoken rule of goldfields not to ask, and not to tell. And only a novice or an ill-mannered lout would break the taboo – so his secret died with him.

Driving towards the little-known Hunker Creek, which was rich in gold yet totally overshadowed by the world-famous Bonanza Creek nearby, I suddenly noticed an old bucket-line dredge, partly hidden among some trees. The seemingly forgotten relic of the last phase of the great gold rush had a melancholy air. Landlocked and abandoned, it sat forlorn, like Noah's Ark after the flood. Entirely clad in sun-bleached grey timber and bigger than the hotels in Dawson, the incongruous giant was a somewhat startling find.

Gold dredges like this one represent the untold story of the Yukon and its gold. They were initially developed in New Zealand in the 1880s, then used and refined in California and Montana. By the time the first of these enormous machines arrived in the

Yukon in late 1899, they had been perfected and were a marvel of the age. At one point, there were 19 of them operating in the Klondike area. While the romantic struggles of the pioneer prospectors during the first two or three years of the rush grabbed all the headlines, the attention of poets and imagination of the world, the huge dredges lumbered on, finding gold in the deep and difficult ground for decades. They brought a new way of life to the Yukon. The gold dredges and the massive crews that supported them kept Dawson alive long after the colourful throng of hopeful miners had moved on to Alaska, or gone home. The last of these awesome machines stopped work and did a final clean-up in 1966.

At first, the dredge working in the region was eager and haphazard. But the buckets struggled with the frozen ground and the gold – locked in chunks of icy dirt – passed straight through the dredge and was lost with the tailings. Gradually, a four-stage system was developed that increased efficiency and reduced breakages. A survey drilling team would 'prospect' new ground and identify the richest areas. Then the second gang stripped away all the vegetation and loose overburden from the chosen sections. Next came the thawing crew, who pumped water down through the frozen earth and made the gold-bearing gravel workable. This could take a couple of months, and ideally was done a year or two ahead of the dredge to ensure a constant supply of workable pay dirt. Occasionally, an old-timer was employed to pan samples taken from the buckets and check for colour. While no doubt grateful for the work, there is something plaintive about a lone figure panning down gravel, old-style, beside a gargantuan, state-of-the-art, gravel-guzzling machine.

These behemoths worked while floating in a small, self-made lake. The digging ladder, an endless chain of manganese steel buckets, clawed up the deep untouched placer gravels to the front of the dredge. The material was then tipped into a hopper that fed the trommel – a slightly inclined cylindrical rotating screen. High-pressure water then washed the pay dirt to break up the lumps and flush the fine gold, small pebbles and sand through the screen's holes and onto the gold recovery sluice tables. All of the material that was too big to pass through the trommel's screen dropped onto the stacker belt – a conveyor that dumped the rocky tailings far behind the dredge. If the ground was expected to yield big chunks of gold, a 'grizzly', a series of parallel iron bars, was placed at the lower end of the trommel over a nugget sluice.

Intrigued by the sight of this abandoned giant, I parked and made my way through the thin woodland that was slowly establishing itself on the stony spoil to get a closer look. Then I stood silently for a while, gazing up in awe of both the machine and the people who had built it. It felt as if a mind-blowing piece of gold rush history had suddenly materialized in front of me.

The gold dredge evoked a feeling of prehistoric animal power. A wood and steel brontosaurus, a long neck devouring the ancient gravels for its innards to digest the nutrient gold. Then far behind, a long tail and fan-shaped heaps of rocky dung. For many years the dredges meandered slowly along the valley bottoms, and the graceful curving lines of their 'droppings' are still evident – like the fossil record of a now extinct beast. As if to lend weight to this imagery, the dredgemen often pulled up the skeletal remains and huge tusks of long-buried mammoths and occasionally the smaller tusks of a mastodon.

I decided to enter the dredge. After all, this wasn't a working claim, with a family's wages, their entire summer's gold unguarded while they slept, but an incredible relic. Warily, I climbed into its shadowy interior. The old wood hadn't perished and seemed sound, and I relaxed a little. The dredge was a patchwork of sunlit deck and deep shadowy recesses, and it was hard to shake the thought that in most parts of the world, it would now be full of venomous creatures – snakes, spiders and scorpions. However, this vessel had been savagely winter-sanitized over many years, and ought to be totally free of such threats. I relaxed a little more, but started whistling after the fleeting thought occurred to me that bears might like to rest in the sheltered interior.

I carefully made my way up to the hopper, where the iron buckets fed the dredge its pay dirt, and looked down into the trommel, now silent and empty. I imagined how staggeringly noisy these dredges must have been – clattering rock on squealing metal, steel buckets banging and rattling – 24 hours a day for the whole season. How much gold had passed through this vast machine? The ground at the mouth of Hunker Creek was particularly rich, and a dredge could recover hundreds of ounces of gold in a single day. One such, Dredge No. 4, is recorded as having recovered 9 tons of gold during its working life.

It is worth pausing to consider what 'to get rich' meant during the Yukon gold rush. By the year 1900 over 34 tons of gold were being mined in a season – and to date, the Yukon has yielded well over 500 tons of gold. That is just under £40 billion at today's values. In the UK the biggest National Lottery win of all time was roughly £200 million, while the average win for the EuroMillions lottery is about £58 million. As I write this, a ton of gold is worth approximately £76 million. It seems likely that each of the dredges found several tons, and so did those miners working the richest claims on Bonanza, Eldorado and Hunker. So during the best years, it was as if the relatively small settlement of Dawson was absolutely packed with lottery winners, many of whom were totally happy to spend their sudden and massive wealth in the town itself – the wild excesses of the time are almost incomprehensible. If several people in my parish won the lottery every year, and spent most of it in the village pub, my home might begin to feel a little like the youthful Dawson City too!

As I reflected on my trip to the Yukon, it felt like a great privilege to have experienced at first hand the shaft made by the very first miners on Jim's claim. Being just off Eldorado Creek, it would have been staked very early in the rush – and I had held one of the few big nuggets that they had missed. And now, to have been able to explore one of the giant gold dredges that kept Dawson alive and vibrant well into the 20th century – a witness to the extreme opposites of gold production in this fascinating and generous land. It seemed incredible to think that the whole extravagant, world-gripping adventure was likely started by someone rinsing a dish, while George Carmack, blissfully unaware of the wealth beneath him and indifferent to the forest's carnivores, slept peacefully beneath a birch.

Most people I met in and around Dawson had a gripping wild animal story. The couple I was staying with were once driving south when the road dipped into a deep cut through a long snowdrift. A flash of yellow eyes caught in the headlights. They slowed down and found themselves among wolves. The pack took off and ran on either side of the car, its speed checked to keep pace with them. They drove slowly on the glittering frosted road, with wolf-breath swirling in the headlights' beam. To have the essence of wilderness itself loping along beside you – what a supreme and primal experience, and what are the odds! As the road climbed up out of the drift and the banks of snow grew smaller, the wolves burst over them, scrambling over the lip in a flurry of white – and then they were gone. The 20 seconds of heart-stopping wonder were over, and normality resumed.

In general the wolves didn't seem to be a problem, but the bears could be. I visited a family who were mining over by Dominion Creek and who told me how they had just sat down to their Sunday roast dinner, when a huge bear appeared and prowled around the house. Hard to enjoy your meal with a loaded rifle on your lap, they said.

A lively man I'd met a few times before, who lived near the Klondike river, also once had a near-miss with a bear and now lived in a shipping container, which he had made look like a neat little cabin by cladding it with timber offcuts – cute and bear-proof. 'I can shut the doors and sleep peacefully,' he said, as if that level of domestic security was a novelty. Given that he was so far from the sea, I always meant to ask him how he got the container up there.

With so much talk of the wonders and dangers of moose, wolves and bears, I felt left out. I hadn't even seen any tracks yet, let alone a living animal. I made enquiries, expecting to be told of a trail, river crossing, wallow or drinking place favoured by the Arctic's star wildlife. But I was quietly advised to try the city dump – at night. This was most certainly not in the tourist literature, so off I went.

Just after midnight, I drove the few miles out of Dawson along the Klondike Highway, and turned off onto the track that led to the rubbish dump. The description 'night' seemed misleading, as it never got darker in summer than a twilit gloom. Here, the rough dirt road swung in a long right-hand curve and finished with an unexpectedly shocking scene. It was as if a theatrical curtain had suddenly been pulled aside by a grubby master of ceremonies. The sprawling dump seemed so out of place in careful, pristine Canada, where fly-tipping and litter are an unknown southern problem, that I stopped the car and gazed in amazement. I had not expected it to be like this.

The rubbish dump was like one of those terrifying medieval visions of hell. The chain-link boundary fence had long since lost its authority and hung loosely from its concrete posts, or not at all; long stretches lay flat and tangled with waste. The city's detritus had formed a landscape of low ragged hills. Some mounds smouldered and cast a thin white mist, adding to the site's unworldly atmosphere. And the whole area was patrolled by bears.

Their dark silhouettes wandered lazily in the gloom, stopping to sift through torn bags and old broken boxes, like despondent refugees from another world. And I was absolutely delighted. I had come to see bears and here they were, loads of them. Mesmerized, I got out of the car to watch. From a distance they seemed pedestrian and calm. But the ever-present danger was apparent as soon as one got too close to another. Then they would both rise up, roaring with indignation. These were wild bears – real, raw and powerful. It was exhilarating to see, like watching a storm in slow motion. A fairly small black bear ambled my way, then stopped and effortlessly flung aside a discarded door. It stood and stared at me over a section of the drooping fence, and I sensed that my audience with these remarkable creatures was over.

The next morning, my hosts severely chastised me for my stupidity. As an Englishman, I obviously knew nothing of bears and had got far too close. And I am sure that they were right. But now I'd had my Arctic wildlife encounter, and loved every minute of it. I was, however, curious as to who else had been at the dump in the dead of night, and had sneaked on me!

And then my glorious first visit to the Yukon was over. I packed and waited anxiously for my promised lift to the airport, but there was a delay and my hopes of getting there early, or even on time, soon faded. As we pulled into the car park, I saw my plane taxiing away from the terminal and out towards the runway.

While I sat miserably, trying to think how to get myself to Whitehorse overnight, in time to catch my next flight to Vancouver, my driver ran to the terminal building and was now waving frantically for me to hurry over. This seemed completely pointless, until the Dakota cut its engines, turned and rumbled back along the dirt runway. I was astonished and my misery flipped to joy as I grabbed my pack and ran to the check-in. This was far beyond anything I had experienced with air travel – no plane had ever come back for me before.

My documents received barely a glance as I rushed through the check-in area and dashed outside. With engines roaring, the leviathan drew up and stopped close by to where I stood incredulous. Then there was a long quiet pause, before the side door suddenly opened and deployed the steep steps. An older man, confident in his smart Air North uniform, looked down at me as I gushed my thanks, still hardly believing what had just happened. He stared at me for a moment longer, almost smiled, and then said in a deep Yukon drawl, 'Son, it's all part of the North.' And so it was.

*

I didn't fly Air North for my next visit to this vibrant outpost, but drove instead – a pity, as the Dakota DC-3 was the most agreeable way to arrive. Once a year, up to a thousand gold prospectors and their families meet somewhere in the world to drink, dance, catch up with the news and hold a competition. The World Goldpanning Association oversees the arrangements, and the nations vote to decide which member country will next be granted the honour of hosting this colourful event. In 2007 Canada beat off all rival bids and secured the prestigious right to host the world championships, which were to take place in Dawson.

Keen to compete in that year's event, and excited at the chance to return to the Yukon with my family, I hired a huge RV and drove the long road from Fairbanks in Alaska. At last, we ambled down the final stretch of the wonderfully named Top of the World Highway to the mighty Yukon river. And there, across the vast eddying water and nestled beneath an ancient landslip, I saw once again the most welcoming of cities. The rattling chain ferry slowly hauled us through the current, and there was plenty of time to relax and admire the neat cluster of sunlit dun- and pastel-coloured buildings on the far bank. I was so pleased to be back; it felt like an old friend was waiting for us. And I knew that Dawson, the greatest of the gold rush capitals, was about to host a brilliant championships.

This was going to be a wonderful, adrenalin-filled week. My family and I would get to meet the eclectic worldwide gold community, and catch up with news of nuggets, deaths and babies. I loved to meet the bright-eyed newcomers and feel the youthful energy of these rising stars. And then there would be a chance to reminisce with veterans I had known since my first world championships in France, back in 1988.

To be honest, I had found that initial event pretty scary at first. I was young, alone and found myself surrounded by a host of rough-looking people: huge bearded men, dressed for the outdoors with knives ostentatiously hung from their wide leather belts, and women who seemed straight from a mountain gold camp, confident, beautiful and strong – nobody would mess with them unscathed. But after three cautious days I began to relax. I had witnessed no fights or trouble, just the uplifting experience of seeing many nations peacefully aligned and all of one mind – a thousand good friends who had gathered together joyfully in an annual migration of goodwill.

Every year, the competition builds through an exciting series of heats and qualifying rounds towards the last day's demonstrations of excellence in the finals. There is an official category for everybody, to allow for a panner's age and experience – beginners, children and veterans are all encouraged to take part. The three most prestigious classes are: proficient men, proficient women and the national teams. There is no limit to how many people each nation can enter, and this is all part of the fun. Anybody who wishes to take part is welcome. The competition's aim is to identify the world's very best gold panners as individuals – and where they are from is almost incidental. The exception to this is the national teams' category. In this case, as with most of the world's sporting competitions, one team is chosen to represent their country and the focus in this event is on the nation.

As would be expected, gold-rich countries such as Canada, the USA, Australia, South Africa and Finland usually field many highly skilled panners. But so too do those lesser-known gold nations with a passion for this sport – the Czech Republic, Slovakia, Poland, Austria and Spain. This year, I was sure that

France, Italy and Germany would be strong too; and Sweden had just raised the bar by inventing the world's fastest gold pan. It was also rumoured that the outstandingly good Dutch gold panners met every fortnight for training.

Among such Olympians, I knew that the odds were stacked against Britain, a nation with limited wild gold and relatively few prospectors. I had been elected the captain of our team, and mindful of the acerbic wisdom once offered by an ironic athlete – 'The more I train, the luckier I get!' – we all trained hard, getting up early each morning and off to the practice area before breakfast. And if the training pools were already crowded, awash with swirling gold pans as steely-eyed competitors sought to knock seconds from their time, we found puddles in the road in which to hone our skills.

The competition's challenge is essentially very simple. Can you wash pay dirt really quickly and keep all of the gold? It's solely a test of a person's skill with a gold pan; there is no element of actual prospecting or luck involved. For this to be fair, each competitor must have exactly the same chance. The arena is built with thirty rectangular troughs of knee-deep water, the washing pools, and the carefully seeded pay dirt is measured into buckets, one per person. The judges know how many tiny flakes of gold, each no bigger than a crushed poppy seed, are in each round, and there is a crippling three-minute time penalty for each piece lost. To have any hope of moving through the heats, quarter- and semi-finals, a person must find most of the hidden gold, all of the time.

Panning for gold is one of the few ancient skills, like axe work, archery or making fire, which is still practised today. These championships should be applauded for keeping the old craft alive, even if there were no interest in the actual races and medals.

Around the dawn of the Bronze Age, gold pans were made of wood in the shape of a shallow dish or trough. A rectangular form of the wooden gold washing 'pan' is still used in Japan – the *yuri-ita*. Then came the familiar steel pans, which were used during the major gold rushes of the 19th century and throughout most of the 20th, but now these too have been superseded by highly accurate moulded plastic pans. However, the washing technique used to settle the gold and wash away the lighter material remains almost unchanged. How wonderful that a miner from five thousand years ago could pick up a modern plastic pan and be comfortable with using it in minutes.

When hunting for natural gold in a river, there is no easy way of knowing how good with a pan you actually are. Whatever gold is found is welcome, and most people imagine that the show of colour remaining in the dish was all of it. The ruthless transparency of a gold panning competition quickly exposes the charlatans, the boastful and those poor souls who were, until now, perhaps ignorant of their limited ability. I once knew a man who styled himself as 'king of the river' for years – until he entered his first competition and lost three-quarters of the seeded gold. He was so crestfallen that we hardly ever saw him again. And then there was the outrageously overconfident man I met at a championship in California. 'I'm the best in the world,' he assured me loudly, while recklessly thrashing his pan about in a great show of flying gravel and white water. He didn't make it through the first heat on day one. If you don't have the courage to show the whole world your true mettle, don't compete, as you will be found out. But if you're ready to learn, be positive and open-minded, then the championships are the best training school on Earth.

The week in Dawson passed pleasantly and too quickly. Each day was a blend of short, nerve-racking qualifying heats, and long quiet periods for conversation, more practice and trips out to the goldfields. We took the chance to visit David Millar at one of his claims. Like Jim, David was an internationally known competitor and well-respected gold miner. I wanted his opinion on whether vibration would increase the efficiency of my sluice box. He said definitely not, it would do the opposite, as all the heavies would lock together. Later that day, when back in Dawson, we went to a riotously lively pub, The Pit. Night had fallen and all were enjoying the band when it suddenly stopped playing, and the whole mass of well-oiled customers poured out into the street. Almost reverently, they fell silent to watch a fine display of ghostly pale-green northern lights that were dancing over the mountains to the north. And I thought again, *this is Dawson, the tiny city of enormous contrasts.*

Perhaps the most surreal of the many interesting moments I had that week was when I joined two friends beside a campfire, Charlie from England and Gerry from Ballarat in Australia. Gerry had brought along his banjo and struck up a jazz-like, laconic version of 'Waltzing Matilda'. It was spellbinding and so hauntingly original that I barely recognized the tune at first. When he finished, he muttered that he was so sick of being constantly asked to play this song that he'd created his own version. Then, suddenly realizing he needed a pee, he asked Charlie to mind his banjo and was gone.

Gerry had barely stepped away from the small fire's glow, when three figures staggered out of the gloom, very drunk and carrying rifles. They could hardly walk, but noticed that Charlie was holding a banjo. 'Play!' ordered the nearest drunk. Charlie tried to explain that the instrument wasn't his, but they spoke very limited English and took this as a refusal. Angrily, one of them staggered forward and poked him with a rifle, slurring more urgently, 'PLAAY!' The situation was rapidly becoming unpleasant, and I turned to Charlie and implored, 'For God's sake play something!' With all the panache of someone who has never held a banjo before in his life, Charlie began playing. He struck two 'chords' with his left hand high on the instrument's neck, then slid his hand down the fingerboard to strum two more. While flashing a generous smile at the threatening trio, he repeated this infantile tune. It worked, and while barely able to stand, they started dancing. Arms and weapons held high they hopped and swayed in time to the music, before finally gesturing their thanks and wandering off back into the darkness. Gerry returned, and Charlie quickly handed the banjo back to him.

At last, the day of the championship finals arrived. The very air buzzed with pent-up excitement and nervous energy. The worldwide gold clan had mustered for the last time to watch their very best fight it out for the title 'champion'! A travelling tourist, newly arrived in Dawson and unaware of what was going on, might have wondered at the sight of such a rabble – a cheerful throng of jumbled humanity, the very old and young, all bunched together with coats and bags and flags. The clean-shaven and bearded, barefoot and booted, hatted or with long hair flowing as free as themselves – and all, so very earnestly, clutching large colourful plastic discs.

I had made it to the final in the proficient men's class before. And some years earlier, when Austria hosted the world championships, a grizzled old prospector who I didn't know assaulted me with his blunt and uninvited advice. He walked up as if to complain about something, then in a deep growl and rolling his Rs impressively, said, 'Yoorrre technique in de heats ees gooed.' Surprised, I puffed up a little, flattered by the admiration of this stranger. But then he continued, 'Yoorrre technique in de finals ees rrubbeesh!' Suddenly humbled, and with my feet firmly back on the ground, I asked him why. He then explained that he had watched me pan carefully to place myself in the upper third of each heat many times, ensuring that I went through to the next round. But then he was disappointed and annoyed to see me show a similar caution in the actual finals. He said that by doing this, I would always achieve a respectable place, but would never win a medal. In the finals you have to be brave, throw caution to the wind and unleash the hunger of your full talent. I wondered now if he was in Dawson, and up in the crowd watching. Not wishing for any more of his fair but abrasive advice, I focused: I had to do better this time.

The national teams' event is run as a relay. The five competitors line up behind their allotted pool, each with a pan and a bucket filled with pay dirt. Seconds count and every movement the team will make is planned and rehearsed. There is one small vial, a clear plastic test tube, seated in a wooden block to one side. This most unimpressive of treasure chests will hold all the gold they find. Once sealed, the team captain will respectfully present the tube to the judges. Although all five arm-straining bucketfuls of dirt won't yield enough gold to cover a pea, each tiny flake slipped into the tube is a joy and a three-minute time penalty avoided. In a race that will last less than ten minutes, any penalties are a hope-wrecking disaster.

As ever, we can learn from children. My favourite niece and nephew had splashed and laughed and gaily panned their way through their heats, lost in the simple joy of taking part. However, although the five-strong British team had made it to the finals, I felt no such carefree levity. The other four were Mike Jones, Malcolm Thomas, my daughter Daisy Thurkettle and Mary Russell, all strong competitors, and I knew that I must not let them down – no slips, no spills, be clear, seem calm – although all the while my stomach churned and rumbled. And then, like lightning in a summer storm, the Tannoy rang out and called the national teams to take their place. The last event, for which we had trained so hard for days, would now test our worth in minutes.

The arena filled up quickly, and teams swapped smiles and handshakes, and called out crocodile greetings of 'good luck!' – they didn't mean it. To have come this far, all knew that they must pan their very best once more, and thrill the happy crowd with world-class panning excellence. Now ready by their allotted pools, every team of five whispered to each other, tense as thoroughbreds at the starter's gate, hearts racing, proud and yearning for the medals that quietly await the favoured few. Silence fell and all was still as stern-faced stewards prowled and made their final checks. And then the starter's gun, and with a mighty bang it all began. As one, the jostling crowd sprang to their feet, waving flags and cheering, or blowing horns and whistles to lift their team to glory.

While grateful for this joyous explosion of support, those panning knew to ignore the din. As if in meditation, they had to keep all their senses focused on the gold. In those few precious moments nothing else should matter – there is nothing else – but mud-stained thrashing water and tiny specks of sun-kissed metal, elusive in the dirt. At last, the pan seems almost empty. The pay dirt's gone and only a slight smudge of black sand remains. Then heart in mouth, the panner stands and gives their dish the slightest tap. This is the moment of truth, of triumph or disaster: will any grains of gold appear from beneath the dark sand's heavy veil?

I glanced up at the timing clock to see how we were doing, and was pleasantly surprised. Our first two panners had finished and were away. Both had found gold and slipped it safely into the little tube. And now the third was wonderfully at work – as if in a dervish trance, swirling the pan in perfect circles, a finger's breadth beneath the muddy water. I watched with pride – this was masterful control – and our many hours of practice were repaid in full. With a final flourish, the panner winnowed golden grains from gravel chaff and placed the precious flakes safely in our tube.

I was the last to pan, and mindful of the judgemental old Austrian's advice, I decided to give it my all. Time stood still and it seemed mere moments later that my turn was over. I stood exhausted and tapped my glistening pan, and from the first riffle four bright colours leapt into view. I touched a finger on my forehead, a little sweat and skin oil helps to pick up the gold. Then like the other four, I slipped these little darlings into the tube and sealed it. We had all found gold in a total time of just over 13 minutes. I knew that this was fairly good and a very respectable team effort.

Calm now, I walked over to the booths where the judges sat ready to verify the gold we had found. The small man before me opened our tube and tipped all the gold flakes into a clean pan to count them. I was shocked to see so many and leant forward to count them with him – there were 19! This was exceptional, as the maximum that could have been seeded in this final was 20. At worst we had lost only one piece, and we might have found all of them! And then, I had a gut-wrenching shock, as he pushed one piece aside, saying that it wasn't gold.

I stammered, unable to believe that my judge was probably the only man in the Yukon who didn't recognize a piece of gold when he saw one. 'It's pyrite,' he said knowingly. To prove his point, he picked up a 6-in nail and rammed the head upon the disputed yellow grain. The gold piece flattened slightly and shone more brightly. 'See, it's pyrite,' he insisted. I was now furious at this display of ignorance and chided him that the test would have shattered any form of pyrite, iron, copper or arsenic, into a greyish dust. His overconfidence wavered, and he called for support from a nearby South African official, who took one look at the tense situation and left. And bless him to this day, he had only gone to fetch a man whose opinion would be indisputable. As I saw him leading fourth-generation miner David Millar to the troubled booth, my desperation eased. David leant in, took one look and without any hesitation announced, 'Of course it's gold!'

My nerves shattered, I wandered off to find the team and tell them of the epic fight – and that our total haul of gold was a wonderful 19 pieces! In the time following a final, the competitors cannot relax. There may yet be a protest of unfairness or about some technicality relating to the rules, and in the worst cases this can even result in the event being rerun. Also, of course, we did not know how much gold the other teams had found. But we landed in the best of all possible places: on 26 August 2007 we were the favoured few, and Britain had won.

I would like to say that we whooped it up on that last night, intoxicated with our unexpected victory. But we didn't. Our Everest had been climbed, the first British team to win at this level, and now we were safely down the other side and perhaps still in shock, we seemed calm, dazed even. All the same, I beamed at everyone like an idiot, danced jigs and waltzed unsteadily to Gerry's banjo, a little embarrassed by suddenly being caught in the winner's spotlight.

Next morning, neither rushed nor hungover, I watched as the gold panning community packed up and said their farewells. Were they all winners? Very few had won medals, yet all were enriched, and it showed in their faces. As in the gold rush itself 110 years earlier, only a handful of people had found glory. Yet everyone who had answered the call of the Yukon had been blessed by the spirit of this land. With heads held high for the rest of their lives, they could say to all those who'd stayed safely at home, 'Yes, I went to Dawson!'

I opened the small blue case to take another look at my medal. It flashed in the sunlight and my heart leapt at the meaningful beauty of this rare golden disc. I knew that it was unlikely I would ever win another, and was perfectly at peace with that realization.

I too had just wanted to be there, medal or none. My growling old Austrian friend had been right – and wrong. To be accepted into this worldwide golden family was victory enough. To be known as a bona fide panner and prospector within the ranks of these earthy, rough-edged and colourful people. To walk tall among these international soulmates, and to see the best in them, and they in me. This is finding gold!

These days, I might still continue to go to gold panning competitions, but not to try to win. Yes, I would be thrilled to make it to the finals, and then salute and cheer the young who climb the champion's podium. But now old and bearded, I might just growl at them, 'If you focus too much on the medals, you'll miss the gold all around you.'

10

HARD LESSONS WITH THE *ROYAL CHARTER*

'No clean dry man ever found gold,
nor had the tale to tell.'

—Mary Elizabeth Russell

In the measured and gentle world of gold prospecting, you rarely have to deal with the dead. The virgin specks of nature's precious metal that are washed and found by prospectors have never been seen nor touched by human hand before – not since the world began. But treasure is another thing entirely, once belonging to people who were cruelly robbed by fate and whose voices still call out to be heard. While hunting for their loss, you are among them every day; their shattered lives surround you. Scattered throughout the gloomy deep – among the starfish, rocks and weed – lie shoes and buttons, cloth and pins, storm-smashed plates and bowls. While you were not the engine of their despair, nor caused their young lives to end at the very cusp of home and glory, the site of a shipwreck is a poignant collage of tragedy and loss, a hieroglyphic story of these people's lives.

In the case of the *Royal Charter*, the wealth and love they carried could have lifted their families and dear friends from all the rigours of Victorian life. I know this, because they said so. In telegrams and letters home, they wrote of hardships, hope and heaps of gold, and how none of them need ever work again! And as I grew to know them, just a little, I listened to the objects that we found on the shipwreck, and heard their voices caught in graceful copperplate and printed text. In the archives in Melbourne I have held the surviving passenger list. I have seen their names, so beautifully written, and felt the spirit of these courageous young people, homeward bound and full of hope. And what I heard I liked. Theirs is a dreamy tale of high adventure, of men and women's courage on the far side of the world. Yet in the end, as in a Greek tragedy, all that remains is heartbreak – as nature in a fury swept them all aside.

I have also heard their names maligned. Some thoughtless gossips say it was their greed that killed them. But I would say to all inclined to that opinion: go hang your heads in shame. This shipwreck was a slaughter of the innocent and hope, and it is simply heartbreaking.

In late October 1859 the *Royal Charter* was close to Liverpool. A three-masted clipper with the advantage of both sail and steam, this state-of-the-art iron ship could make the voyage from Melbourne in Australia to England in fewer than sixty days. It was thought a wonder of the age, much like the *Titanic* would be 52 years later.

At the time, the gold rush in south-eastern Australia was in full swing, and huge amounts of gold were still being discovered.

Many miners and their families were content with what they had found and were bringing their wealth back home. Banks were also loading every homeward boat with a fortune in bars, nuggets, coins and sacks of gold dust.

The *Royal Charter* alone had taken on board over forty thousand gold sovereigns and fifteen thousand half-sovereigns. Together with the bullion bars, nuggets and gold dust, the shipment would be worth over £190 million at late-2025 spot prices. But even this colossal figure was not all the wealth on board. It is believed that the passengers possessed a further huge sum of gold between them, perhaps to the extent of another £72 million.

For discretion, and perhaps the avoidance of tax, a good deal of personal gold was hidden – sewn into clothing, or worn beneath skirts and shirts in money belts. One man never left his cabin during the whole voyage; paranoia perhaps, but more likely justified by what he guarded. Children were used too. A painted doll, dressed but never played with, would hardly have drawn a second glance – even if she were cast in solid gold. I have heard tell of a similar ornament in the shape of a supposedly wooden coach and horse. The ship's manifest was lost, but the newspapers in Melbourne gave daily reports of the many strong boxes that were loaded before she sailed.

Close to midnight on 25 October 1859, a shrieking gale increased to hurricane force and swung to blow from the north-east across the Irish Sea. The captain gave up trying to reach Liverpool and ordered the massive anchors to be dropped. He hoped to ride out the storm well offshore of Anglesey, but within two hours both anchor cables had parted. Now at the mercy of the sea, the ship drifted broadside towards the coast's low cliffs. But then, while still

some way offshore, the hull touched and caught on a sandbank –
and there was hope. The captain announced that the tide was going
out, and they might yet all be saved. But while he was an excellent
and experienced seaman, in this he was wrong: the tide was coming
in. The rising water soon lifted the ship off the sand and onto the
rocks. While pounded by gigantic waves, the crew got a man ashore
and rigged a line to try to set up a boatswain's chair and get the
passengers to safety. The sailors were joined by 28 local men from
Moelfre, who heroically did all they could to save the survivors. But
the ship-to-shore rescue had hardly started when the ship's iron
hull broke, and the sea flooded in.

The final list of passengers and crew was lost, but it is known that
39 people survived, and a parliamentary report some years later
said that a total of 497 men, women and children died in the tragedy.

This was in the age just before weather forecasting was
invented. Indeed, the *Royal Charter* Storm (as it became known)
and the total loss of 132 other ships to the hurricane that night
caused such an outcry in confident Victorian Britain that one man
decided to act. Admiral Robert FitzRoy was an excellent seaman,
who had achieved fame as the captain of HMS *Beagle* on Charles
Darwin's voyage. FitzRoy believed that winds were related to
atmospheric pressure and moved in circles, and he was familiar
with a wondrous new form of communication: the telegraph. He
felt sure that these two could be combined to send out a warning
to shipping of a storm's approach. Had he achieved this a few years
earlier, the *Royal Charter*'s name would perhaps hardly be known.
But his story too came to a tragic end.

The very first shipping forecast was sent out on 31 July 1861,
yet there were many in power who ridiculed FitzRoy for trying
to anticipate the hand of God. They argued that the weather was

an act of the Divine, and it was close to heresy to think otherwise. Such was the ferocity of his opponents' public attacks that FitzRoy was driven to despair and depression – and in April 1865 he cut his own throat with a razor. Nevertheless, tens of thousands of people were saved from a watery grave by his tenacity and genius, and his legacy led to the modern shipping forecast.

The story that Ken Williamson had told to me in his farmhouse kitchen – of how he had watched a fortune in gold dust fall back into the sea – had fastened upon my mind. The salvage team with which he'd dived on the *Royal Charter* in the early 1980s had been fixated on finding bars of gold bullion, huge nuggets and fistfuls of gold sovereigns. They'd scoffed at the very idea of trying to recover the humble gold dust. Their equipment sucked up the seabed and passed everything across a tough steel screen. This was why Ken had implored me to kit up for the lost dust, and to go and make my fortune.

'After all,' he'd said, eyes sparkling, 'there is more gold in that tiny patch of sea than in any river you'll ever prospect.'

I relayed Ken's tale to nearly everyone I knew, looking for support from any sub-aqua divers who would join this adventure. Meanwhile, I researched the shallow water salvage techniques being used by treasure hunters in the Caribbean while searching for wrecked Spanish galleons. I was drawn to the propwash deflector, or 'mailbox' as it is also known. This large bent tube is attached to the back of a boat and deflects the current from the boat's propeller down to the seabed. Light coverings of sand are quickly blown away, as if at the base of a waterfall, but all the heavier material stays put.

To use the deflector, we would need a boat with at least an 80-hp engine, so I was blown away when a friend phoned to say, 'You know you wanted 80 horsepower. Well, what would you say to 420?!'

He had found us an ex-military NATO Combat Support Boat, and it sounded perfect – a tough 8.4-m terrier of a boat, with twin 212hp Ford Sabre marinized diesels, driving twin 12-in Dowty hydro-jets. The two jets could be tilted downwards at any angle, and could act as our propwash deflectors. The whole high-powered treasure-hunting package was fitted within a twin-walled, marine-grade aluminium hull.

In went all of my savings and a week later, the boat was delivered to a cheerful old boatyard on the ominously named Gallows Point, a small headland in the sheltered Menai Strait – the channel that separates the island of Anglesey from the Welsh mainland.

My new team gathered on a farm campsite on the north-east of the island, beside the ancient village of Moelfre, where our tents were pitched in a large field that sloped down from the milking parlour to the rocky shoreline. Across the sea, a scatter of perhaps a dozen boats rocked comfortably on their moorings in the small, east-facing bay. Moelfre is quaint but not overly so. Facing a small pebbly beach where a few boats bobbed in the water, the tightly packed stone houses were wrapped around a pub and a café. A narrow road curved down between the old buildings and the sea, before rising up and over the limestone cliffs that protected the bay. A small stream weaved between the buildings and over waterfalls, before finally ducking under the road and flowing out across the beach. While beautiful, there was also a rawness there, a feeling that Moelfre sits cheek by jowl with nature. A recent easterly gale had covered the road with pebbles that were still being cleared away. And the sobering silhouette of the Moelfre lifeboat station dominated the small bay, a reminder that the sea is indifferent to humans.

The next morning, we headed back to Gallows Point and watched as a creaking old hoist launched our impressive boat. The huge engines finally roared into life and enveloped the launch slip in a cloud of white smoke. Our equipment loaded, we headed up the Menai Strait towards Puffin Island, where gannets dived into the waves. Once at sea, we pushed up the revs and thundered along the coast to Moelfre, skimming over the waves while the deep-throated engines roared 'success!'

I was elated and honestly thought we might all be rich by the end of the week. I was experienced enough in gold prospecting to know that sudden wealth was staggeringly unlikely while panning in rivers, but we were headed for a treasure-filled shipwreck, a different thing entirely.

The site of the *Royal Charter* wreck is no secret. Here, the shoreline is a series of low cliffs, like a giant's steps rising up from the sea. Tourists hiked the coastal path that ran along the clifftop, while hardy sheep grazed the salty turf, and contentedly ignored them. There too, on a rise above a clump of wind-sculpted thorn bushes, sits a small memorial stone 'to commemorate the loss of the steam clipper *Royal Charter*'.

Between each rise of the cliffs were large, gently sloping platforms of fossil-rich limestone. And above the limestone, a thin band of oily shale separated it from a band of white quartz conglomerate. This mass of pale rounded pebbles was studded with pyrite and looked for all the world like the 'white channel' gravels that line the Bonanza Creek in the Yukon. North Wales and Anglesey are rich in minerals, and there was very likely natural gold in that rock. What were the chances – a treasure ship and a band of ancient quartz pebbles, both shedding gold onto the same beach?

When we arrived at the wreck site and dropped anchor, I couldn't wait to dive and discover first-hand what the seabed was like. I had read that it was sandy, while another report said there were rocks and weed; some said the wreck was visible, others said not. I needed to know the truth about the conditions as soon as possible so that we could set to work.

Safe in my sub-aqua gear, I went down and finned slowly across the area, imagining the unimaginable. And there, among a tangle of weed and boulders, a small section of the ship's bow was clearly visible. The long iron ribs stretched out incongruously through the tumbled rocks that surrounded and partly buried them. I was shocked at how close to shore the bow lay – barely six paces. No wonder the people on board were determined to get themselves and their hard-earned gold to safety. My heart went out to them.

Two days later, we readied the hydro-jets to blow our first hole. It was to be located near midships and shoreside of the wreck. Soon the plumes of rising seawater were sand-free, and we knew the hole had been made. A slight current cleared away the last of the clouded water and my friend Charlie and I descended to collect the treasure.

But there was none. While I hadn't expected gold bars or a clichéd chest full of riches, I had been sure that there would be a scattering of gold dust, or a coin or two. How else could Ken have seen a wealth of gold grains glitter as they fell back into the sea? On the morning of the wreck, it was said that storm-scattered bright gold sovereigns lay on the shore as thick as seashells. But search as we might, our hole yielded only disappointment.

That evening, we went to eat and think some more in Moelfre's tearoom, Ann's Pantry. There, we met a young man who was surprised to hear that we had left our boat out in the bay on a mooring.

'Do you not know an easterly is due?' he asked.

I said that the boat would be fine, as the wind wasn't expected to be strong.

His curt answer seemed straight from a mariner's textbook: 'Why would you take the risk if there is no commercial advantage?'

I knew that he was right. I was being lazy. There is a lovely old adage that goes something like, 'Neither the reckless nor timid should go to sea, for both will be found out.' Tired and frustrated, I finished my meal and stared out into the darkness; my cosy tent and sleeping bag would have to wait. We had only just started, but now we had to take the boat all the way back to the moorings at Gallows Point and safety.

On our first day at the wreck site, we found that as the *Royal Charter* was so close to the shore, it was tricky to set a stern anchor. We decided to leave the boat on the mooring at Gallows Point for a day or two, and to make things easier for ourselves by fixing two rock anchors up in the low cliffs. Offshore, the seabed rapidly became sandy, and the bow anchor wasn't a problem. But early on the third morning my mobile phone rang.

It was a man from the boatyard, sounding flustered and angry: 'Your boat has sunk! Is this an insurance job?'

In shock, I replied that the boat was not insured, as I hadn't been able to find a company that would cover a Combat Support Boat. We hurried across the island, racing along the winding hedge-lined lanes. Why, I do not know, for there was no rush – all was surely lost.

We arrived to find that the place where the boat should have been was empty – the sun-rippled surface of the water gave no clue of what lay beneath. The tides around Anglesey can be enormous, often over 7m high, and we had to wait for hours before the water was low enough to see what had happened. When it finally receded, there she lay, still upright and full of seawater. At least the hull had not been holed, or the water would have drained out with the tide.

Sullen and still in shock, we joined a few curious men from the boatyard and squelched out through the shallow estuarine mud and weed to examine our wreck. There were no clues as to what had happened. This tough little boat, which had survived God knows what throughout a long military career, had sunk on a safe mooring during a calm night. There is always some tension concerning others who may have treasure fastened upon their minds too, and whether this was a fluke accident or sabotage I will never know. Perhaps now feeling pity for us, the boatyard men offered to bring the sodden hulk ashore.

Back in Moelfre, a Land Rover was impatiently waiting for us. Nigel, one of the lifeboat crew and a skilled engineer, had heard our news and wanted to help. He quickly explained that, even as we spoke, the two huge engines were being eaten away by corrosive salt water and if I were to have any hope of the boat ever being seaworthy again, we must go and get started on saving the engines – now!

I'm not an engineer and I was grateful to someone else for taking the lead, and agreed. We worked all through the night and well into the next day. The engines were stripped, and all the salt water was flushed out with fresh water. This water was then replaced with diesel oil, which in turn was replaced by engine oil. With the engines saved, we then focused on the dozens of electrical parts. Dials, switches, alternators, starter motors, batteries, relays – the list went on and on – and all must be washed, dried, oiled and tested. It is perhaps enough to say, and give some measure of the scale of the task, that it took 11 days to recover the boat fully.

Finally, with some trepidation, I watched the boatyard's creaky hoist gently relaunch our craft. It was like seeing an elderly relative coming out of a hospital's intensive care: *Are you OK now? Will you ever walk again? Can you talk yet?* With great relief, we watched the battered old veteran sit comfortably in the water and stay afloat – the ultimate confirmation that there was no hole in the hull.

I climbed aboard and pushed hard on both starter buttons. Had days of care and Nigel's clinical engineering worked? The restored diesels turned and coughed, then fired up and grumbling, poured out clouds of thin white smoke. My Lazarus! With revs kept low, I waited while the engines warmed and the pistons polished their salt-poisoned cylinders, and valves refound their seats. I listened happily to the rumbling earthy growl – a sound I'd never thought I would hear again.

The weather changed and the wind blew from the south-west. This was good for diving, as the cliffs now protected the wreck site and the sea was calm. But with the change came constant rain, which was very wearing. As we were living in tents in a field and were out on a boat all day, there was no chance to dry anything out.

On the disappointing earlier dive, we had found that the seabed was not littered with bars, nuggets, coins and dust. And I now thought that any heavy treasure might have worked itself down into cracks and fissures in the seabed, in the way that natural gold does in rivers. To wash out these potential gold traps, we developed a new piece of equipment. It would be impossible to hold a straight jet of high-powered water while weightless as a diver, so we created a 'T'-shaped steel nozzle. Water from one of the hydro-jets was piped down and then burst out of the nozzle, with equal pressure, in opposite directions. But we soon found that if there was any tidal current, it caught the long feed pipe and dragged the struggling diver away. And if there was no current, the black muck that filled any possible gold-catching depressions arose in clouds, blotting out any chance of seeing what gold might have been uncovered.

Yet this was the least of our problems. The damage caused by sea salt now crept through our boat like an unrelenting cancer. I had thought we were clear of the problems caused by the sinking, but almost every day some different piece of equipment would fail, and we would have to head back to Moelfre to mend or replace it. The most humiliating failure was when a dead short flattened all four of the engines' batteries. Helpless, we had to wait to be rescued. The other divers walked back to Moelfre, while Charlie and I waited sheepishly for the lifeboat. Besides Nigel, we were friends with some of the crew by then, and I think they enjoyed the chance to tow this tatty old wreck of a boat around the headland and into the full view of the whole village, curious about why we were being towed back to our mooring.

I was starting to realize I had badly underestimated the difficulties of working a shipwreck – even one close to the shore in fairly shallow water. No half-baked salvage mission would be successful. Sometime further on in our expedition, Charlie wryly observed that the *Royal Charter*'s lost treasure was protected by seven 'padlocks'. To triumph, each must be in line and open, or the gold stayed where the 1859 hurricane had hidden it. In no particular order, the padlocks were:

1. The boat and diving equipment must be of good quality and working.
2. The crew must be fit, rested and capable of working, day or night.
3. The weather should be calm, with no wind or only a gentle southerly blowing.
4. The sea must not be too deep, and can only be worked through the low tide.
5. The underwater visibility must be good enough to see gold, not clouded with silt or an algal bloom.
6. The seabed sand layer is a barrier that has to be moved.
7. The layer of boulders and iron shipwreck below the sand is another barrier that has to be moved.

While it helped to understand *why* it was so difficult when we stratified the issues in this way, this didn't make the problems go away. There was a night, late in the fifth week, where I was ready to give up. I lay alone in my tent, wrapped in a rancid, damp sleeping bag that stank of diesel oil. Rain lashed the shuddering canvas as the cloud-laden westerlies continued to spoil the summer. I knew the military adage that no battle is lost until the leader thinks it so.

But I also knew that there is a time to give up. Not to quit too early, but have the wisdom to know when you are beaten.

Unable to sleep, I pulled out my phone and texted all my woes to my partner, Mary. A few minutes later, her short reply lit up my screen: 'No clean dry man ever found gold, nor had the tale to tell.'

Those few words captured the very essence of what I was trying to do. With great bravado, I had left the comfort and short days of office life, to opt for this. Not really knowing what lay before me, but happy to embrace the adventure.

There are always the opposites in life: hope and fear, feast and famine, success and failure. And while hoping for the best, we must be ready for the worst. I was certainly now familiar with the rough adventure that failure offers. And had exponentially evolved my own acceptance of risk. My lovely office with two windows would never sink and have to be hauled out of the corrosive sea by the staff; rather, a bad day might be when we ran out of photocopier toner.

I flopped back onto my awful bed, thinking more about Mary's words, and found that I was suddenly content – as if enlightened. These weeks had been extraordinary. We had been tested and found weak; not yet worthy of reward. It's said that nothing worth doing in life is easy, and that was now understood. Hard lessons learned, next time we would do better.

11

SHIPWRECK REVISITED

'There is something in a treasure that fastens upon a man's mind.'

—Joseph Conrad, *Nostromo*

If the winter passed slowly, it was still not slowly enough. Spring arrived early and there was so much to get ready. Once again, providence stepped in as my commitment became absolute. I would throw everything I had into finding the sunken gold this year. Even if all of the salvors before me, in the 19th and 20th centuries, had found 99 per cent of the gold, the 1 per cent left was still worth a fortune. And nobody could have found 99 per cent of the lost gold on that shattered wreck. Some reassuring words by Henry Ford seemed to endorse my decision to revisit the shipwreck, 'Failure is simply the opportunity to begin again, this time more intelligently.' Precisely!

The five resources in all such projects are: people, time, money, machines and materials. The people would be family and friends, who always make the best teams, and I would double the time we spent in Moelfre to 12 weeks. The money part was going to be tricky, as my few savings were all spent. As for machines, we had learned that blowing with hydro-jets alone did not uncover the gold, so this year we would use suction dredges as well.

The Californian mining company Keene Engineering made well-respected 6-in dredges, and we needed two of them. With one mounted on either side, the boat would be balanced, and whenever the conditions were right we could work really quickly. The technical capacity of a 6-in dredge is around $17yd^3$ per hour ($13m^3$/hr). In theory, we could blow away the lighter sand with the jets, and then sift through up to $50yd^3$ ($38m^3$) of the heavier ground with the dredges during a typical 90-minute dive. Finally, getting our air cylinders filled was never easy, so I would add an on-board compressor to the list.

The spectacular leap in our technical ability planned for the second year was absolutely thrilling. And why not dream? Dreams are the magic that drive projects forward. However, I was struggling to dream up the money I needed to make it all happen. I didn't want to have a wealthy investor breathing down my neck at every setback. And I knew there would be problems – they go with the territory.

I considered the neat little cottage I lived in: did I dare to use my own home to raise the funds? At what point does courage become recklessness?

My father had always advised me that when considering a venture, first ask yourself, 'Is it reversible?' And next: 'Can I cope with it failing?' There is an inherent expectation of success, or you wouldn't even be thinking about it. Knowing this, stay grounded and don't let yourself be dazzled by flattering visions of your own ability.

Mindful of this advice, I stopped imagining the fortune in gold that might lie waiting for me, and contemplated failure instead. If I lost my home, I would probably have to live in a caravan in the field with my Christmas trees. Helpfully, I rather liked the idea!

After all, I had been part-raised in a caravan in a clifftop field, and it would not be the end of the world if I ended up back where I started in life.

Using my home as collateral, I borrowed all I could from the bank, and it was still not enough. So I sold my entire lifetime's collection of natural gold to top up the expedition funds – after all, commitment is everything, and now everything was committed.

For that commitment to be rewarded, we now needed a new boat. The old vessel had been scrapped, but I couldn't think of a better machine for the task ahead than another of NATO's excellent Combat Support Boats, as long as it avoided sinking this year. So now I just had to find one – and luckily I had my family to help. After leaving the Royal Navy, my father became a boat builder. He had worked with hydro-jets for many years and took on the task. Amazingly, he soon found one in Holland. It was a beauty, and had been maintained with the utmost care. This CSB was a huge step up from our first one. The owner agreed to deliver it, and the deal was done.

In early May, I packed my car meticulously and set off for the biggest project of my life. About halfway to Anglesey, I stopped at a motorway services and rushed up onto the bridge that spanned the four carriageways. There, I waited for the Dutch driver who was trailing along some distance behind me. Finally, like a tank transporter, his low-loader trundled into view. The moments as it passed beneath me were sheer joy. All depressing memories of last year's many failures were crushed beneath the haulier's 18 wheels. A fabulous 8 tons of first-rate boat and matching olive-green trailer would soon be arriving at Gallows Point. I knew the boatyard men, who had tried so hard to help us rescue last year's sickly vessel, would chuckle as this pristine monster pulled into their yard.

In Anglesey, we were blessed with superb weather and not a breath of wind. The distant mountains of Snowdonia shimmered in the heat, and the azure lapping sea looked positively Mediterranean. Red-faced tourists, flummoxed by the heatwave, sat eating ice cream and wishing they'd worn sunscreen. The other divers arrived, and we raced to unpack and get the boat ready to be launched.

It was dusk before we were finished and the new boat was in the water – full of fuel, engines warmed and loaded with a mountain of equipment. Eager to make an early start at the wreck site the very next morning, we opted to take the boat from Gallows Point up along the coast to Moelfre that night. I didn't want to waste a moment in case the wind blew up, turned east and stopped us from working before we had even begun. Last year's harsh lessons had been well learned. Now, with near-perfect weather conditions, we took the boat for a nocturnal pleasure cruise.

By the time we reached Puffin Island and the open sea, it was pitch dark, yet a faint green glow began to light up the boat. I had seen bioluminescent plankton before, as tiny fairy sparkles in breaking waves. And once, during a night dive on a sub-aqua training course in the Canary Islands, my instructor had lit up as we finned through a patch of this magical plankton. For those few minutes, she seemed like an elemental being – flying just above me, her dark silhouette outlined by a thousand tiny lights. But the plankton bloom that we had just entered by Puffin Island was absolutely immense, far larger than any I had ever seen before.

As we motored forward slowly, our bow wave made a strip light of bright green neon on either side of the boat. The vessel and everything within it glowed an eerie green, and we moved like playful apparitions in the warm spring night. Then, in the darkness off to my right, I was shocked to see a bow wave as large as ours suddenly approaching. Fearing a collision, I strained my eyes yet couldn't see the craft that made it. The luminous green 'V' shape swept on towards us and I confess the hairs on the back of my neck rose – for there was no boat. When a collision with the spectre seemed imminent, the ghostly bow wave faded to a ripple and was gone. To this day I do not know what approached us that night and then dived beneath our boat – perhaps a whale shark feeding on the plankton banquet.

Unbelievably, the plankton mass increased in brightness until it became so amazing that we stopped the boat to watch and play with the cold green light. We found that if a bucket of water was thrown overboard onto the calm surface, a huge area of the sea flashed green, like silent otherworldly lightning. And if a thin stream of water was flicked out in a wide arc, long waves of green, glowing light formed briefly, resembling an infant northern lights. We travelled at night on the sea many times after this, but never saw such bioluminescence again.

The good people of Moelfre seemed pleased to welcome us back. While I suspected that it was mostly for our entertainment value, I was told reassuringly that it was because we had gone about the whole thing quietly last year – the Welsh are not impressed by show and boasting, especially not from a rabble of mostly English divers.

The boat alone could draw a crowd. We fitted a frame of steel scaffold poles across the deck and then hung the 6-in gold dredges out on either side. A lightweight roof of stout bamboo poles and white marine-grade canvas was built to offer some protection from the sun or rain. Soon the olive-green military boat's sleek, no-nonsense, simple lines were lost, its graceful design buried beneath a mass of sailcloth, sticks and pipes, fuel cans, an air compressor and large heap of diving equipment. People chuckled and said that we looked like a cross between Humphrey Bogart's *African Queen* and the river patrol boat in Coppola's movie *Apocalypse Now*. I laughed with them as they were right, we did! But everything aboard the ugliest boat in the bay was necessary and fit for purpose.

The first two weeks passed quickly. No gold was found, which was fine as each day our technique improved – and we had the luxury of time. The 12m-long dredge pipes seemed enormous, but even this length still restricted us to working only at low tide. Each day was simple and determined by the wind that blew and the rhythm of the tides. If low water was at 5am, we were out on the sea at 4am, and then again roughly 12 hours later for the next low tide. Our lazy days were when there was a midday low and only one dive was possible. This year, the team and I were staying in a static caravan and a large house that a forester friend had generously lent me. We slept so much better than in last year's tents – and good sleep was important on a long trip like this.

Nevertheless, some of us still had rough nights. If the first boat really had been sabotaged, I couldn't let that happen again, so I organized a guard-duty rota. Each night, two of us would sleep aboard our boat, bedded down on top of the engine covers – whatever the weather. And just in case it hadn't been sabotage, and these boats did sometimes sink without human help, we slept with one arm out of the sleeping bag. Best not to wake up trapped while sinking.

We had started diving at the Moelfre end of the shipwreck, as the *Royal Charter*'s strongroom had been located in the stern. At first, the holes we made by blowing the sand away with the hydro-jets were ragged and not good enough. With only a bow and stern anchor, the boat swayed from side to side. We needed precision and experimented for a while before settling on a plus-sign-shaped ('+') anchoring pattern. The four anchors were left in place, and the lines were marked with electrical tape and attached to a buoy. This saved a lot of time, and gave us the ability to start each new day exactly where we'd left off the day before. The jets worked best when set to blow slightly astern, not vertical. This created a powerful 'waterfall' that blew the sand, shells and small stones into huge mounds well behind us, and left a neat oval hole to dive. On good days, the hole could be the size of a small bungalow, and the debris mound formed a new island.

One morning, I was sitting on Moelfre beach when, to my surprise, a local fisherman joined me.

'They know how you're getting the gold ashore,' he whispered earnestly. 'They've seen the small grey bag that comes in each day – the one that's handled with care and is always guarded.'

I thanked him, as it wasn't the first time that he had helped us, and told him that anybody considering a raid was going to be sorely disappointed, as we hadn't yet found any gold: the coveted bag only held Charlie's dry shoes, tobacco and roll-up papers. Nevertheless, it was helpful to have the warning that we were being watched.

The seabed to the *Royal Charter*'s stern was a surprise, being both flat and barren. I had been expecting rocks and scattered wreck, but instead uncovered a level plain of sticky glacial clay. The clay's surface was pebble-dashed with myriad tiny stones and rounded lumps of a pyrite mineral. We followed the empty plain towards the shore, and finally found a heap of limestone boulders that storms had swept across the clay and up against an undersea cliff. This was more promising, a place where the sea had deposited heavy things.

The jets soon blew away the covering of blond sand, and a dredge pipe was taken down to clean out from between the rocks. As we went deeper, the ground turned dark and black silt swirled up into the nozzle, revealing jagged shards of broken crockery. At last, debris from the shipwreck. Deeper still, we uncovered chunks of concreted iron and torn fragments of brass, copper and lead.

My cousin David was diving with me that day, moving the smaller rocks so that I could work the dredge nozzle forward. Beneath one boulder, I noticed a small black disc lying on the pebble-dashed clay and picked it up out of curiosity. It looked a little like a lead washer, but as I lifted it towards my face mask I saw that it had a milled edge. This thrilled me, as I thought it might be a tarnished silver coin. I swept my thumb lightly across its surface to clean away the black silt, and the piece turned mustard coloured. For two or three seconds, no more, this puzzled me. I took my thumb away and suddenly I was holding solid gold; there was Queen Victoria's beautiful young face smiling up at me and whispering, 'Well done!' A sovereign indeed. We had worked so long for this moment, and yet, when it came, it was a total surprise.

Eager to share my elation and this thrilling find, I turned to face David and held up the wonderful coin. He grinned, took out his demand valve and cheered – streams of tiny silver bubbles burst from his mouth and rose in tumbling triumph. This pivotal moment happened during the middle of our fifth week. Counting the awful six weeks of the previous year, it had taken eleven weeks of hunting before we'd found our first gold coin. If perseverance is the key to most endeavours, I would say none more so than when exploring a shipwreck.

Managing the people who came to dive with us was a tricky logistical problem. Most of the friends and family who volunteered to help could spare only a week or two, and there had to be an ongoing balance in the team. Achieving this over the full 12 weeks called for the utmost care – working with 10 people one week and then none the next was unthinkable. Similar to when I worked in an office, I used a wall planner to schedule our time and people. There were 16 names neatly interlocked across the board, and I stopped to look at it one day and think.

On the face of it, the planner simply showed *who* was with us and *when*. But I found myself asking *why* they were coming . . . It was already clear that the seabed was not paved with gold. I felt a growing warmth for this chart of names written in felt-tip and squeezed into small rectangular boxes. It was a touching statement of goodwill. These people were not joining the project for riches, but for the sheer delight of taking part and sharing in my dream of finding gold. My first wife once said a lovely thing: 'I like being with you, as you make things happen.' How wonderful that so many others felt the same. I couldn't possibly have done this without them and was so grateful to them all. Together, we had built a great adventure to share and a memory that would live on into old age.

And it was not only the 16 names on the chart that mattered. Moelfre has a love for all things *Royal Charter* and the village people gave us what help they could. The lifeboat crew who had towed last year's boat to safety now visited us for news, and helped us to find anchors, chain and moorings. And the farm where we stayed gave us all the help they could too – even if old Mr Evans nearly always finished a conversation with an awful story about a headless body that was once found offshore. (According to this grisly cautionary tale, a mass of feeding whelks had clustered where the poor lost diver's head should have been.)

You don't need anybody's help to go prospecting in a river with a gold pan, when being alone is fine although it can be lonely. But I needed so many people to do this, and working with a good team was a real joy. I felt like a solitary musician who had recently joined an orchestra – and found that the music we all made together was awesome.

Having found our first gold sovereign among the boulders heaped against the undersea cliff, we made that area our focus for a while. Being situated away from the wreck and close to the shore, the area was untouched by the Victorian salvors. The underwriters at Lloyd's of London had insured much of the gold on board and within weeks of the tragedy, hard-hatted divers were pulling up a fortune for them. Contemporary newspapers printed gripping reports of the good days: on 17 December 1859 the *North Wales Chronicle* described 'a further discovery of gold from the wreck of the *Royal Charter*, namely, 540lbs of gold coin, 40 ingots of gold, 286 sovereigns, 47 rupees, 38lbs of gold dust, five bars of gold and one cup ingot'. Once the underwriters were satisfied that their losses had been recovered, the wreck was sold to Gibbs, Bright & Company, who continued the salvage work.

More than a century later, we worked steadily, alone if the ground was easy or in pairs if it wasn't. We usually needed one diver to move the smaller rocks with a crowbar, while the second diver manoeuvred the dredge nozzle. It was important to work slowly. If too much material was sucked up at once, the stones might jam in the pipe and form a plug-up. Anticipating this problem, our pipes were made of clear, food-grade polyurethane plastic. These were good, as we would be able to see any plug-ups quickly. They were also very strong, being ribbed and reinforced with a steel spiral helix. Finally, the pipes were smooth on the inside to allow the dredged material to flow easily up to the sluice.

Beneath the boulders, the heavier material had formed a dark, at times anaerobic, layer that sat just above the ancient pebble-dashed clay. I was working through a patch, thick with shattered crockery, when a small nugget appeared and gleamed from among the black dirt. The shining, bean-shaped piece grabbed my attention: this was our first nugget and I knew that the other divers would be so pleased that we were, at last, in good ground. Then, while focused on the nugget, I almost absent-mindedly noticed that a short length of dark 'string' was hanging down the slope of the working face. I had not noticed any string or twine before, as along with even the largest ropes, all of these natural fibres had long since rotted away. To satisfy my curiosity, I reached over and pulled the string gently towards me. The dark ground slipped in a mini-avalanche and to my amazement, a solid gold, full-hunter pocket watch slid into view. It was magnificent, with patterned engraving and a full heavy guard chain.

Soon another wonderful find was spotted, but I wasn't quick enough this time and lost it. I had spotted a fist-sized chunk of rough white quartz, but as I reached to grab it, the dredge's suction caught it. The suction from the 6-in dredges was very powerful and material whooshed into the nozzle as soon as it got close – as it did now. The quartz rolled and flashed a patch of gold spread like butter across one surface, and vanished up the pipe. I couldn't believe that I had just missed this fabulous specimen.

Thinking that it would roll through the boat-mounted sluice box and fall out, I quickly finned over to where the tailings were falling down through the water like black snow to form a large mound. But it was not there. I waited, gazing upwards to see it fall, but still nothing came, and I assumed that the piece was so heavy with gold that it had stayed in the sluice. Believing that it had been safely caught, I carried on dredging to see if there were any more. But when I surfaced, I was saddened to find that the chunk of exquisite quartz had not lodged in the sluice after all. The best gold ore specimen I have ever seen had rolled past me and slipped through my fingers – and returned to the sea.

Not long after losing the specimen quartz, a small gold watch was snatched out of the clay by the dredge's powerful suction. But I had learned my lesson not to assume that it would stay in the sluice box. Fearful of another loss, I raced to the surface. Without taking off my fins or weight belt, I struggled aboard and clumsily made for the sluice. Heart racing, I pulled back the heavy rubber splash mat and sighed with relief. The ladies' gold pocket watch was still there, gleaming like new under the flow of rushing water.

Once back dredging, a fracture in the clay caught my eye, as I could see the edge of something very dark trapped within it. Using my dive knife, I dug beside the fissure and gently levered the piece out. It was a large coin, made of silver and unlike anything we had found before. On one side was a beautiful portrait of the young Queen Victoria, but the other side was a surprise: it read 'One Rupee'. When I brushed off the loose black-stained silt the date 1840 became clear, and then the words 'East India Company'. The coin was an enigma. It bore the monarch's head, but was clearly a form of token issued by what was once the most powerful corporation the world has ever known – one with its own army and navy and, at times, controlling more than half of all the world's trade. To my delight, I soon discovered that there were more of these fascinating coins trapped within the long clay fracture. I learned later that the East India Company had been operating for 259 years at the time of the *Royal Charter* shipwreck, but was dissolved only 15 years later.

Of all the many beautiful and poignant artefacts recovered, the most telling for me was a tiny child's ring. I was working with an ever-cheerful and very capable diver, Neil, to clear out the area between a group of armchair-sized boulders, when he pointed to a patterned scrap of gold that was just about visible in a patch of blue-black clay. I teased the piece out and we were amazed to find ourselves looking at the smallest jewelled ring we had ever seen, so tiny that it wouldn't even begin to fit on the end of my little finger. It was stunning, finely crafted and set with an opal and a tiny diamond; the second matching diamond was missing. We raked up a bucketful of the ground that had held the ring and carefully panned down the dirt, hoping to recover the lost diamond, but it wasn't there.

A few years later, while in Melbourne making a television documentary about the shipwreck, we showed the ring to an expert jeweller. She was enchanted by the richness of the unhallmarked gold and declared that it must have been made locally during the gold rush for the child of a seriously rich miner, as the diamonds were from India and the opal was Hungarian. I've mentioned how, while in Australia, I had the opportunity to see the surviving ship's passenger list. There was only one small girl travelling on the *Royal Charter* in first class, and I am very much minded to think that this fabulous ring was hers.

There was one dive, a few days after finding the tiny ring, when I thought that we had hit the jackpot. I was sucking up a gritty mass of very dark muck and had glimpsed an occasional speck of gold – *good ground*, I thought. At the end of the dive, with only a modest amount of expectation, I went to the sluice and pulled back the rubber splash mat. A glowing carpet of gold filled the area where the dredge pipe flare feeds into the sluice. I gasped: if this was all gold, it would be worth a fortune. I savoured the possibility that we had found real wealth for a few moments, before digging my fingers into the layer. But alas, it was only heavies of pyrite, iron concretion and lead – with a very thin coating of gold dust that had been concentrated by the water's flow.

As I'd spent a vast amount of time and money to finally uncover the ship's gold, uninvited guests were not welcome. I was working with my daughter Daisy in a large hole when I noticed shadowy figures on the far side. The water was misty with plankton, and I couldn't work out who they were. I told Daisy to stay with the dredge nozzle and finned over.

I was staggered to find two pairs of unknown divers, busy poking about for gold. Using scuba diving hand signals, I asked them what the hell they were doing there, and they just shrugged, the thoughtless idiots – the 'sluice robbers' of the diving world. We had made such an enormous effort to be here, yet they seemed to feel it would be fine to just pop down and take our gold – unbelievable!

I suggested they leave, immediately. Their total lack of any normal courtesy was an issue, but more importantly, they had put their own safety at risk by blundering about under a working salvage boat. If we had been about to blow with both jets when they arrived, the surge of thrusting water would have tumbled them into a huge mound of sand, possibly affording me a spell in prison and them the fame of being the last people to perish on this shipwreck.

The domestic trials of being on a small spartan boat all day were challenging. And there was always a minimum of six of us to consider: two divers in the water, one person watching them as surface safety cover, someone at the helm managing the engines, a person checking the sluices were running well (the 'dredge ferret') and lastly, a 'runner' – the dogsbody who fetched and carried and minded our food.

We had evolved a routine with an enviable kitchen arrangement by using a small stove, Thermos flasks and the engine. Pies were taped to the engine's heat exchanger and tins of soup fitted nicely beside the manifold, which warmed them up perfectly. As soon as a diver surfaced and had passed up their weight belt, they were invited to choose from the day's fare before they were even aboard. It was a wonderful thing to effect the tone of a pleasant waiter and ask a tired and thoroughly chilled diver, 'Now, what can I bring you today? Tea or coffee? And we have cream of vegetable or tomato soup. The pies are chicken and mushroom or beef and ale.' I spoiled them and they deserved it. Although this level of service never happened during my own dive training, I had kept in mind that sergeant's maxim: any fool can be uncomfortable!

The toilets, however, were trickier. The women were invited to take a gold pan up onto the small forward deck at the bow, while the men respectfully cast their eyes astern. The men, when the need arose, would move back onto the dive platform, above the hydro-jets, and request a little privacy. I once commented to my mother that it was interesting how much more the men seemed to pee. She answered that it was because they could, nature having provided them with convenient little hoses! An informed appraisal, but still shockingly blunt coming from one's mother.

I had opted to wear a semi-dry wetsuit this year, rather than a fully sealed drysuit. This allowed me to follow a different routine. Each morning, I placed two large water bottles in the engine compartment to warm up, and then stayed in my semi-dry all day. I felt it was a terrible waste of time to have to surface, mid-dive, for this fairly trivial call of nature. Instead, at the end of each day, I would stand on the dive platform and pour the wonderfully refreshing lukewarm water down into my suit from the neck. The steady flow of fresh water then worked its way down, flushing through my suit, before finally trickling out at my feet. It worked and felt time-efficient as well as good; the pulse of warmth alone made it worth doing. I was surprised that none of the others took to this routine; in fact, there were even hints of disapproval. As a footnote, I would add that I had tried not drinking all day, to reduce the need to pee. But it gave me an incredible headache and isn't safe or healthy. If the toilet urge was more serious, the person was put ashore to sort themselves out.

Dolphins frequently joined us on the journey from the Moelfre Bay moorings to the wreck site. We learned to hold the boat at a speed that they seemed to enjoy, and it was wonderful to be so close to these perfectly adapted creatures. The experience was even better when my brother and his children were aboard. Like laughter, the youngsters' excitement at the dolphins' arrival was infectious. This euphoria reached a peak when we convinced the little ones that the dolphins had come to see them – that in fact, they could call a pod to the boat.

The marine life fascinated me because I know so little about it. And of course there were those reverberating, deep-seated echoes of my own happy childhood, spent close to the wild Welsh coast in Glamorgan and Pembrokeshire. It was hard not to anthropomorphize the little sea creatures that came and went while we dived. The nimble olive-brown shore crabs seemed brave, threatening a pinch if I got too close, whereas the larger, reddish, edible crabs seemed lazy or wisely stayed hidden. Nature has played a cruel joke on the poor edible crab – its shell having a piecrust-shaped edge! The cautious dark-brown lobsters also stayed hidden deep within overhanging rocks and crevices – at least until dusk, when they came out in droves. And there was a time, while I was diving with Ed, another member of the lifeboat crew, when an octopus, its reddish body the size of an orange, suddenly appeared and sat on top of a rock, obviously watching us. It was the only one I saw during the whole trip.

We did take some razor clams home to eat, but only once. They struggled as we prepared them for the pot and, having only one leg, made pitiful attempts to escape the kitchen table. When the whole sorry murderous business was over, they weren't particularly good to eat anyway. I could perhaps have learned to cook them properly, but chose not to.

When my boyhood favourite, a hermit crab, got too close to the dredge nozzle, I stopped work to turn the little creature around and send it safely on its way – they leave little mouse-like tracks in the sand. But this compassion wasn't extended to jellyfish.

For over a week, the whole bay was engulfed in a vast swarm of stinging lion's mane jellyfish. From time to time, I got up onto the cockpit roof to count them; there were never fewer than 14 around the boat. These large, rusty-brown jellyfish have long tentacles that drift along slowly and stretch out far behind them. When you're diving, they look like thin lines of semi-transparent wire hanging in the water. And for me, the pain of getting stung felt twice as bad as a stinging nettle.

One of the men who had trained me to dive had once swum up into a lion's mane, and his head and face had gone right into its body. He said that he took out his breathing demand valve and tried to rub off the sticky tentacles, as his lips were hurting badly. But he couldn't clear them, and even more tentacles drifted in and stuck to the mouthpiece. When he had to put his air supply back into his mouth, the pain was ten times worse. I had been warned, and mine stayed firmly in my mouth. The lion's manes' tentacles stuck to everything – equipment, suits and any hose or line that had been in the sea. To our surprise, we discovered that a rope that had been out of the water for three days, and seemed completely dry, could still sting too.

One morning, we found a man waiting for us on the cliffs. He waved and shouted that he would like to speak with someone. The boat dropped me ashore and he made his way down to me, smiled and introduced himself as Pete the Dowser. Then, with what seemed like the utmost sincerity, he told me that we were in the wrong place. The gold, he assured me, was all around the headland, on the other side of Moelfre Bay. I gently pointed out that we could see the *Royal Charter*'s wreckage, had already found some gold and were working in the area below the actual clifftop monument to the shipwreck. But he persisted, brushing aside what I had felt to be compelling arguments that we were, most certainly, in the right place.

I have always found dowsing to be a curious conundrum – dismissed by science, yet supported by a wealth of hearsay and anecdote. At school, our biology master once surprised the class by setting up a test. We were all sent from the room and then invited back in, one at a time. When my turn finally came, he thrust two bent metal rods into my hands and told me to walk past a bucket in the middle of the room. Baffled by the whole thing, I did as I was told and was actually frightened when the rods moved, then crossed when I passed the water-filled bucket.

'You can dowse,' he said authoritatively, and sent me to stand with a small group of classmates. The lesson then proceeded with no further explanation (he was a touch eccentric).

The formal teaching I have long since forgotten, but that dowsing demonstration has always stayed with me. So whenever

I met people such as Pete, or old Mary Ellen in Ireland's Wicklow mountains, with her tales of 'withy stick' dowsing for gold, they received a sympathetic ear.

There was another reason why I agreed to meet with the dowser later that evening. A woman who'd lived in Moelfre all her life had told me about a wonderful day many years earlier when she was out in a boat, and the sea was calm and crystal clear. She said that they were enjoying the rare opportunity to peer into the depths, when suddenly a huge anchor came into view. As she described it to me, it had to lie in the area that Pete was so excited about. In the natural sciences, like measuring forests and navigation, this sort of thing is called a 'convergent approximation' – and I love them; absolutes are boring. It's often a string of tiny random clues that leads to big discoveries, such as when an Armada shipwreck was once found in Ireland in a place it shouldn't have been, simply because a diver was curious as to why an isolated spot on the coast was called Spanish Point.

When Pete the Dowser and I did meet up, we agreed a deal should I find gold on the unknown wreck he believed he had found. Then he used two metal rods to lay transects out from the shore and give me the location. A few days later, I returned with Charlie at low tide to hunt in gullies for any traces of shipwreck. We found none. While this wasn't conclusive, I decided this was a treasure for someone else to find. After all, I already knew of a wooden ship laden with silver and gold, wrecked against low cliffs, of which there was now barely a trace that it had ever been there either.

When we'd finished exploring the easy ground close to the shore, we moved back towards the actual shipwreck. The *Royal Charter* does not lie parallel to the shore cliffs, but at an angle of about 30 degrees. The bow is close to land, almost touching at low tide, while the stern is much further out. Our earlier work had led me to expect to find an almost level seabed of the pebble-dashed clay under the pale sand. And so it was to start with. But then the dredges uncovered a lip, a straight fault line where the clay suddenly descended vertically. Hoping that this was some natural anomaly, possibly a shallow fissure lined with gold, we set about clearing it out. But down it went, so deep that we could only dredge it at the lowest point of the tide. A massive iron post appeared that we initially thought might be a cannon – so, unimaginatively, we called the place 'Cannon Hole'.

I was baffled by how the huge pit had formed. It extended up to the massive iron hull of the *Royal Charter* itself – right to the point where the whole stern section had tragically broken away from the rest of the ship, and doomed the rescue that was being organized at the bow. At first, I assumed that the colossal waves that had been pounding the ship had poured through the breach and thundered down onto the clay, blasting it away to form this hole. The thought that we may be the first divers to get to the bottom – and a carpet of gold – spurred us on. But the more of Cannon Hole that we uncovered, the more it became obvious that this was wishful thinking. It was a vast rectangular pit that was obviously man-made. Nevertheless, having invested so much effort in trying to empty the hole, we pushed on. When we finally reached the bottom, it was interesting but a complete disappointment. There was not a single speck of gold to be seen; instead, the pit was lined with rounded lumps of the glacial clay.

I later read that the Victorian salvors had cut and lifted all of the ground that was close to where the ship's strongroom had been. During the storm, gold had poured out through the broken hull and been churned into the seabed clay. The precious dirt was then taken ashore somewhere, so that the bars, coins, nuggets and dust could be washed out. Before it became the barren Cannon Hole, this patch of reddish mud must have held gold worth tens of millions. It would make a good project to find the place where they did the clean-up afterwards, as wherever the washing was undertaken, some gold would have been lost, even if only a little of the dust.

If I have an open mind about dowsing, it is fully made up with regard to the miracle of ethereal help. Twice I have been saved by something that I do not understand. The first time was in my early twenties while hiking at Christmas in the Italian Alps. Nobody else wanted to come with me, so I set off alone. Although I'd been determined to be careful, I took a shortcut and was caught in a small avalanche. While the snow slip didn't sweep me very far, the slope was too steep to climb back up again, and I found myself trapped on the north side of the mountain in waist-deep powder snow. It was late afternoon, and my pleasant hike had suddenly turned into a life-threatening situation. I had moments of near panic as the severity of my position became clear to me.

I quickly got a grip of myself and reasoned that if I couldn't get back up the incline to safety, I must go down. With trepidation, I looked at the immense, snow-covered mountain slope that fell away before me. I set off and soon found that moving my feet in circles, as when pedalling a bicycle, worked best to push my way through the snow. But I made very slow progress and before long I was suffering with the cold. My left leg had taken a huge bash in the initial fall and, while I was relieved that it wasn't broken, it was painful and increasingly difficult to move. I pushed into the snow with my left hand to take some weight off the damaged leg, but soon lost the feeling in my fingers. I remember wondering if I should be worried about losing my left hand, but then thought to myself, *you're dying, it doesn't matter.* With the comical sense of an Englishman's not wishing to embarrass anyone, I pushed on, wretched yet driven by imagining how my freezing to death would spoil Christmas for everyone.

Finally, in the evening's twilit gloom and totally exhausted, I knew that I was beaten – there was nothing left in me. I stopped and simply asked for help. Not a prayer, not targeted at anyone or anything, really; it was as if I were asking the mountain itself to assist me. And then, with a sudden rush, help came. A sparkling golden warmth started in my chest and flowed out into my limbs. The feeling came back to my left hand, and I was filled with renewed energy. Now able to push on, I continued wading down through the deep powdery snow and eventually I found a track that ran along the mountain's contour and back to where I was staying.

I have no idea what happened to me that day, nor what force enacted the amazing physical rescue. I do know that I had felt finished and had given up trying to save myself. In quiet, penitent desperation and with all of my self-conscious ego gone, I had humbly opened my mind and asked for help – and it came.

The second time I was saved by something miraculous was while diving on the *Royal Charter*. The two instances were similar but very different. I was working on the seabed with Charlie – me on the dredge nozzle and him moving rocks. We were both breathing air fed down to us from the boat compressor through long, yellow, reinforced hoses. Charlie signalled that he was going up to have a cigarette break, and left. It had already been a long dive of just under three hours, and I knew that we would want to stop work soon. I carried on without him, to get a little more done before he came back.

Almost immediately, I was struck by an intense compulsion to unclip the air hose from my waist belt. The clip is for safety, to prevent the diver from losing the surface air supply. Like an internal voice, it railed at me to act. 'The clip is a nuisance! It'll get tangled in the dredge,' it implored, then shouted, 'It's a mess – get rid of it!' Next came its urgent final demand: '*Unclip it now!*'

The sudden clamour of a voice in my head shocked me, and I remember trying to reason against it. After all, I had been working like this for hours without the air hose getting tangled, or the clip being any trouble. Purely to silence the irritating voice, I stopped work and unclipped the hose from my belt. With the safety tether now gone, I gripped the demand valve firmly with my teeth so as not to lose it. Moments later there was a slight tug on the line, I bit harder, then the air supply was ripped from my mouth. Even when using surface air, we carried an air bottle on our backs in case of a problem, so I switched to breathe from that. But I couldn't carry on working, as I was angry now. Thinking that somebody on the boat had been totally careless, I surfaced to chastise the culprit.

Yet they were all innocent. I discovered instead that my airline had gone under the boat and been sucked into the jet intake. The demand valve, which only a few minutes before had been in my mouth, was now rammed between two buckled bars of the strong protection grille and the yellow airline was wrapped tightly around the impeller's drive shaft. I hung in the gloom beneath the boat, numb with shock. I had acted on the prescient warning with such bad grace, and had almost been rude to the life-saving voice. If still clipped to the airline, I would probably be dead by now; hauled up by the waist so quickly that my ear drums burst, my face mask smashed into the metal hull, filling my eyes with broken glass, and my whole body trapped firmly against the intake. And with no air, I would have had only a minute or so before drowning. I had just been spared a truly horrible death.

When I got trapped in the avalanche, I had respectfully asked for the help that I so wondrously received. But this second time, I hadn't even been aware that I was in danger. I have no idea where the phenomenal help came from, but in both instances it was very real and it saved me. I find it pleasing that while living in an age which arrogantly thinks it understands everything, wonders like this can still occur. For me, the realization that there is an unknown power out there, which can help in times of great peril, is like finding gold for the soul. I am now careful to listen for any whispered advice, and believe that my hunches will keep me on the right track in life. However, I also live in hope that, whatever this transcendent phenomenon is, it doesn't have to save me again.

The stern section of the *Royal Charter* was gone. It had been lifted and taken away to be broken up and searched for gold in the 1860s. But the deep impression the hull had made as it sank down into the clay seabed was still there. After finishing with Cannon Hole, we moved up onto the lip beside where the massive stern had been. The vessel's enormous weight had squeezed out the clay like thick cream extruding from a hastily bitten cake. If the Victorian salvors had made such a huge effort to excavate Cannon Hole, then the ground beside it could still yield a little gold.

We took two days to blow away the sand and uncover the clay lip's great rolled slabs of fractured mud. I dived with my partner, Mary, to examine the newly exposed area, and see if it was worth bringing down a dredge pipe. My eye was immediately caught by a narrow channel that zigzagged across the broken surface. I dropped closer to see if it had caught any heavy material, and was delighted to discover about a spoonful of grainy gold dust scattered along it. This was very promising and well worth dredging. I continued checking along the crevice to a point where the sides pinched together, and I could see that a little further ahead of me the fissure opened up again.

I spotted the golden glow before I saw the nugget itself. The clay sides of the crack were shining as if a yellow light were set within it and I approached in awe, as if witnessing magic. With breath held and heart racing, I looked down to see a most beautiful chunk of natural gold nestled in the ancient clay. Most big nuggets are thick with embedded quartz – but this piece was almost pure gold. I lay quite still for a while, staring at this sensational find, and sensed that it liked the attention. I nodded my respect, removed my demand valve and mumbled, 'I have only ever seen something like you before in a museum.' I swear it glowed even brighter. But still I did not touch it. I wanted to savour this sweet success, this triumph that it had taken the whole team's Herculean effort to achieve. I drank in the moment, committing to memory every joyful second of when first making the nugget's acquaintance.

Perhaps predictably for a prospector, these noble feelings soon faded, and I began to wonder just how big the nugget actually was. . . If I was looking at the top of an oval-shaped piece, it might be enormous. But then again, it might only be several smaller pieces locked together. With base avarice now steering my thoughts, it was time to reach in and allow the glowing mass to reveal itself. I realized that I was, of course, the second person to do this and hoped the nugget had given as much pleasure to the 1850s miner who'd first found it on the other side of the world. Perhaps the nugget had been trapped in clay back then too, albeit in the rock-hard, sun-baked, rusty earth of Australia.

My fingers closed around the egg-sized lump, and I lifted it out. Suddenly aware that I had not looked over at Mary for a while, I glanced around and found her hanging in the water above me, watching. I laid the nugget, for it was one piece, in my palm and gestured wildly with the other hand. She shrugged in that dismissive, arms-out gesture that says, 'What are you on about? It's nothing.' In the boat later, Mary explained that she couldn't understand why I was so excited about a piece of brass – it was obviously far too big to be gold!

I surfaced and called to Lorna, the diver who was watching us as our surface cover. As she crouched on the dive platform, I locked eyes with her and said quietly, 'I am about to pass you something wonderful. But don't react at all, as we are always being watched. Just calmly take it from me and put it in the grey bag with Charlie's tobacco.'

Life is so much better if you keep the inner child alive. With a foolish desire to just go wild, I waved goodbye to Moelfre and roared the boat out to sea. I wanted the rumbling 400-hp growl to be heard by everyone who had helped us: it was a salute, a farewell with respect. I wondered if we would be missed – although who were we to the villagers anyway? Even just being a footnote in the *Royal Charter*'s long story would be nice. But my 12 weeks of responsibility and pressure were now over. And once clear of the bay's shelter, I crashed through the choppy sea, sending plumes of sparkling white spray high above the boat. I knew that this might be my last time as skipper of this much-loved ex-military gem, and I was determined to enjoy every thrilling second of the long trip back to Gallows Point.

The present moment is so precious. It represents our only chance in life to create the treasured memories that all too soon become 'the good old days'. I think my father spoke for the whole team when he told me later, 'I have only one regret about this trip. That I was not there every single day – it's the best thing I've done in years.'

The gold coins, dust, nuggets and jewellery we found were all declared to the Receiver of Wreck – including the evocative nugget retrieved from the clay crevice. This specimen piece was later reported as being the largest gold nugget ever found in the UK. This openness with officialdom appalled many people who, perhaps through experience, thought that I was best advised to keep quiet and stay away from the authorities. However, I had worked for a government department for 28 years and trusted official systems. Perhaps even more than that, I wanted to be able to tell the gut-wrenching story of the five hundred brave young people whose hopes and sudden wealth were shattered on the rocks, along with that fabulous steam clipper, the *Royal Charter*.

12

THE UNDISCOVERED

'Normality is a paved road: it's comfortable to walk,
but no flowers grow on it.'

—Vincent van Gogh

I had no expectation of getting old, and yet, here I am. My Irish grandmother would no doubt have chided me for saying such a thing, warning me not to tempt fate. But should relentless destiny choose to seize me now, that's fine; I am content. I have had several near misses in life, besides that early incident in the mine shaft, getting caught in an avalanche and my air hose being sucked into the hydro-jet intake, and I do feel very fortunate to still be here – on borrowed time, perhaps? Knowing that my name might appear on the Grim Reaper's to-do list at any moment is helpful: it's like being prodded with a sharp stick to keep moving. I think that it was only when I truly accepted my own mortality that an absolute passion for living developed.

Since diving on the *Royal Charter*, I have designed and built a cottage. Snug, traditional and massively insulated, it's a joy to live in and I hope will provide a much-loved home for all those who follow me. With that fascinating project now complete, I am, once again, free to go hunting for undiscovered gold. And not wanting to waste a precious minute, I have already made a start. My golden journey has already taken me from dustbin lid to military combat boat, so where next, I wonder . . .?

Still mindful that procrastination is the thief of time and mediocrity the thief of life, I have put together four extraordinary possibilities. Each will need the skills learned during decades of prospecting. Helpfully, as I have noted once before, during the 20 or so years since leaving the pleasant and sheltered world of office life, my acceptance of risk has soared.

I have also always strived for the widest possible network of friends and acquaintances – and then, most importantly, I have listened to them. Each of the new possibilities on my to-do list has sprung from hushed conspiratorial conversations with kindred spirits and agreeable scheming with gold-fevered friends. OK, here we go – welcome to my world!

The British Goldpanning Championships are an excellent place to catch up on prospectors' gossip and pick up any hint of a newly discovered location for gold. Which is what happened at the last competition when two unusually furtive conversations set me a challenge that marks the first opportunity of the four possibilities to explore. Hours apart, two well-informed friends separately confided in me that a new Bonanza had been found. The details were predictably sketchy, but the overlap in their accounts was intriguing. I believed that this new and exciting find was real, and not the fancy of a gold-fevered imagination. And I also sensed that a most timely and welcome convergent approximation was forming – the dawn chorus of so many adventures.

The gist of the rumour was that three men were working in the mouth of a Scottish river where they were finding ounces of gold. Wisely, they had been able to keep their find a secret by working quietly during the hours of darkness. Nonetheless, eyebrows had been raised, and their clandestine operation became compromised when they sold some of their gold. Neither of my informants knew the men personally, but I had enough information to make a start. Helpfully, I knew someone who was skilled at finding people.

About three months later, I had a phone call from him, saying that he had some good news. Not expecting much, I was delighted to hear that he had found the three individuals. He chuckled, saying, 'I have even more good news! They want to meet you.' Acting as my intermediary, he arranged a get-together, and I took a morning flight up to Inverness and hired a car to the address I had been given. Once there, I was welcomed in and invited to take a seat at a large dining-room table. This was completely empty, except for a small white china saucer filled with an impressive heap of unusually bright gold dust. These men had done exceptionally well.

We talked politely and positively for almost two hours, each trying to get the measure of the other. However, I had an early evening plane to catch, so finally pushed for us to reach a conclusion. I said that every single thing that they had told me sounded true, although they still nursed the mistaken idea that their gold was pure. All wild gold is a natural alloy with a touch of other metals, usually silver. But this didn't matter. The gold they were finding was a fabulous rich yellow colour and obviously of good quality. I paused before asking my last question. I wanted to be upfront with these men, and I knew that what I was about to say might exclude me from ever working with them: 'Why on earth are you talking to me?'

I made the point that they had found an outstandingly good gold location, and had managed to keep it a secret. And, by whatever method, they were successfully extracting heaps of gold. Surely, there was no need to involve anybody else now?

Good men, they were immediately candid in return. Their point, in agreeing to meet me, was that they had worked quietly at night for two freezing winters, and they were sick of it. Their hope was that a new man, with fresh ideas, might come up with a better way of recovering the gold.

This was music to my ears, as I was already formulating a plan. I explained that we would need to be discreet and keep the location free of rival panners for as long as possible. To that end, we could use electric sub surface dredges – silent and invisible. And what is more, we could create some form of decoy that would allow us to work during the warm summer months – in broad daylight.

Finally, I wished them well and left. It is inspiring that people are still finding gold in new locations. Whether they choose to involve me or not, it was great to have met them and sat around their proud saucer of radiant gold.

The second of my four extraordinary possibilities concerns an ancient Irish book, *The Annals of the Four Masters*. Compiled in the 1630s by monks, the work is a chronicle of Irish history stretching from the early 17th century back to the very earliest of times. Of particular interest to me is what it says about ancient gold mining. This, and other references, record that the gold of the Irish kings was found and worked in the hills and forests south of the present capital, Dublin – in particular, 'in the woods to the east of the River Liffey'.

There was a well-recorded and fascinating gold rush to the very south of this mountainous area in 1795. The initial discovery was made by a local boy who found a gold nugget while fishing. This was assumed to be lost property, and the rush didn't start until many years later, during which a few thousand ounces of gold were recovered. It's said that a 24-oz nugget was found as late as 1856. However, it is the social aspects of this rush that are especially interesting. A wonderful cat-and-mouse battle went on for decades between the local people and the authorities, who were trying to control the goldfield. The Wicklow gold rush remains a fine example of a very small district containing a large quantity of rough and readily accessible gold.

While Irish history is always colourful and thought-provoking, what really brought it to life for me was when I happened to be staying with a friend near Dublin. The telephone rang and an acquaintance of his asked if he could call by to show us something.

A big, rough-looking yet unexpectedly polite man arrived in the early evening with a beer glass half-full of dark sandy gravel. He passed it to me and invited me to pan it down. I did, and an arc of coarse, rust-stained gold appeared in my pan. We stared at it, me delighted and him still full of doubt. When I asked how he had found it, he replied, 'Panning with a washing-up bowl!'

I wondered how much more of this gold there must be. Then came the shock. He paused thoughtfully for a moment, reached into his pocket and pulled out something rolled up in kitchen paper. 'What about this?'

I took the small, heavy bundle and stared into his eyes. 'I don't even need to unwrap it,' I said. 'This is gold!' The weight confirmed what he had found even before we took the piece out of its wrapping. It was fantastic – a sandwich of thick gold squeezed between two thin bands of water-worn quartz.

But such is life that the revelation seemed to puzzle him, and perhaps he still doubted his discovery. With a quick thanks, he muttered that he had to go as he was due at a bingo session that evening. Before he left, he turned and added that he would show me his pineapple-sized piece one day. He never did, and I have since heard that it was sold.

'One swallow does not make a summer', or so the saying goes. However, there was a second, completely separate incident that compounded the first. An acquaintance who enjoyed metal detecting explained how, while meandering across a field of cows, his detector rang out. He was expecting to unearth old shotgun cartridges, bits of lead or the odd copper coin. Not in his wildest dreams did he ever imagine finding gold, yet a few minutes later, dumbstruck, he was brushing the last of the dirt from a fist-sized chunk of gold-rich quartz.

This too was not a Walter Mitty-style fantasy; I have seen the find with my own eyes. The man invited me into his house and showed me where the family's footwear was lined up. Then he lifted a wellington boot and gave it a firm knock – and the rock that fell out was breathtaking. Rough and iron-stained, the ferruginous quartz was riddled with gold veins: butter-yellow metal ran through every part of the specimen. He was pleased to have impressed me, and quickly pushed the lump back into its very rural and unlikely hiding place.

If these two examples weren't comfortably enough to make the point that the Irish gold is still there to be discovered, there is a third. A farmer was ploughing up a grass field when he clipped the bedrock beneath the thin soil; later, after it had rained, he spotted something bright lying on the surface. Again, the piece is exceptional. The white quartz has a water-worn top edge and is sharp underneath, where it was ripped from the vein. The gold is very thin, but shines as if already polished. Since then, the farmer has learned to pan, and has now washed dirt in all the ditches surrounding the field. Apparently, there are traces of gold everywhere.

One find could be happenstance, two a coincidence, but three is definitely a pattern.

Dipping back into history for a moment, there is more interesting evidence that supports the view that while England has very little natural gold, Ireland is awash with it, and it comes from the late 12th century. After the Anglo-Norman conquest, Ireland was commanded to pay '400 marcs of gold', while the exchequer didn't require England to supply any gold at all. A marc was roughly equivalent to 8 troy ounces.* And lastly, there is the absolutely fabulous and unparalleled collection of Bronze Age and Iron Age gold ornaments in the National Museum of Ireland. While a puzzling piece of research from 2015 suggests that the Irish Bronze Age goldsmiths were actually using English gold from Cornwall, I strongly doubt this, and consider the huge weight of historical evidence and modern practical experience testifies firmly against that view.

Nevertheless, it's difficult to know quite where to start with exploring this idea. It requires a thorough survey of the whole

---

* A troy ounce weighs the equivalent of 31.1g and is the unit of measurement used to weigh gold and silver; whereas an avoirdupois ounce is the equivalent of 28.3g and is used for everything else, such as cooking ingredients.

area, something more suited to a mining exploration company. But on the other hand, just imagine how tremendous it would be to find one of these very small but staggeringly rich gold veins – after all, I know three people who already have.

Much is said about how to get on in life, yet there is one simple key: talk to people. When selling Christmas trees in December, I meet many interesting people. And if there is time, I always mention my interest in gold.

One day, a customer listened to me for a few moments before unexpectedly declaring that he too had found treasure. I was surprised by how casual he was about it, and asked him to explain. He obliged and gave a gloriously detailed account of finding silver coins – actual 'pieces of eight' – on a Caribbean beach. He spent a part of each winter there, and said that a few of the coins washed up with every storm. It struck me that these coins represent the ultimate prize, quintessential treasure from a shipwrecked Spanish galleon – the very stuff of *Treasure Island*.

While we were speaking, other customers began to ask for my help, so I scrabbled about for a scrap of paper to jot down some notes and the man's contact details. When I found a paper napkin left over from lunch, I asked him to draw the island on it – which he did. The next step was pure Long John Silver: I asked him to put a cross on the map where the pieces of eight had washed up – and he did. I now had a roughly drawn paper-napkin treasure map, with X marking the spot.

It seemed that my excitement was still not obvious to him. When handing me the map, he said that he was already fairly rich, and had no interest in hunting for treasure. I chided him for his blunt materialism, saying that this was nothing to do with making money, but wholly for the sheer life-affirming thrill of experiencing a storybook adventure.

At home that evening, I used an internet site with satellite images to check the nature of the land and sea around his 'X-marks-the-spot' beach. The water was shallow for a long way offshore. The hurricane that caused the wreck would have bumped and rolled the ship all along its path of destruction, scattering the debris in a more or less straight track. To try to discover this line, and at what angle from the shore the ship came in, I would need to sample the seabed in stages. I think that at this initial reconnaissance stage, the equipment I'd need would be no more than scuba gear, an under-sea scooter and a crowbar. Keeping a fairly low profile at first might be wise. I have since checked to see if this wreck is already known, but there is no record online of a shipwreck being there . . .

How wonderful! Simply by talking to a man who was buying a Christmas tree, I am now fixated on the exhilarating possibility of finding ancient silver.

And lastly, there is possibly the most difficult project of the four. Not long ago the owner of a small quarry asked me to visit him. Giving nothing away, he simply said that he had a job for me. My heart sank, as I assumed it was tree work – manual planting or felling, the sort of thing that I don't really do any more. But once safely past his two menacing Alsatians, and sitting comfortably with a coffee, he explained that treasure was on his mind.

He had met two men who believed they knew the location of a ship that had gone down two hundred years ago, with five boxes of gold and nine chests of silver aboard. The men needed help with the salvage, and the quarryman had very generously suggested me. I was only given a mobile telephone number to contact, there being a reluctance to trust me with an address at this point. I called the number and, heartened by the cheerful nature of the conversation, agreed to fly over to Dublin the next day.

I was met at the airport by a well-dressed, middle-aged man who led me out to where his new, top-of-the-range car was parked. With its cream leather seats and slightly tinted windows, the vehicle afforded a level of comfort that was unfamiliar to me. However, while easy and directionless, our small talk was less comfortable in that I still didn't know who this man actually was, nor where we were going. As we left the city, I tried to memorize the names of the places that we were passing. But it was hopeless. While having some Irish ancestry, I struggled to commit the Gaelic names to memory and Cionn Átha Gad soon merged with An Bóthar Buí, or An Muileann gCearr. My desire to know roughly where I was being taken on this beautiful island now relied wholly on my wristwatch. By knowing the time and where the sun was, together with our speed and how long we had been driving, I could make a basic 'dead reckoning' calculation of our final location.

We finally pulled up outside a large, impressive house and I chastised myself for my misgivings. But on entering the front door I was taken aback, as the television was tuned in to a Russian channel. Two beautiful young women were chatting in Russian at the kitchen table and, giving them a smile, I corrected myself, thinking, *be as paranoid as you like!*

Before long the second man arrived, who seemed pleasant enough, hearty, with big blue eyes and an obvious passion for finding gold. We discussed the possibility of working together – they with their knowledge of the treasure's location, and me with the know-how to recover it.

If the project were to go ahead, it would be the first time that I have ever teamed up with complete strangers and I am still wondering whether this extraordinary possibility is worth the risk. If it does go ahead, I will insist that we keep the whole thing above board and seek the Irish Government Authority's consent. At a recent gathering in London, I was introduced to the Irish ambassador and thought that it would be a good start to secure his support. But I was only halfway through explaining the endeavour to him, when he gave me his card and left. I am not sure how to interpret that; obviously, he is a very busy man.

I sometimes feel that the more I know, the less I am certain of. Am I finding the gold, or is the gold finding me? Humans have enjoyed a special relationship with this enchanting metal since prehistory. It has whispered softly to me and cast its spell over me from the very first moment I saw that Welsh prospector's collection of wild gold almost 50 years ago – formed in a star before the Earth even existed, and now temporarily entombed in blocks of clear resin and displayed on the dresser in his kitchen.

There are moments when I feel tuned in to this divine element, on its frequency as it were – a priest to the eternal metal. And yet, for me, this is not about a form of dowsing. It's more like a sixth sense, as with the uneasy feeling that some people get when being spied on, or when we somehow know that a loved one is in trouble – an ancient understanding, not yet understood by science.

I had a particularly memorable instance of sensing where the gold was, or it me, in 2019. A very determined young woman had asked me if I would take her out gold panning. She had been given a terminal diagnosis, and panning was on her to-do list. We met in a high mountain valley, where the narrow road runs right alongside a gold-bearing stream. While she learned how to use a gold pan, I kept absent-mindedly wondering where we could find a good sample of gold. I had already taken dozens of people to this accessible panning spot and had found very little with them – just an occasional speck. I desperately wanted her to do much better.

Three times I glanced upstream, and each time a rock no bigger than a loaf of bread caught my eye. When the panning lesson ended, we paddled over to it and broke the fractured bedrock open. Disturbed silt clouded the water, but we both instantly saw the glow of gold. When she reached forward to pick up a piece, I snapped 'Stop!' so quickly that she jumped back as if recoiling from a snake. I had not meant to frighten her, and quickly explained just how staggeringly rare it is to see gold unaided through coffee-coloured water. We stood watching the radiant light for a few moments, then cheerfully gathered up the bright little nuggets.

This amazing find left me almost speechless. In a heavily overworked place, where, at best, I had hoped to find a few specks of gold dust, I had been instinctively drawn to a rock hiding nuggets. Whatever this sixth-sense intuition phenomenon was, it had just happened. And in many ways, I feel that I gained more than she did during our short day together. She was an inspiration. I have never met anybody so assuredly seizing each day and living it to the full.

Finding gold is a journey. It's not about striving to reach a summit, it's solely for the sheer adventure that can be found in an old way of life. I have evolved and am now content to embrace this somewhat feral existence. I travel with chance and am not overly concerned by the societal requirement to conform. And in doing so, my life has become exponentially richer, and I walk where the flowers grow.

To reflect for a moment upon the wisdom I was once offered by one-legged Ian as we sipped coffee in his campervan; and I mean this to be inspiring not melancholy. If you will take the advice of an old man, I would say this – find your passion in life and get on with it, you are mortal and don't have long – go find your gold!

ACKNOWLEDGEMENTS

You can go out prospecting for gold alone – but not so when writing a book. I have had panfuls of help from the most caring and supportive publishing professionals, and a river of endless patience from my family and close friends. Their unerring encouragement, guidance and readiness to help were vital and hugely appreciated. This was a fifty-year journey, and I can only pick out and name a handful of those fine people that I met scattered along my life's trail.

To start with the book itself, I would first thank Jane Turnbull, my agent, who persuaded me to write *Finding Gold*. After the success of *The Wood Fire Handbook* I had wanted to write my next book about gathering sticks and kindling – Jane said 'No! People will be far more interested in your search for gold'. And from that moment, she has kept me on track and guided me through the quite bewildering and often lonely process of writing and publishing.

I then had the extraordinarily good fortune to work with the team at Short Books – again within the Octopus Publishing Group. I would thank those involved for their craft and endless cheerfulness in transforming my rough manuscript into a thing of beauty and bringing it to the market.

This book was carefully created by Publisher: Jo Morrell; Commissioning Editor: Katie Forsythe; Project Editor: Rimsha Falak; Copy Editor: John English; Creative Director: Mel Four; Editorial Assistant: Sarah Ramnath-Budhram; Production

Controller: Sarah Parry; Sales: Lucy Helliwell & Natasha Photiou; Marketing & Publicity: Chloë Johnson-Hill, Charlotte Sanders, Erin Brown, and Karen Baker; Legal Reader: Nicola Thatcher; and Developmental Editor: Sue Lascelles.

And at home, I would heartily thank my partner Mary for her readiness to help with the many drafts. And for her quiet acceptance of my hiding somewhere for hundreds of hours, tapping away on a laptop, while reminiscing my world of gold. My daughter Daisy, whose English is so much better than mine, patiently cast her eye over my pages and nudged me to improve and correct any waywardness in my prose or grammar. My father and two sons' steady confidence that the whole project would succeed was also hugely appreciated.

From the long shadow of a lifetime's gold-fevered passion, I would ask a few exceptional people to step forward and take a bow. My distant past, the early years, were instructed and enriched by the company of the following fellow panners – all remembered, in no particular order, with great fondness: Alf Henderson, Mike Gossage, Mike and Colleen Jones, Geraint and Fran Evans, Glyn and Janet, Ken and Denise Williamson, Trevor and Yvonne Chesters, Colin Kimberley, Meirion Thomas, Les Farmer, John Krenc, Peter and Yvonne Dallas, Barbara Copley, John Wilcox, Terry Mahony, Bob Galloway, Staffon Feron, Chris Engel, Bob Sutherland, Tim Curtis, Leon Kirk, John Hooper, Richard and Chris Deighton, Mark Gregory, Charlie Smart, Rex and Norma Bingham, Ian Stephen, Greta and Charlie Clark, Eddie Bell, Mark Bell, Jamie Shepherd, John McDowell, John Swinbank, Alan Souter, Nigel Blayney, Geoff Brown, Kieron Moorman, Tom Taylor, James Ogilvie, Richard from Tasmania, Fred and Gloria Olsson, Peter Gower, Gerry Tobin, Henry and Ann Doran, Chris

Halls, Rob Chapman, Simon Camm, Kauko Launonen, Inkeri Syrjanen, Pirjo Muotkajarvi, Seppo Mauno, Pentti Hongisto, Esko Orava, Vesa Luhta, Jim Archibald, David and Lorraine Millar, Art and Noreen Sailor, Akio and Suzanne Saito, Cesar Castano, Ken and Ulla Karlsson, Geraldine McCrossan, Veronika Stedra, Pierre Guide and Dirk Mehlhorn. Gems within the world's 'golden family' of prospectors.

My patient brother, Paul joined me on many of my gold prospecting trips, as did my ever-smiling three children – who suffered rather as they wanted to go to Disneyland in Florida, but got taken to midge and leech-infested rivers instead!

A special thank you goes out to the dozens of generous landowners that have allowed me to follow my dream and seek specks of wild gold on their farms and estates.

If my gold panning trips were enriched by the company of the excellent people above, the following were invaluable during treasure diving projects: Charlie Field and Lorna Barker, Louis Field, David Headon, John Tewson, Derek Duffy, Brian Perrott, Neil O'May, Chris Andrews, Chris Holden, Chris Kernic, Chris Battye, Bruno Van Eerdenbrugh, Jiri Dunovsky, Cameron Murray, Ed Griffiths and Laura Pritchard-Griffiths, Nigel and Sarah Musgrave, Vince Jones, Mr and Mrs Evans of Nant Buchan farm, Roy Thomas, Dave Jones at Gallows Point and Diana MacMullen who lent me her father's huge house on Anglesey for 12 weeks. My fearless cousin David Blanchette, Mary Russell, daughter Daisy Thurkettle, boat engineer father Gordon and adventure-loving mother Jean all gave their endless and vital support.

Leaving the safety of my office and a wonderfully secure job was a monumental step. I would thank those who encouraged my boldness, in particular: Richard Smith, Tony Penrose, Thomas

Black and Bob West. And those who facilitated the definitive 'Rubicon' party that handsomely marked the biggest transition of my life. Of the 142 people who attended to cheer me on my way, I would highlight Jim Lyon, Steve Scott and their staff at the Forestry Commission who, possibly against civil service rules, allowed the use of the offices and lawns for this wonderful and noisy celebration.

There are too many solid gold people that deserve a mention to include here. To all of those lives touched, loved and respected, but whose names are absent, I would simply say – you are my treasure. And now, I need to get out and meet the new generation of young prospectors!

SELECT BIBLIOGRAPHY

Adamson, G F S, *At the End of the Rainbow: Gold in Scotland*
Berton, Pierre, *Klondike: The Last Great Gold Rush, 1896–1899*
British Sub-Aqua Club, *Sport Diving*
Calvert, John, *The Gold Rocks of Great Britain and Ireland*
Camm, Simon, *Gold in the Counties of Cornwall & Devon*
Chisholm, Cecil, *Retire and Enjoy It*
De Lorenzo, Lois, *Gold Fever and the Art of Panning and Sluicing*
Engel, Chris, *In Search of Yukon Gold*
Hall, G W, *The Gold Mines of Merioneth*
Holden, Chris and Lesley, *Life and Death on the 'Royal Charter'*
Johnson, Samuel, *The History of Rasselas, Prince of Abissinia*
Launonen, Kauko, *Gold in Finnish Lapland*
Lee, Laurie, *As I Walked Out One Midsummer Morning*
London, Jack, *The Call of the Wild*
———, *White Fang*
Maclaren, J M, *Gold: Its Geological Occurrence and Geographical Distribution*
McKee, Alexander, *The Golden Wreck: The Tragedy of the 'Royal Charter'*
May, Philip Ross, *Gold Town*
Palmer, Lee Gary, *Gold Occurrences in the UK, A Gold Prospector's Guide*
Pough, F H, *A Field Guide to Rocks and Minerals*
Service, Robert, *The Spell of the Yukon and Other Verses*
Shackleton, E H, *Lakeland Geology*
Shaw, W T, *Mining in the Lake Counties*
Strodach, G K, *Epicurus, The Art of Happiness*
Thoreau, Henry David, *Walden*
Thornton, Matt, *Dredging for Gold, The Gold Divers' Handbook*

Taking a book from manuscript to market is a team effort. This book was carefully created by

Publisher: Jo Morrell
Commissioning Editor: Katie Forsythe
Project Editor: Rimsha Falak
Copy Editor: John English
Creative Director: Mel Four
Editorial Assistant: Sarah Ramnath-Budhram
Production Controller: Sarah Parry
Sales: Lucy Helliwell
Marketing & Publicity: Charlotte Sanders & Karen Baker

RAISING READERS
Books Build Bright Futures

Dear Reader,

We'd love your attention for one more page to tell you about the crisis in children's reading, and what we can all do.

Studies have shown that reading for fun is the **single biggest predictor of a child's future life chances** – more than family circumstance, parents' educational background or income. It improves academic results, mental health, wealth, communication skills, ambition and happiness.[1]

The number of children reading for fun is in rapid decline. Young people have a lot of competition for their time. In 2024, 1 in 10 children and young people in the UK aged 5 to 18 did not own a single book at home.[2]

Hachette works extensively with schools, libraries and literacy charities, but here are some ways we can all raise more readers:

- Reading to children for just 10 minutes a day makes a difference
- Don't give up if children aren't regular readers – there will be books for them!
- Visit bookshops and libraries to get recommendations
- Encourage them to listen to audiobooks
- Support school libraries
- Give books as gifts

There's a lot more information about how to encourage children to read on our website: **www.RaisingReaders.co.uk**

Thank you for reading.

---

[1] OECD, '21st-Century Readers: Developing Literacy Skills in a Digital World', 2021, https://www.oecd.org/en/publications/21st-century-readers_a83d84cb-en.html

[2] National Literacy Trust, 'Book Ownership in 2024', November 2024. https://literacytrust.org.uk/research-services/research-reports/book-ownership-in-2024